created & written by

BR

art by

NATE WATSON

ANDREW DALHOUSE
colorist

MARSHALL DILLON
letterer

MAT SANTOLOUCO
cover artist

MARK WAID
editor

CHAPTER 1

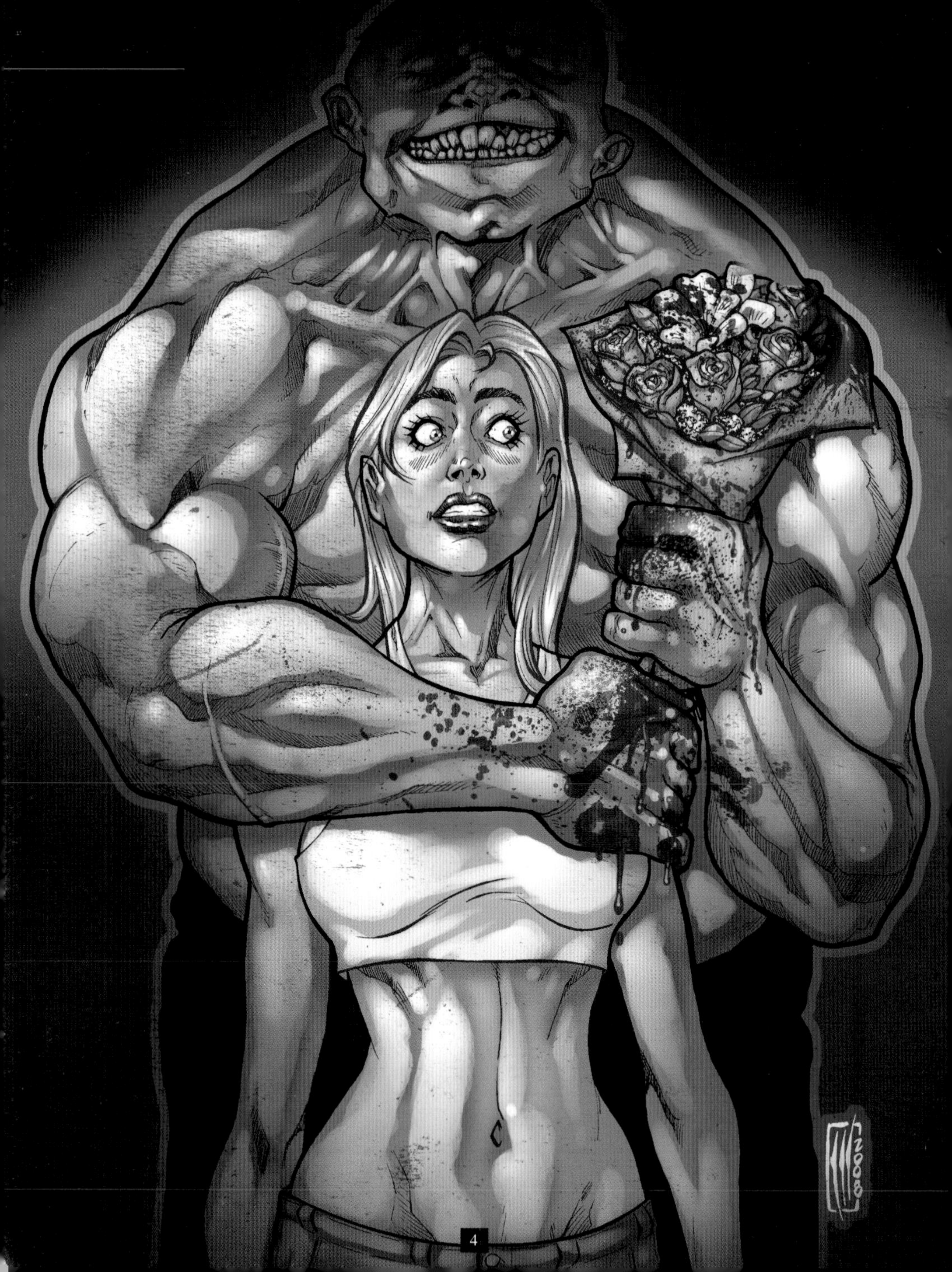

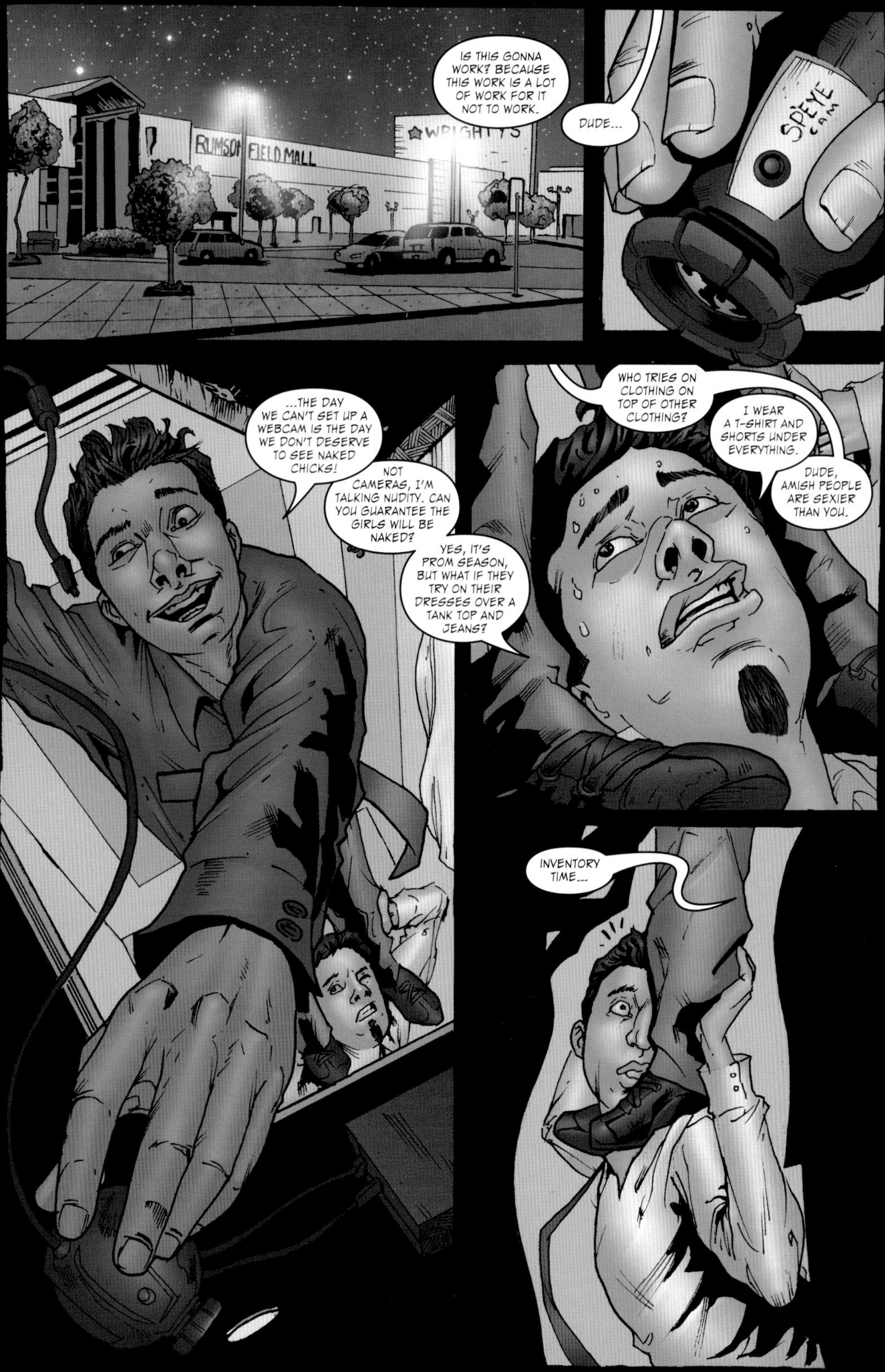
RUMSON FIELD MALL
WRIGHTYS
IS THIS GONNA WORK? BECAUSE THIS WORK IS A LOT OF WORK FOR IT NOT TO WORK.
DUDE...
SPEYE CAM
...THE DAY WE CAN'T SET UP A WEBCAM IS THE DAY WE DON'T DESERVE TO SEE NAKED CHICKS!
NOT CAMERAS, I'M TALKING NUDITY. CAN YOU GUARANTEE THE GIRLS WILL BE NAKED?
YES, IT'S PROM SEASON, BUT WHAT IF THEY TRY ON THEIR DRESSES OVER A TANK TOP AND JEANS?
WHO TRIES ON CLOTHING ON TOP OF OTHER CLOTHING?
I WEAR A T-SHIRT AND SHORTS UNDER EVERYTHING.
DUDE, AMISH PEOPLE ARE SEXIER THAN YOU.
INVENTORY TIME...

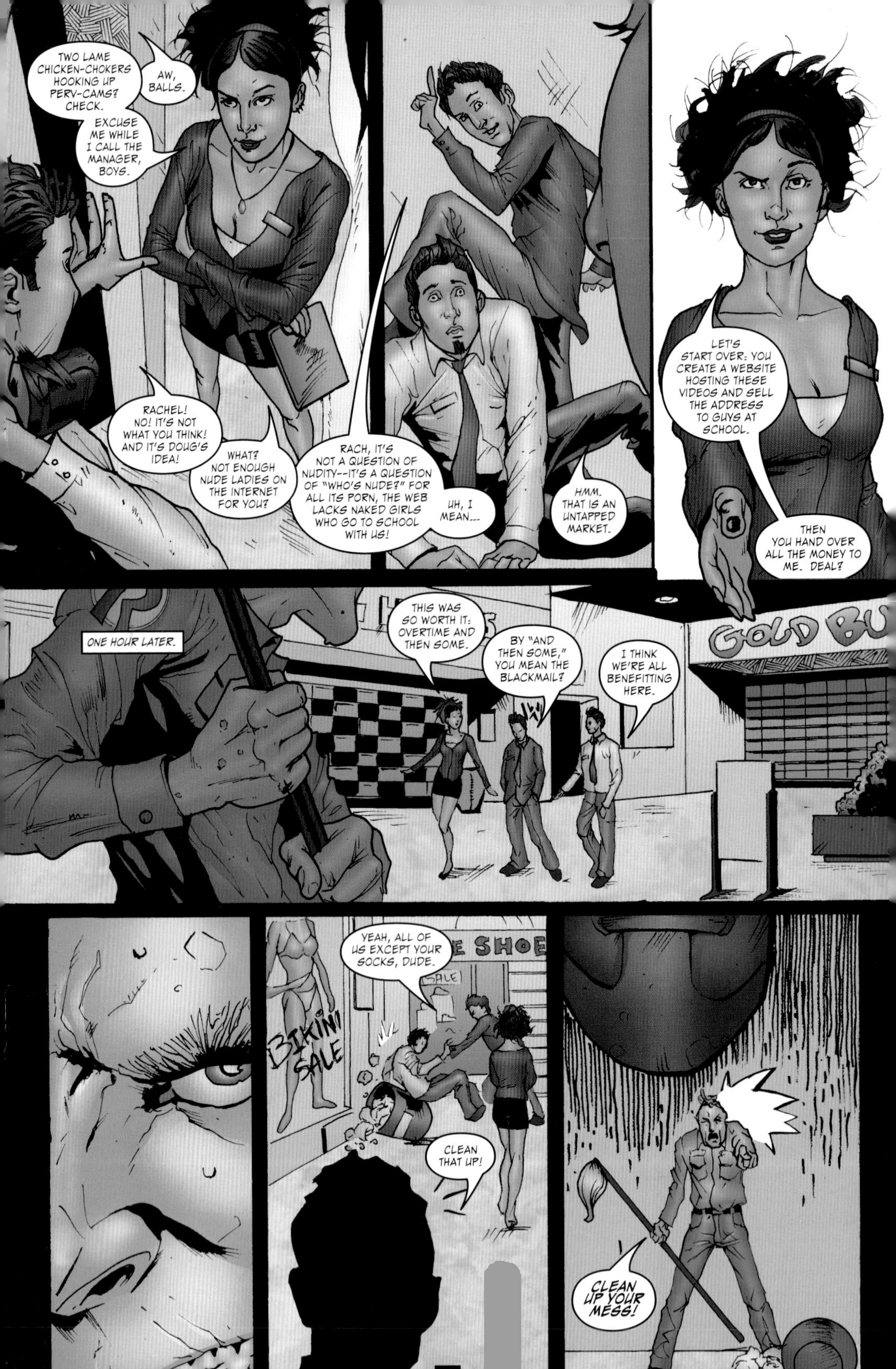
TWO LAME CHICKEN-CHOKERS HOOKING UP PERV-CAMS? CHECK.
AW, BALLS.
EXCUSE ME WHILE I CALL THE MANAGER, BOYS.
RACHEL! NO! IT'S NOT WHAT YOU THINK! AND IT'S DOUG'S IDEA!
WHAT? NOT ENOUGH NUDE LADIES ON THE INTERNET FOR YOU?
RACH, IT'S NOT A QUESTION OF NUDITY--IT'S A QUESTION OF "WHO'S NUDE?" FOR ALL ITS PORN, THE WEB LACKS NAKED GIRLS WHO GO TO SCHOOL WITH US!
UH, I MEAN...
HMM. THAT IS AN UNTAPPED MARKET.
LET'S START OVER: YOU CREATE A WEBSITE HOSTING THESE VIDEOS AND SELL THE ADDRESS TO GUYS AT SCHOOL.
THEN YOU HAND OVER ALL THE MONEY TO ME. DEAL?
ONE HOUR LATER.
THIS WAS SO WORTH IT: OVERTIME AND THEN SOME.
BY "AND THEN SOME," YOU MEAN THE BLACKMAIL?
I THINK WE'RE ALL BENEFITTING HERE.
GOLD BU
YEAH, ALL OF US EXCEPT YOUR SOCKS, DUDE.
E SHOE
SALE
BIKINI SALE
CLEAN THAT UP!
CLEAN UP YOUR MESS!

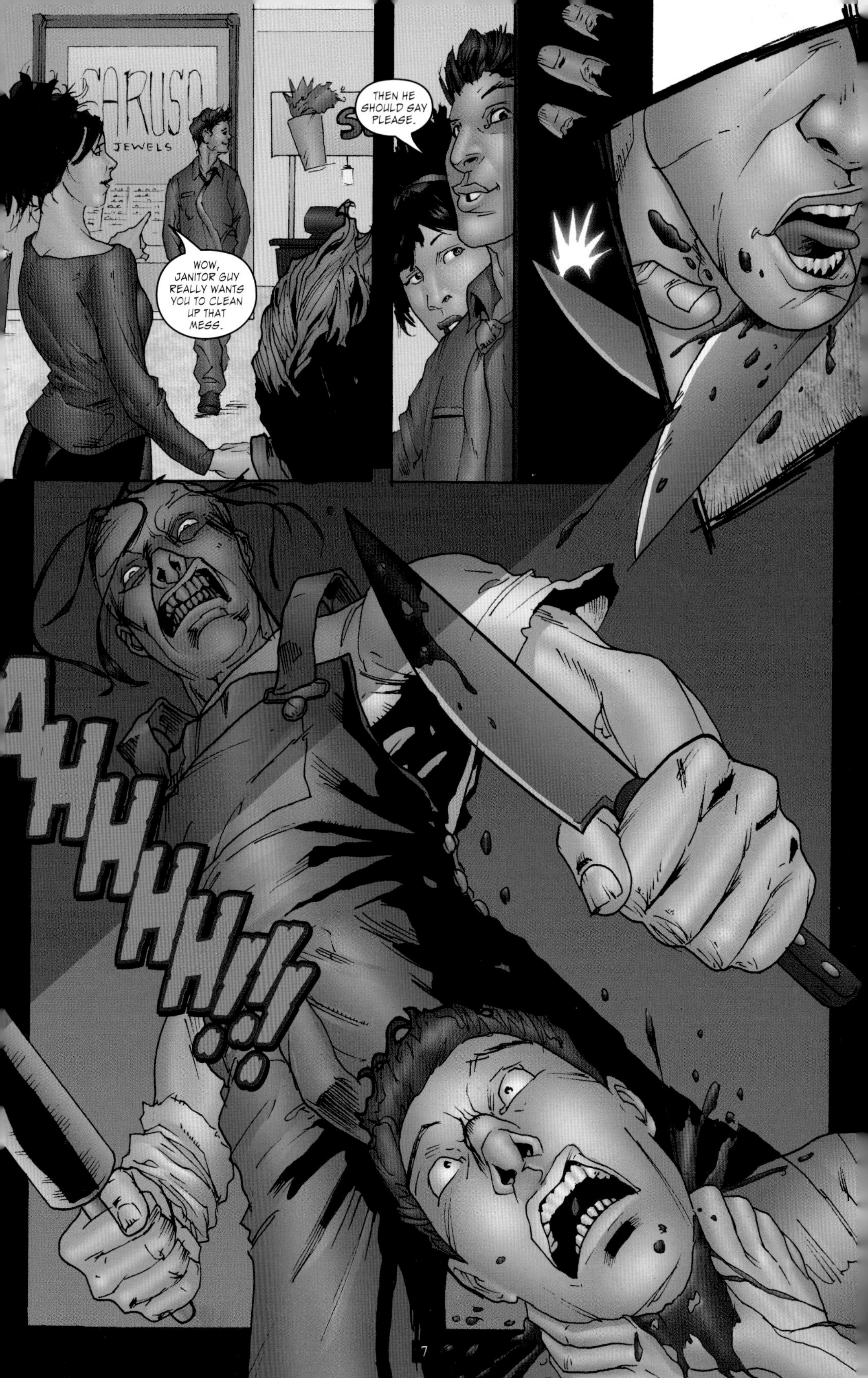
CARUSO
JEWELS
WOW, JANITOR GUY REALLY WANTS YOU TO CLEAN UP THAT MESS.
THEN HE SHOULD SAY PLEASE.
AHHHHH!!

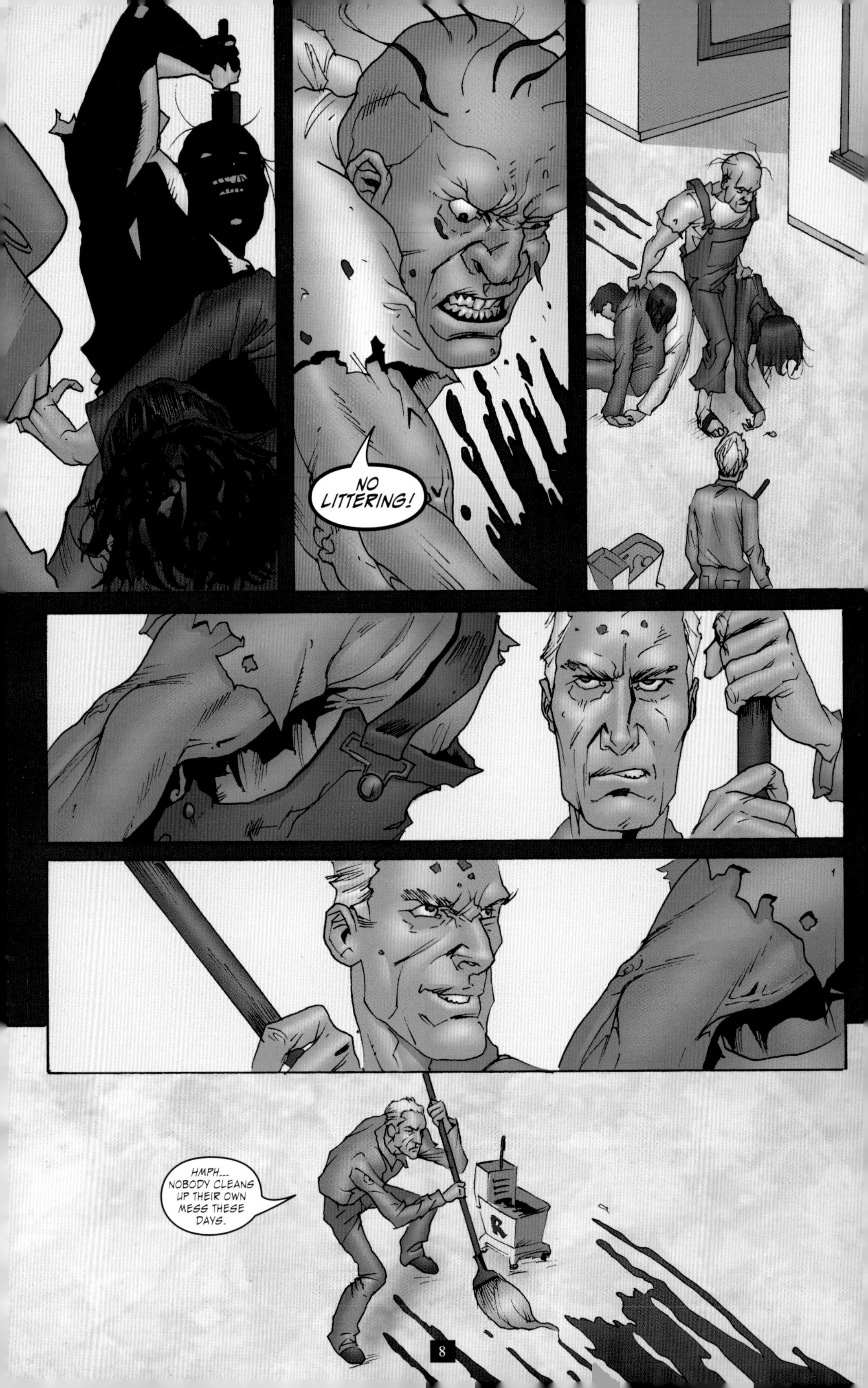
NO LITTERING!
HMPH... NOBODY CLEANS UP THEIR OWN MESS THESE DAYS.

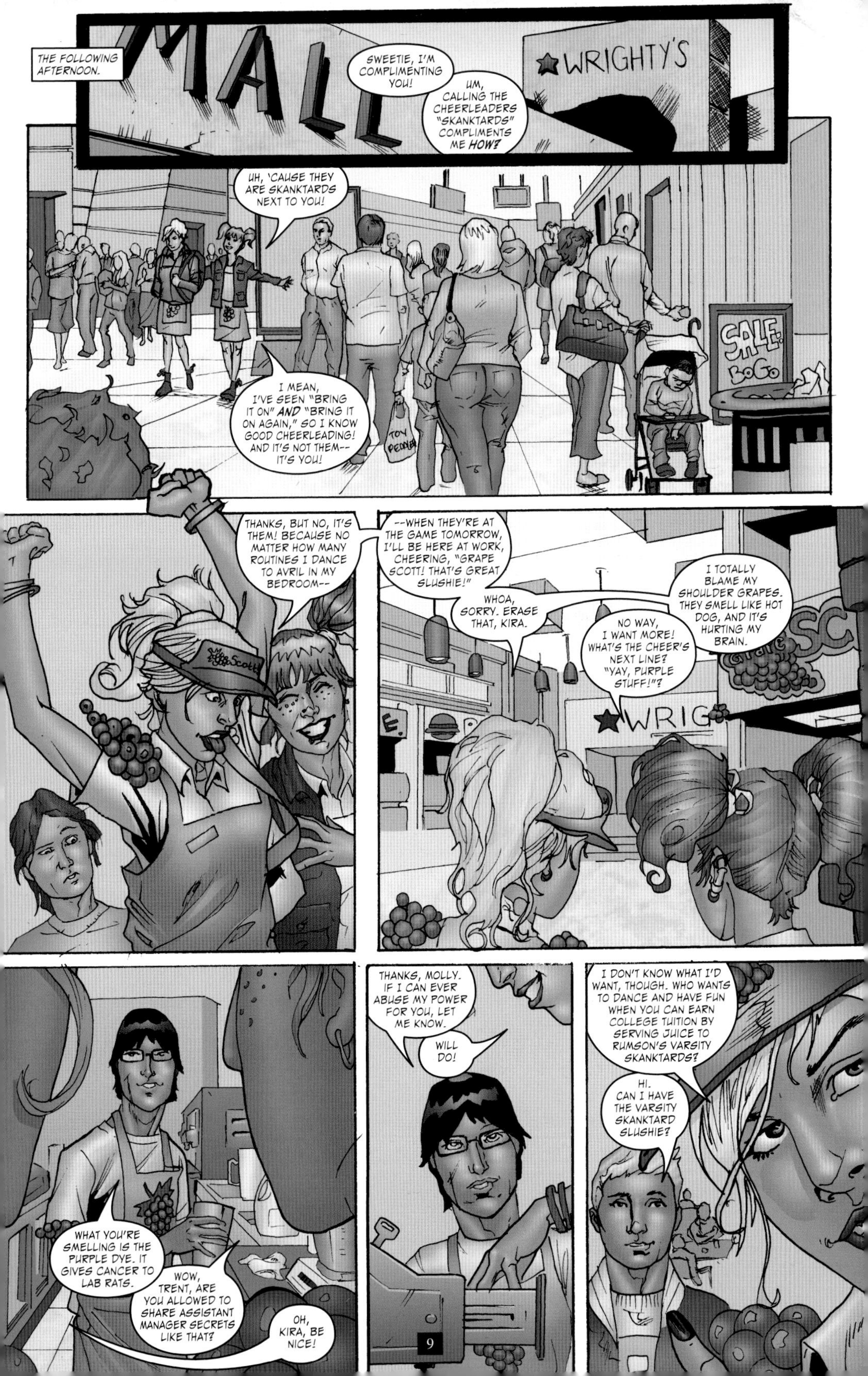
MALL
WRIGHTY'S
THE FOLLOWING AFTERNOON.
SWEETIE, I'M COMPLIMENTING YOU!
UM, CALLING THE CHEERLEADERS "SKANKTARDS" COMPLIMENTS ME HOW?
UH, 'CAUSE THEY ARE SKANKTARDS NEXT TO YOU!
I MEAN, I'VE SEEN "BRING IT ON" AND "BRING IT ON AGAIN," SO I KNOW GOOD CHEERLEADING! AND IT'S NOT THEM-- IT'S YOU!
SALE BoGo
TOY PEDDLER
THANKS, BUT NO, IT'S THEM! BECAUSE NO MATTER HOW MANY ROUTINES I DANCE TO AVRIL IN MY BEDROOM--
--WHEN THEY'RE AT THE GAME TOMORROW, I'LL BE HERE AT WORK, CHEERING, "GRAPE SCOTT! THAT'S GREAT SLUSHIE!"
WHOA, SORRY. ERASE THAT, KIRA.
I TOTALLY BLAME MY SHOULDER GRAPES. THEY SMELL LIKE HOT DOG, AND IT'S HURTING MY BRAIN.
NO WAY, I WANT MORE! WHAT'S THE CHEER'S NEXT LINE? "YAY, PURPLE STUFF!"?
WRIG
WHAT YOU'RE SMELLING IS THE PURPLE DYE. IT GIVES CANCER TO LAB RATS.
WOW, TRENT, ARE YOU ALLOWED TO SHARE ASSISTANT MANAGER SECRETS LIKE THAT?
OH, KIRA, BE NICE!
THANKS, MOLLY. IF I CAN EVER ABUSE MY POWER FOR YOU, LET ME KNOW.
WILL DO!
I DON'T KNOW WHAT I'D WANT, THOUGH. WHO WANTS TO DANCE AND HAVE FUN WHEN YOU CAN EARN COLLEGE TUITION BY SERVING JUICE TO RUMSON'S VARSITY SKANKTARDS?
HI. CAN I HAVE THE VARSITY SKANKTARD SLUSHIE?

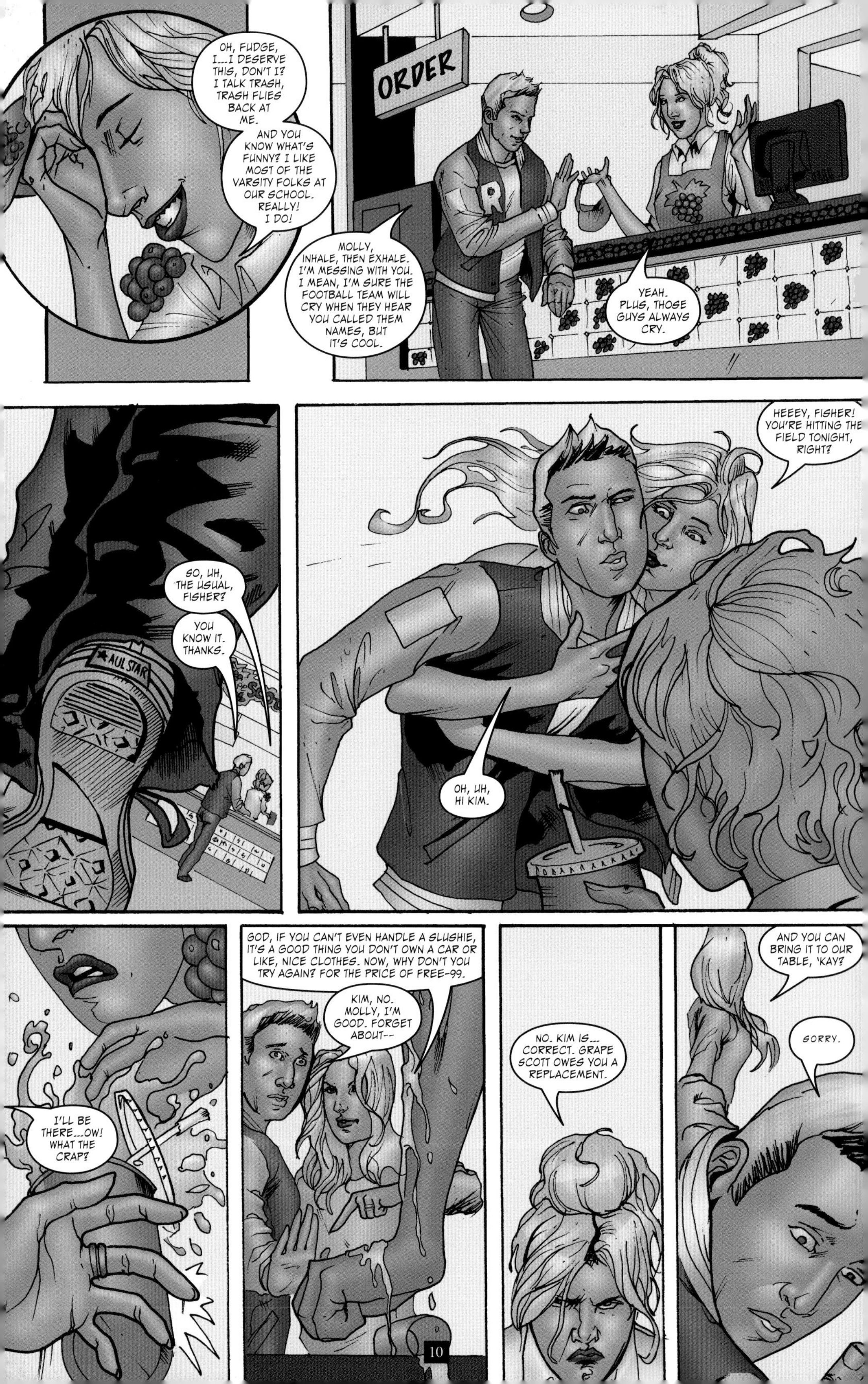
OH, FUDGE, I...I DESERVE THIS, DON'T I? I TALK TRASH, TRASH FLIES BACK AT ME.
AND YOU KNOW WHAT'S FUNNY? I LIKE MOST OF THE VARSITY FOLKS AT OUR SCHOOL. REALLY! I DO!
ORDER
MOLLY, INHALE, THEN EXHALE. I'M MESSING WITH YOU. I MEAN, I'M SURE THE FOOTBALL TEAM WILL CRY WHEN THEY HEAR YOU CALLED THEM NAMES, BUT IT'S COOL.
YEAH. PLUS, THOSE GUYS ALWAYS CRY.
SO, UH, THE USUAL, FISHER?
YOU KNOW IT. THANKS.
AUL STAR
HEEEY, FISHER! YOU'RE HITTING THE FIELD TONIGHT, RIGHT?
OH, UH, HI KIM.
I'LL BE THERE...OW! WHAT THE CRAP?
GOD, IF YOU CAN'T EVEN HANDLE A SLUSHIE, IT'S A GOOD THING YOU DON'T OWN A CAR OR LIKE, NICE CLOTHES. NOW, WHY DON'T YOU TRY AGAIN? FOR THE PRICE OF FREE-99.
KIM, NO. MOLLY, I'M GOOD. FORGET ABOUT--
NO. KIM IS... CORRECT. GRAPE SCOTT OWES YOU A REPLACEMENT.
AND YOU CAN BRING IT TO OUR TABLE, 'KAY?
SORRY.

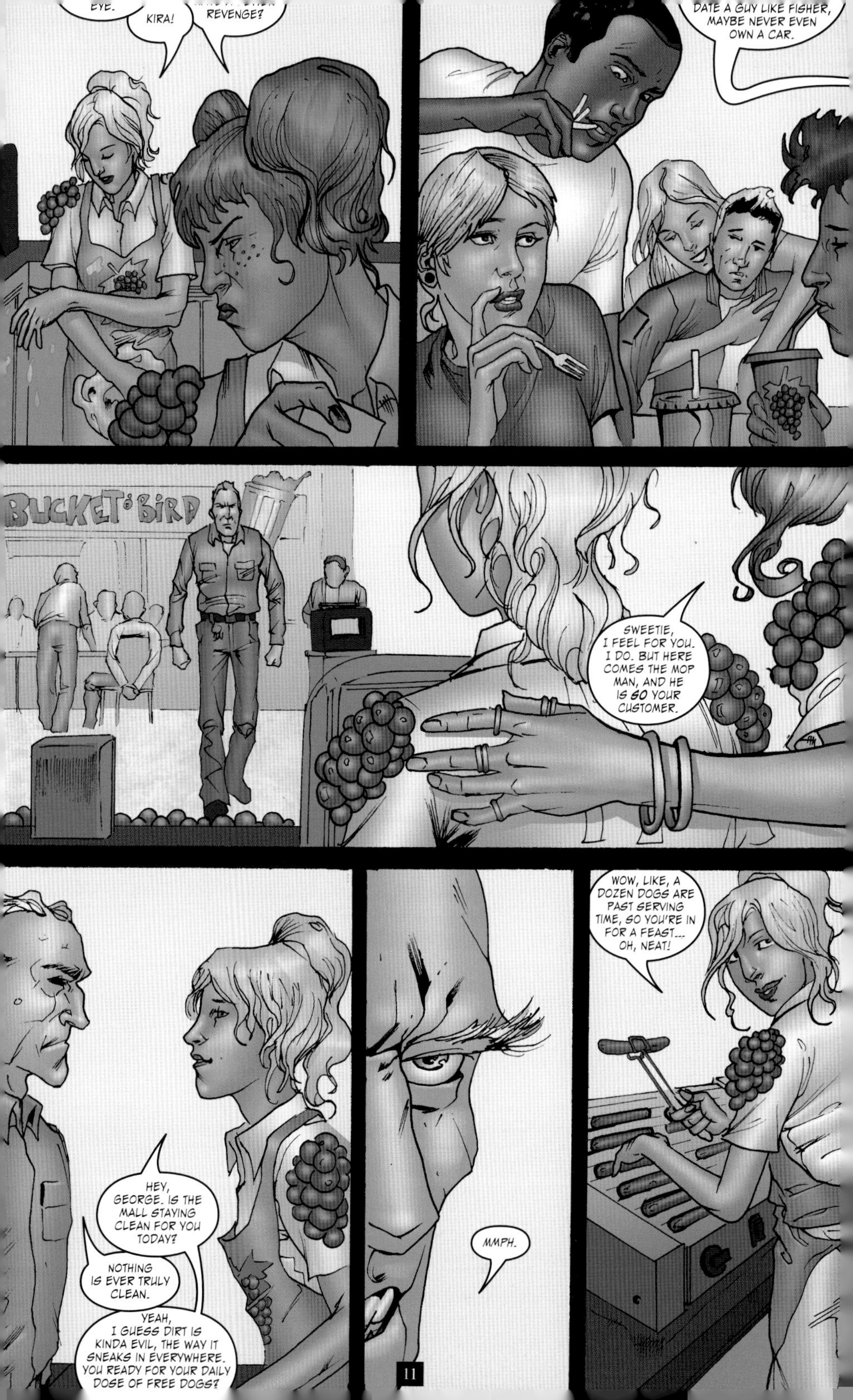
EYE.
KIRA!
REVENGE?
DATE A GUY LIKE FISHER, MAYBE NEVER EVEN OWN A CAR.
BUCKET O' BIRD
SWEETIE, I FEEL FOR YOU. I DO. BUT HERE COMES THE MOP MAN, AND HE IS SO YOUR CUSTOMER.
HEY, GEORGE. IS THE MALL STAYING CLEAN FOR YOU TODAY?
NOTHING IS EVER TRULY CLEAN.
YEAH, I GUESS DIRT IS KINDA EVIL, THE WAY IT SNEAKS IN EVERYWHERE. YOU READY FOR YOUR DAILY DOSE OF FREE DOGS?
MMPH.
WOW, LIKE, A DOZEN DOGS ARE PAST SERVING TIME, SO YOU'RE IN FOR A FEAST... OH, NEAT!

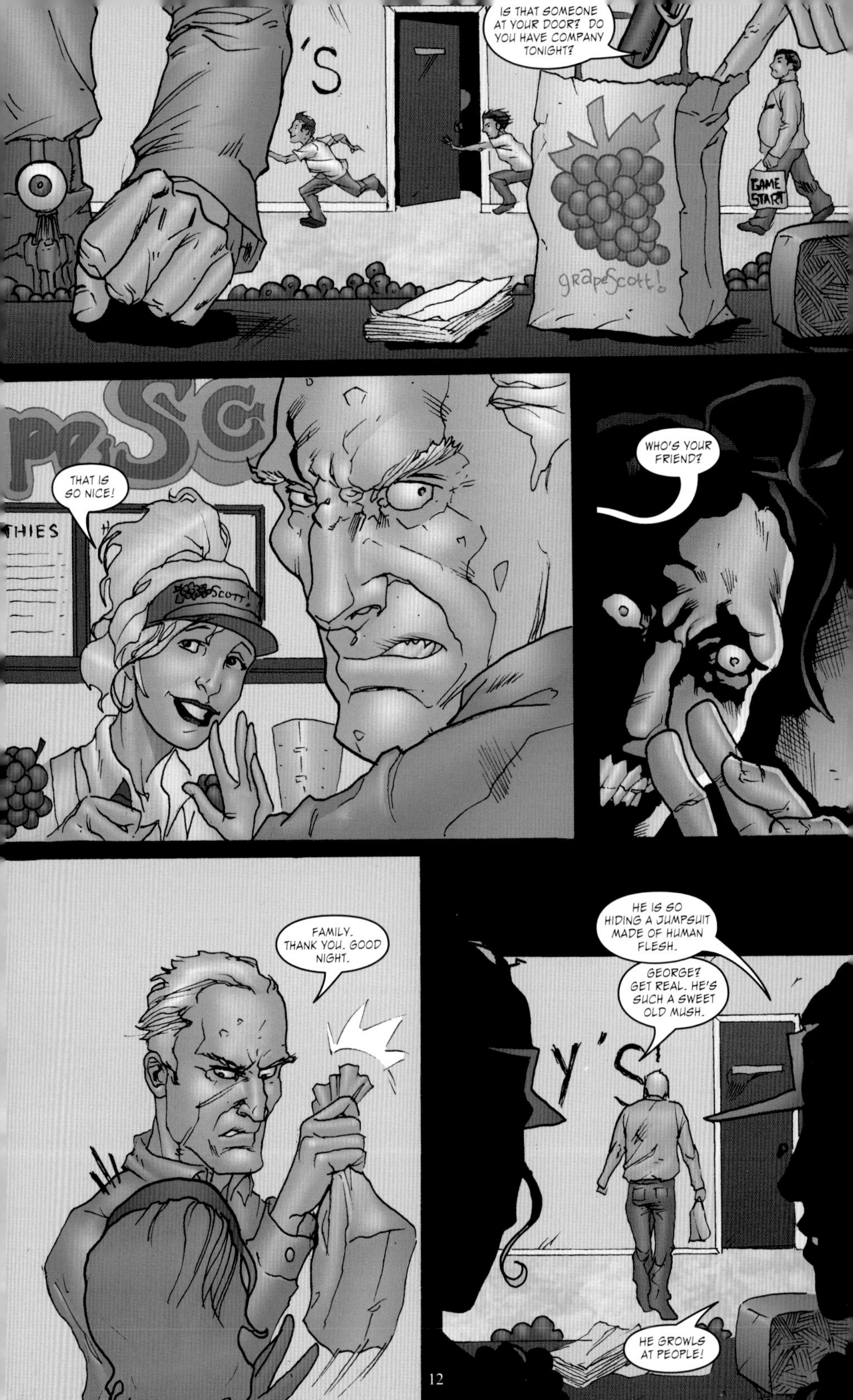
IS THAT SOMEONE AT YOUR DOOR? DO YOU HAVE COMPANY TONIGHT?
'S
GAME START
grapeScott!
THAT IS SO NICE!
THIES
WHO'S YOUR FRIEND?
FAMILY. THANK YOU. GOOD NIGHT.
HE IS SO HIDING A JUMPSUIT MADE OF HUMAN FLESH.
GEORGE? GET REAL. HE'S SUCH A SWEET OLD MUSH.
Y'S
HE GROWLS AT PEOPLE!

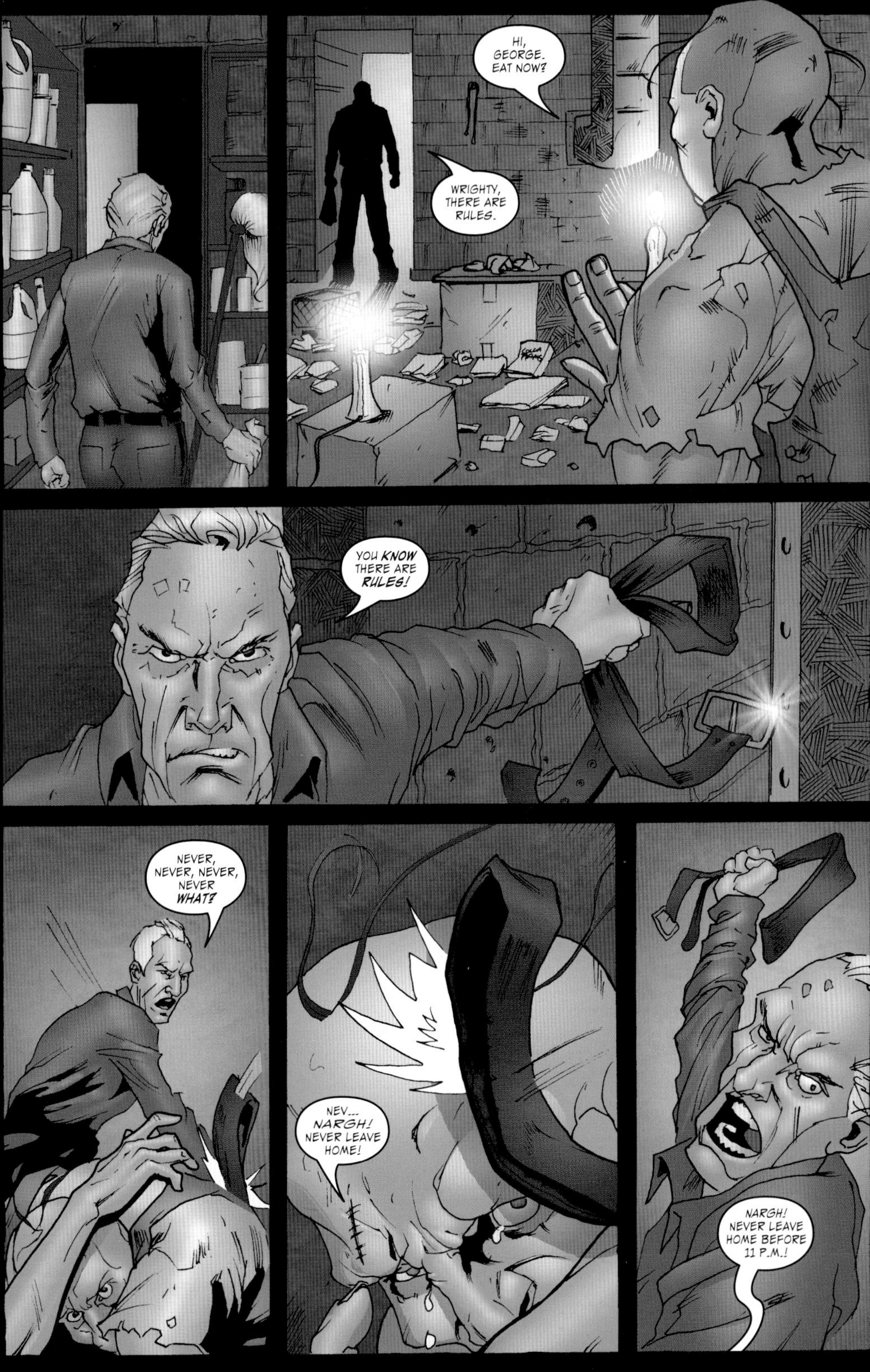
HI, GEORGE. EAT NOW?
WRIGHTY, THERE ARE RULES.
YOU KNOW THERE ARE RULES!
NEVER, NEVER, NEVER, NEVER WHAT?
NEV... NARGH! NEVER LEAVE HOME!
NARGH! NEVER LEAVE HOME BEFORE 11 P.M.!

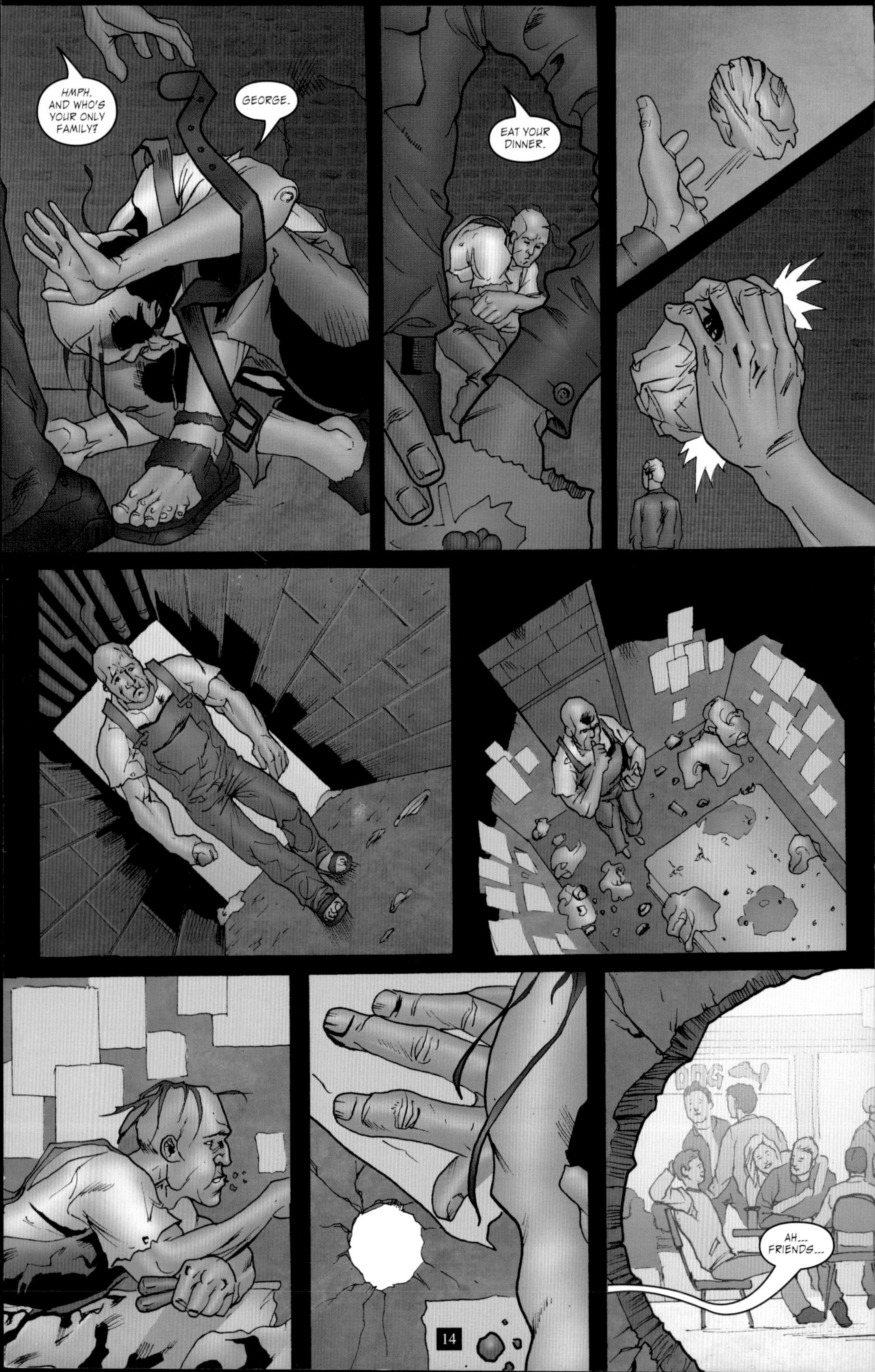
HMPH. AND WHO'S YOUR ONLY FAMILY?
GEORGE.
EAT YOUR DINNER.
AH... FRIENDS...

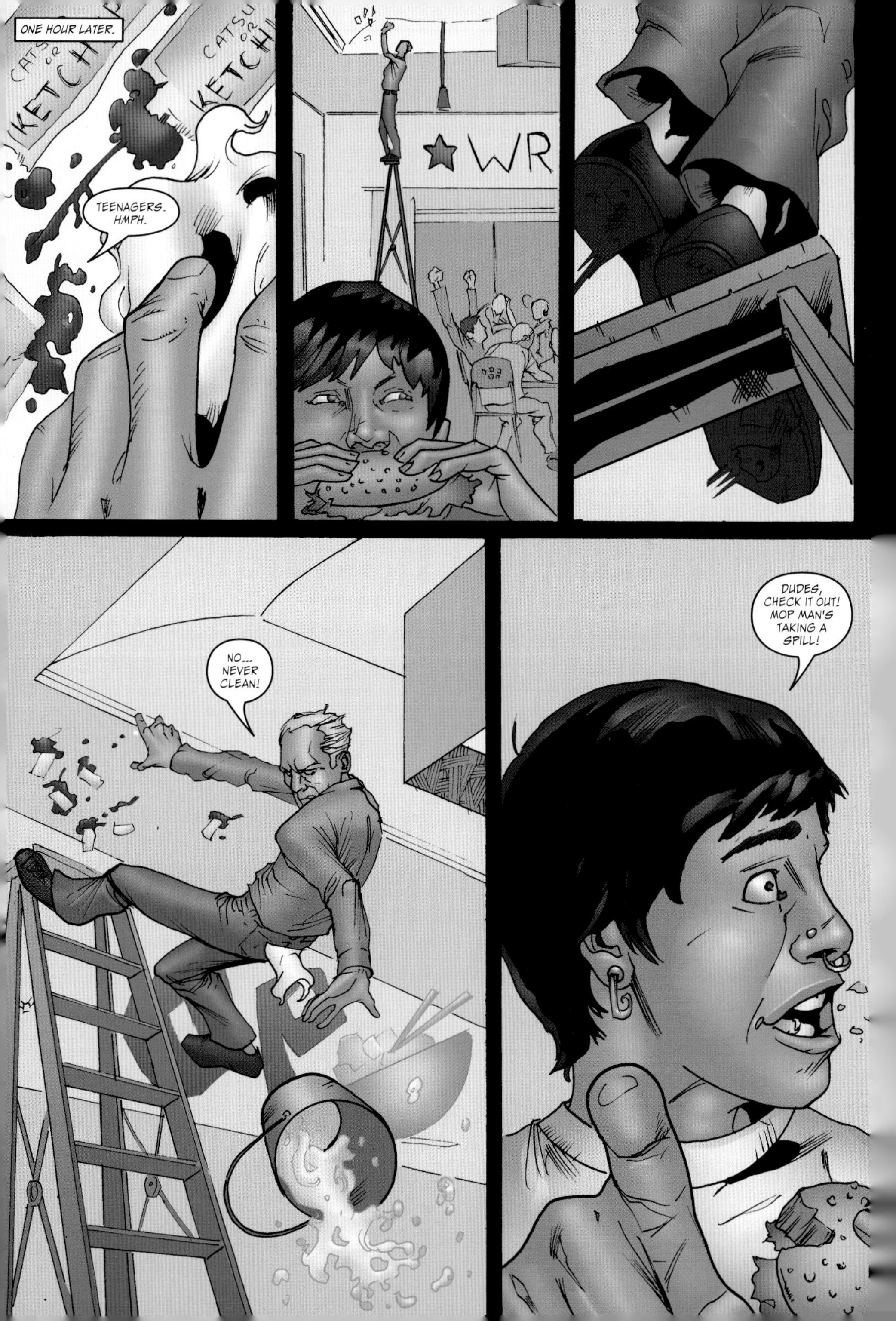
ONE HOUR LATER.
CATSUP OR KETCHUP
TEENAGERS. HMPH.
WR
NO... NEVER CLEAN!
DUDES, CHECK IT OUT! MOP MAN'S TAKING A SPILL!

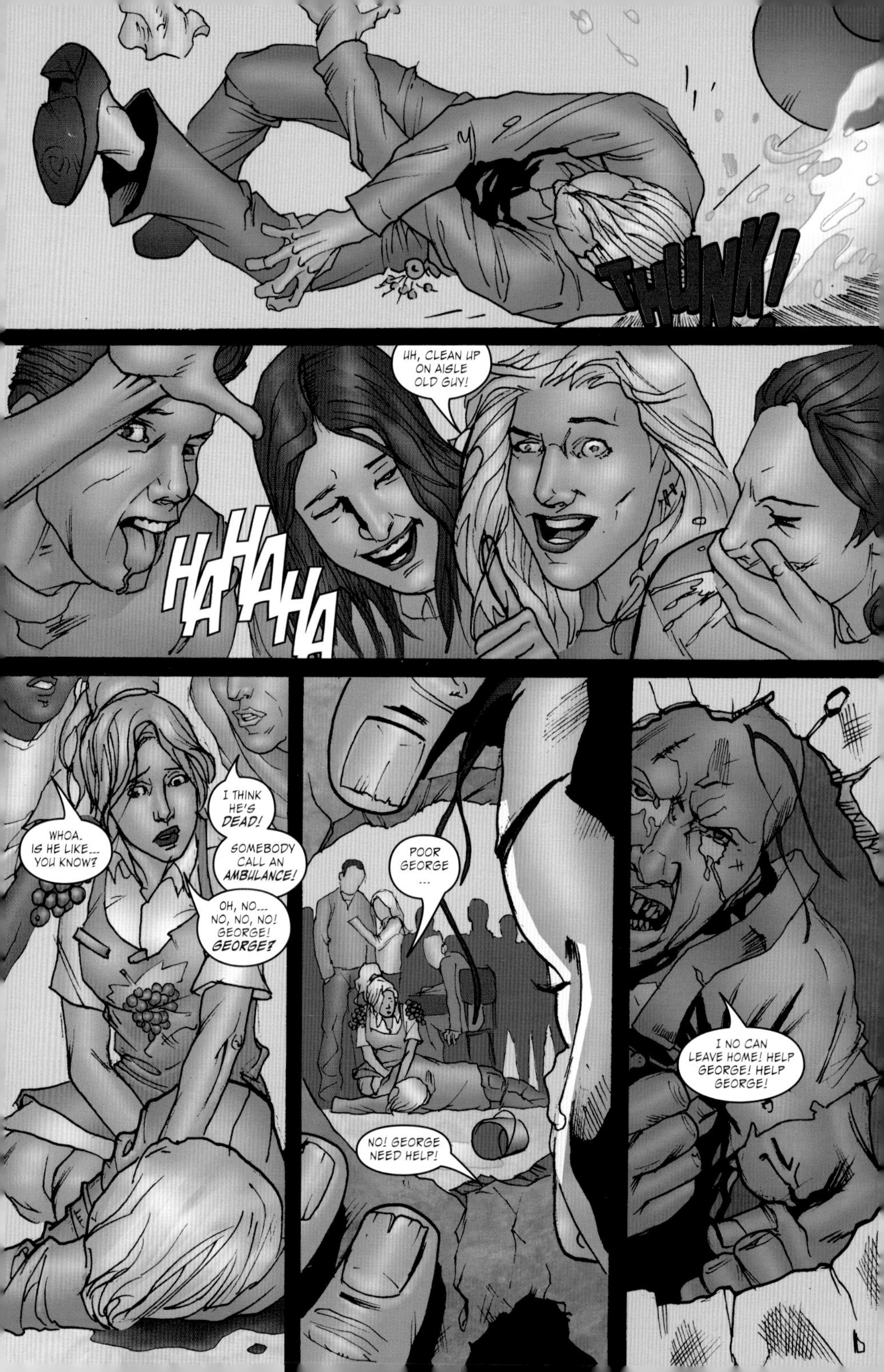
THUNK!
UH, CLEAN UP ON AISLE OLD GUY!
HAHAHAHA
WHOA. IS HE LIKE... YOU KNOW?
I THINK HE'S DEAD!
SOMEBODY CALL AN AMBULANCE!
OH, NO... NO, NO, NO! GEORGE! GEORGE?
POOR GEORGE ...
NO! GEORGE NEED HELP!
I NO CAN LEAVE HOME! HELP GEORGE! HELP GEORGE!

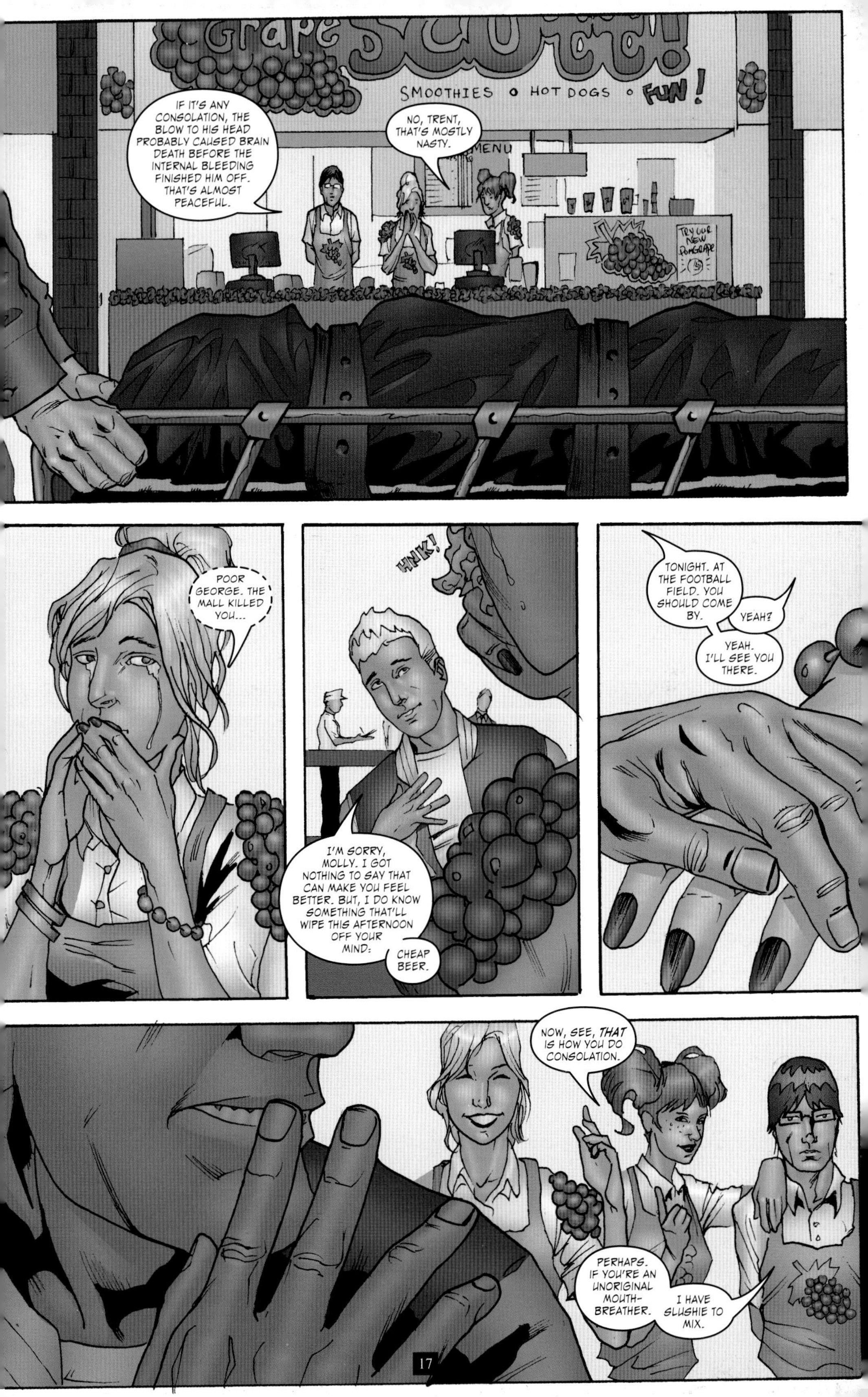
Grape SCUTTLE
SMOOTHIES HOT DOGS FUN!
MENU
TRY OUR NEW POMGRAPE
IF IT'S ANY CONSOLATION, THE BLOW TO HIS HEAD PROBABLY CAUSED BRAIN DEATH BEFORE THE INTERNAL BLEEDING FINISHED HIM OFF. THAT'S ALMOST PEACEFUL.
NO, TRENT, THAT'S MOSTLY NASTY.
POOR GEORGE. THE MALL KILLED YOU...
HNK!
I'M SORRY, MOLLY. I GOT NOTHING TO SAY THAT CAN MAKE YOU FEEL BETTER. BUT, I DO KNOW SOMETHING THAT'LL WIPE THIS AFTERNOON OFF YOUR MIND:
CHEAP BEER.
TONIGHT. AT THE FOOTBALL FIELD. YOU SHOULD COME BY.
YEAH?
YEAH. I'LL SEE YOU THERE.
NOW, SEE, THAT IS HOW YOU DO CONSOLATION.
PERHAPS. IF YOU'RE AN UNORIGINAL MOUTH-BREATHER.
I HAVE SLUSHIE TO MIX.

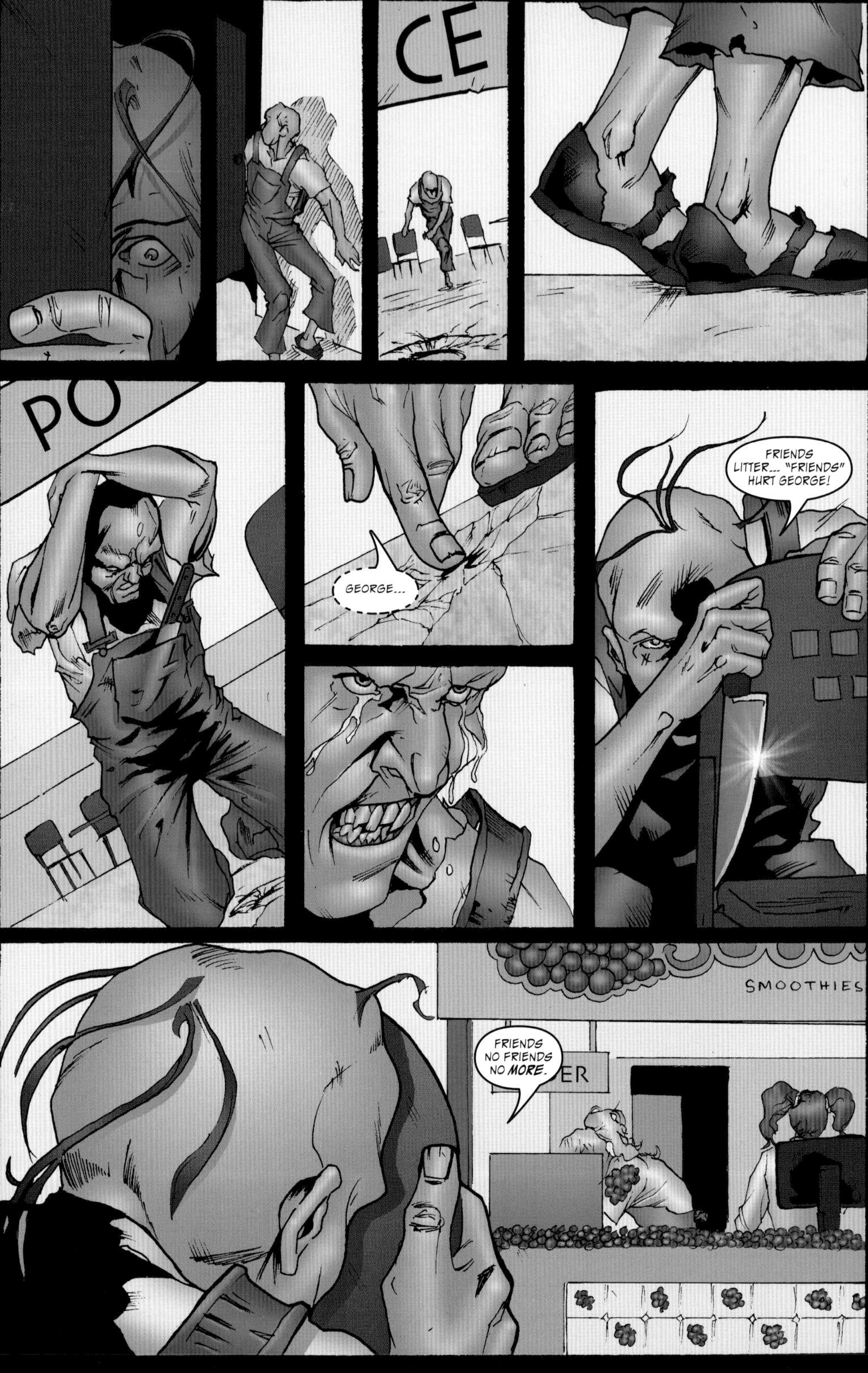
CE
PO
GEORGE...
FRIENDS
LITTER... "FRIENDS"
HURT GEORGE!
SMOOTHIES
FRIENDS
NO FRIENDS
NO *MORE*.
ER

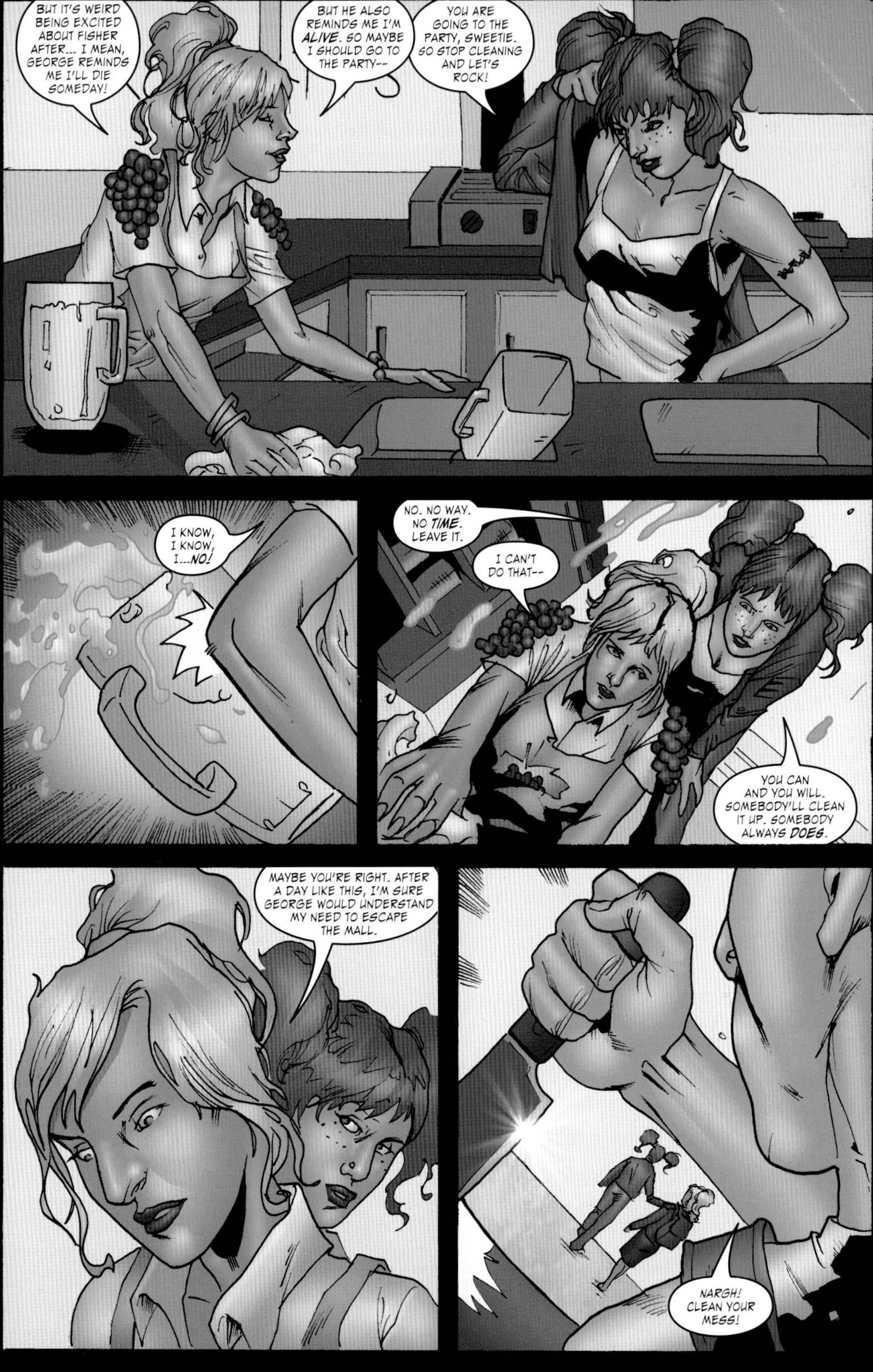

BUT IT'S WEIRD BEING EXCITED ABOUT FISHER AFTER... I MEAN, GEORGE REMINDS ME I'LL DIE SOMEDAY!
BUT HE ALSO REMINDS ME I'M ALIVE. SO MAYBE I SHOULD GO TO THE PARTY--
YOU ARE GOING TO THE PARTY, SWEETIE. SO STOP CLEANING AND LET'S ROCK!
I KNOW, I KNOW, I...NO!
NO. NO WAY. NO TIME. LEAVE IT.
I CAN'T DO THAT--
YOU CAN AND YOU WILL. SOMEBODY'LL CLEAN IT UP. SOMEBODY ALWAYS DOES.
MAYBE YOU'RE RIGHT. AFTER A DAY LIKE THIS, I'M SURE GEORGE WOULD UNDERSTAND MY NEED TO ESCAPE THE MALL.
NARGH! CLEAN YOUR MESS!

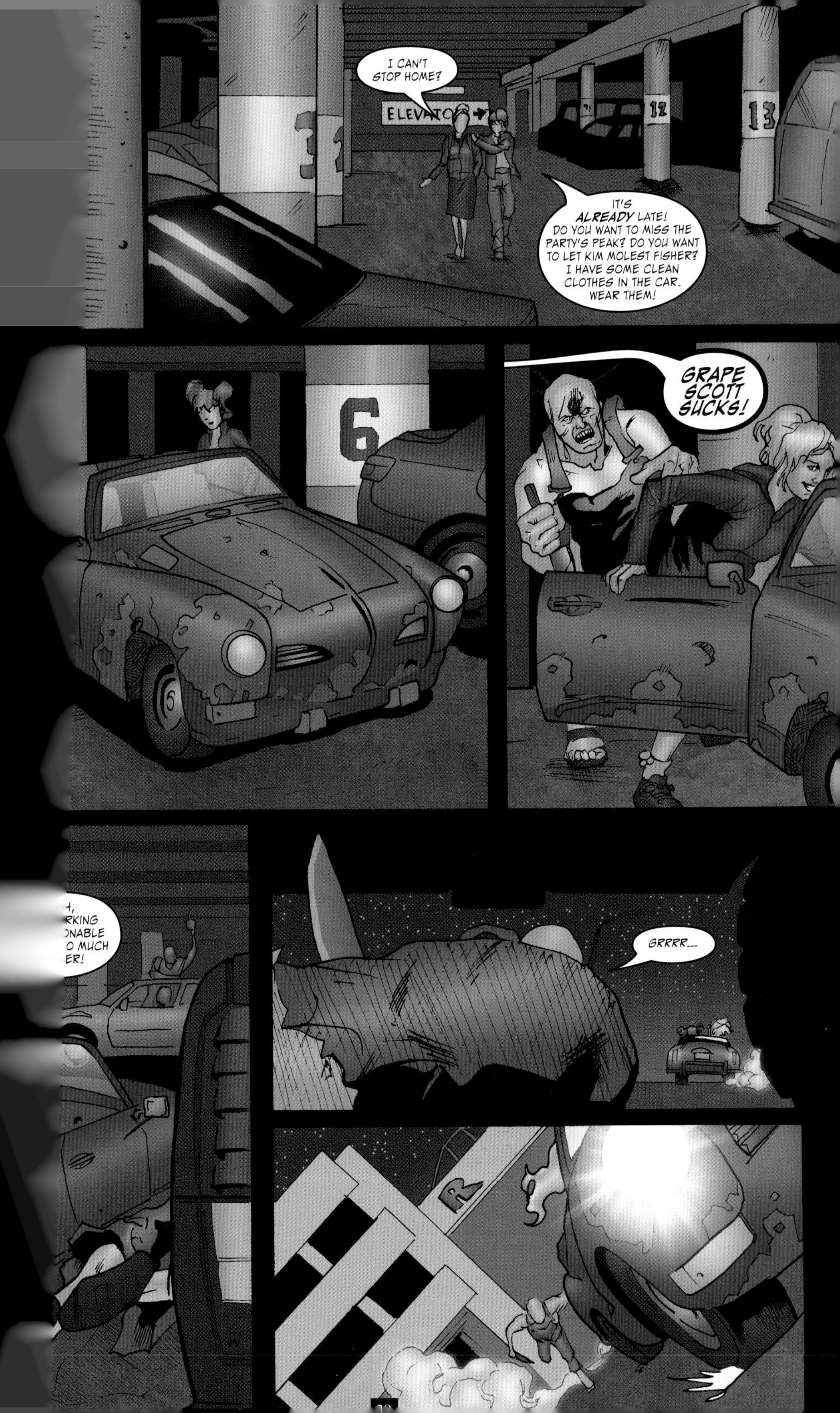
I CAN'T STOP HOME?
ELEVATO
IT'S ALREADY LATE! DO YOU WANT TO MISS THE PARTY'S PEAK? DO YOU WANT TO LET KIM MOLEST FISHER? I HAVE SOME CLEAN CLOTHES IN THE CAR. WEAR THEM!
GRAPE SCOTT SUCKS!
GRRRR...

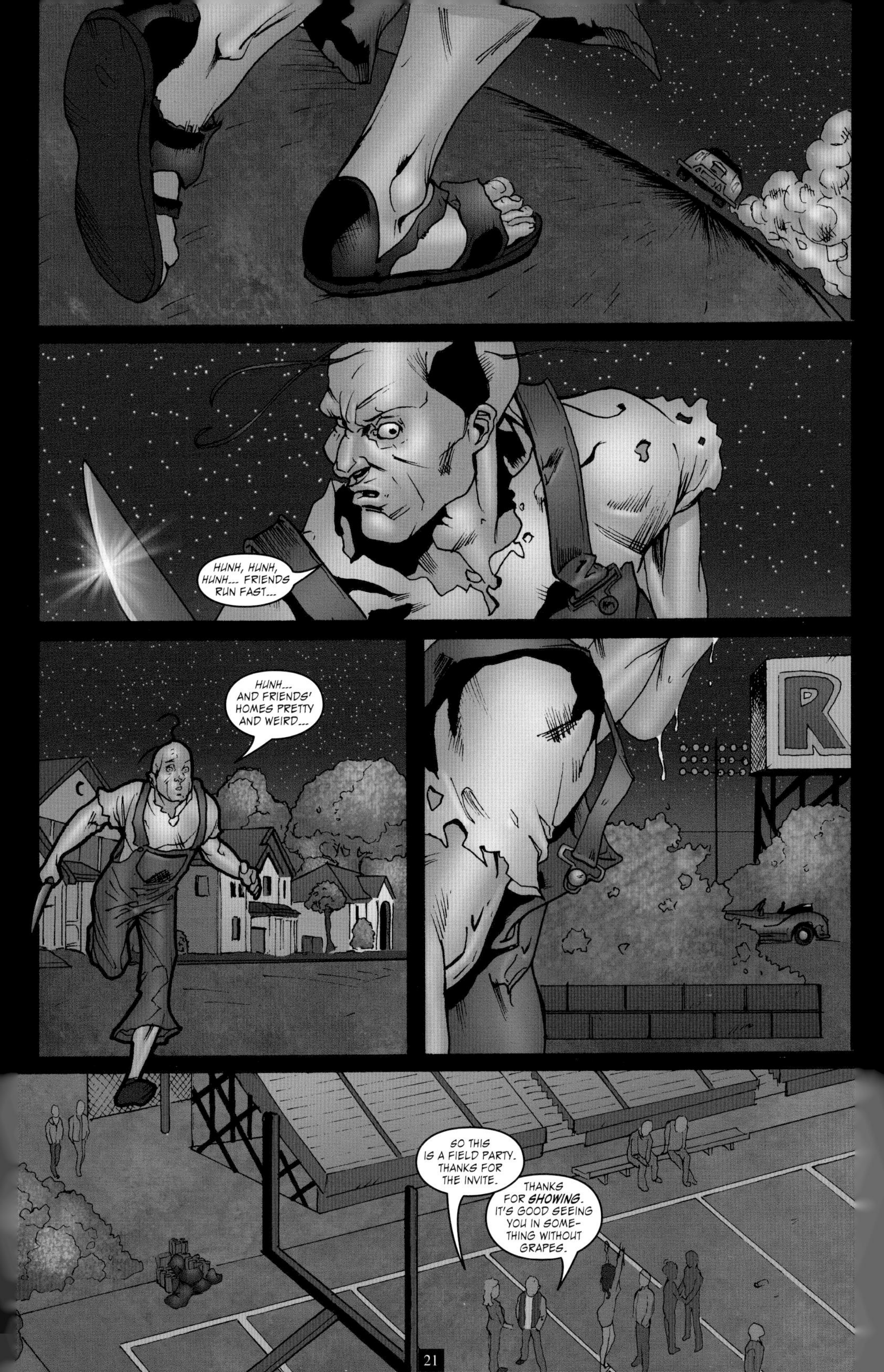
HUNH, HUNH, HUNH--- FRIENDS RUN FAST---
HUNH--- AND FRIENDS' HOMES PRETTY AND WEIRD---
R
SO THIS IS A FIELD PARTY. THANKS FOR THE INVITE.
THANKS FOR *SHOWING*. IT'S GOOD SEEING YOU IN SOME-THING WITHOUT GRAPES.

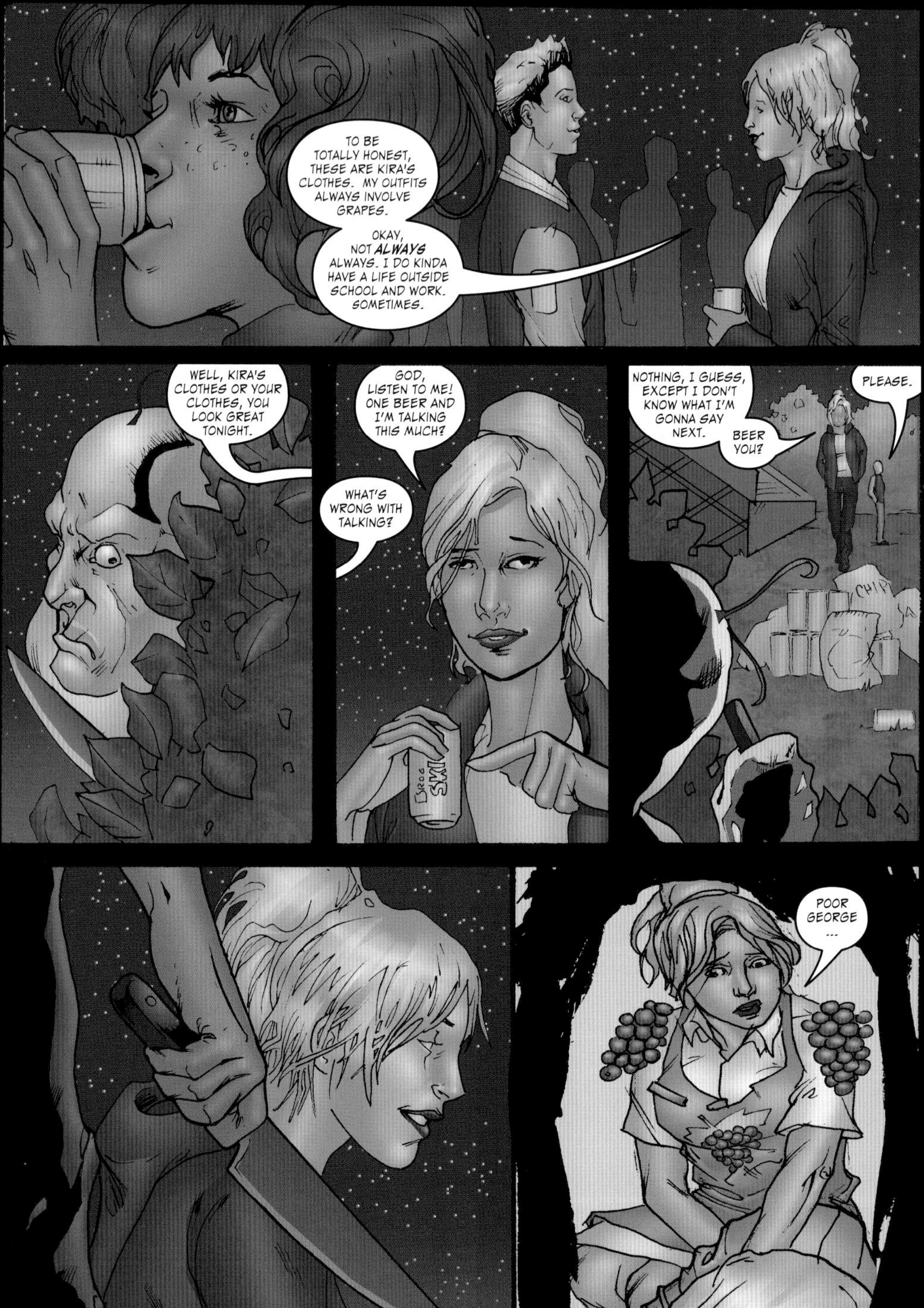
TO BE TOTALLY HONEST, THESE ARE KIRA'S CLOTHES. MY OUTFITS ALWAYS INVOLVE GRAPES.
OKAY, NOT ALWAYS ALWAYS. I DO KINDA HAVE A LIFE OUTSIDE SCHOOL AND WORK. SOMETIMES.
WELL, KIRA'S CLOTHES OR YOUR CLOTHES, YOU LOOK GREAT TONIGHT.
GOD, LISTEN TO ME! ONE BEER AND I'M TALKING THIS MUCH?
WHAT'S WRONG WITH TALKING?
NOTHING, I GUESS, EXCEPT I DON'T KNOW WHAT I'M GONNA SAY NEXT.
BEER YOU?
PLEASE.
POOR GEORGE ...

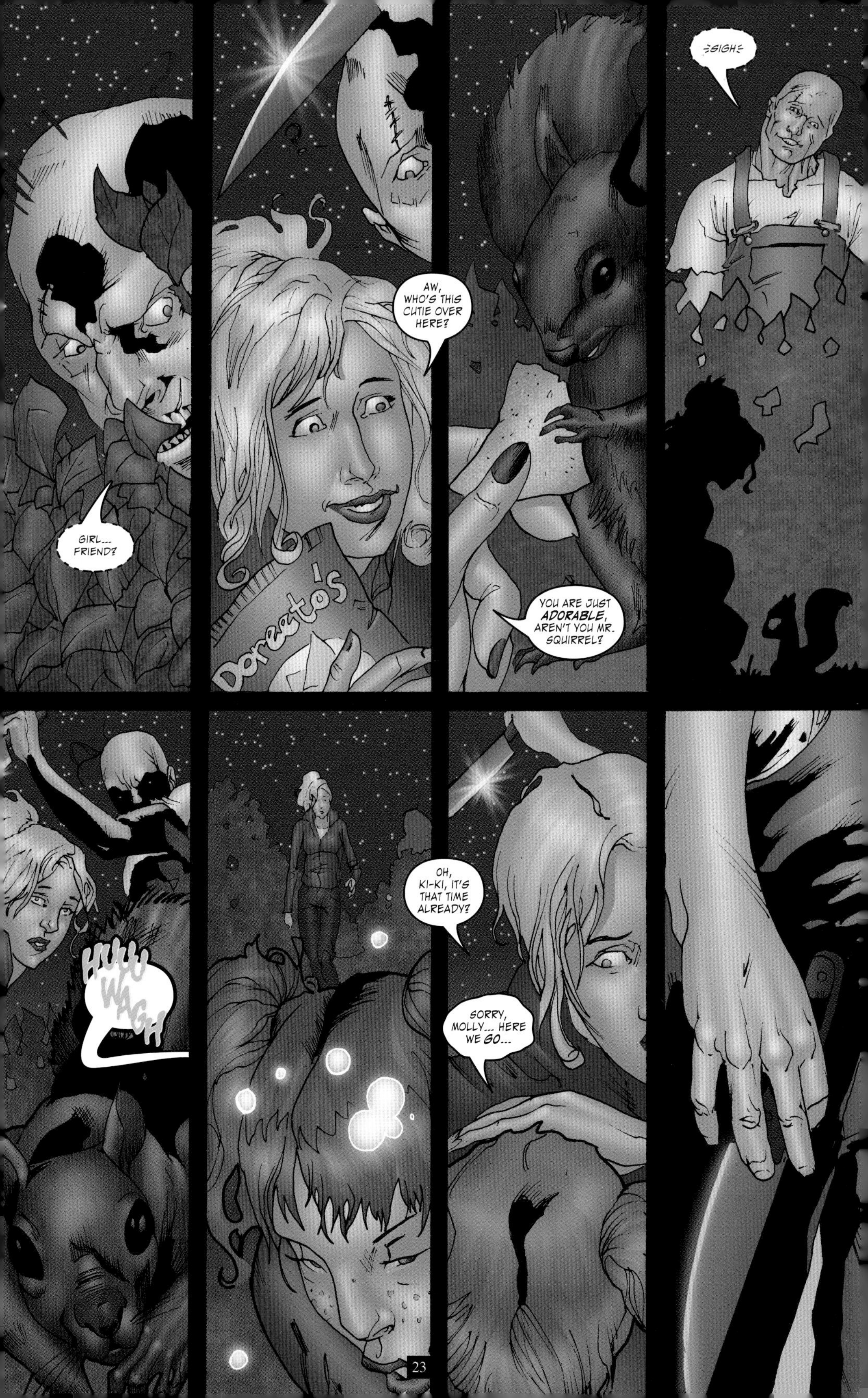
GIRL... FRIEND?
AW, WHO'S THIS CUTIE OVER HERE?
Doreeto's
YOU ARE JUST ADORABLE, AREN'T YOU MR. SQUIRREL?
~SIGH~
HUUU WAGH
OH, KI-KI, IT'S THAT TIME ALREADY?
SORRY, MOLLY... HERE WE GO...

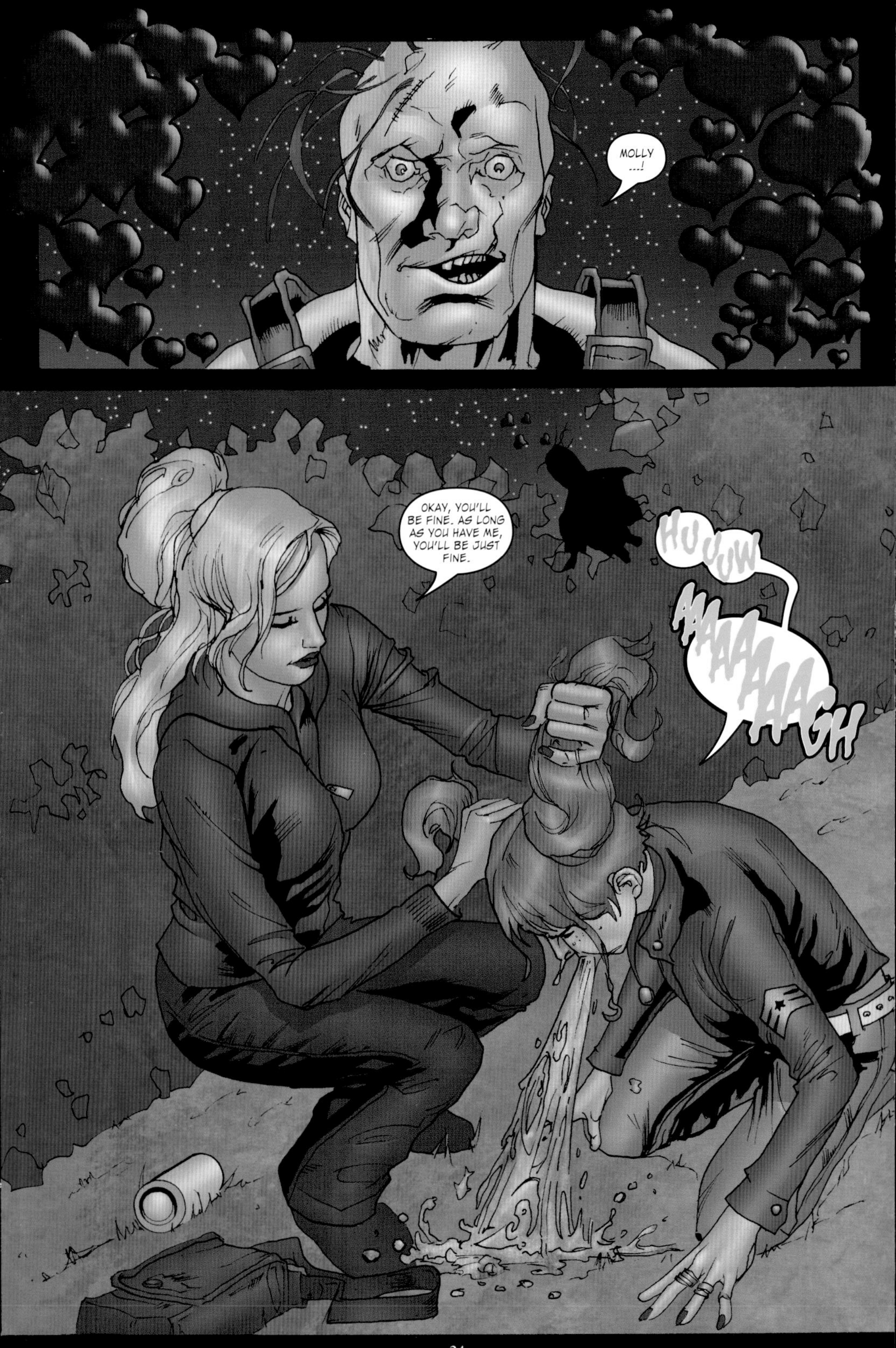
MOLLY ---!
OKAY, YOU'LL BE FINE. AS LONG AS YOU HAVE ME, YOU'LL BE JUST FINE.
HUUUW
AAAAAAAAAAGH

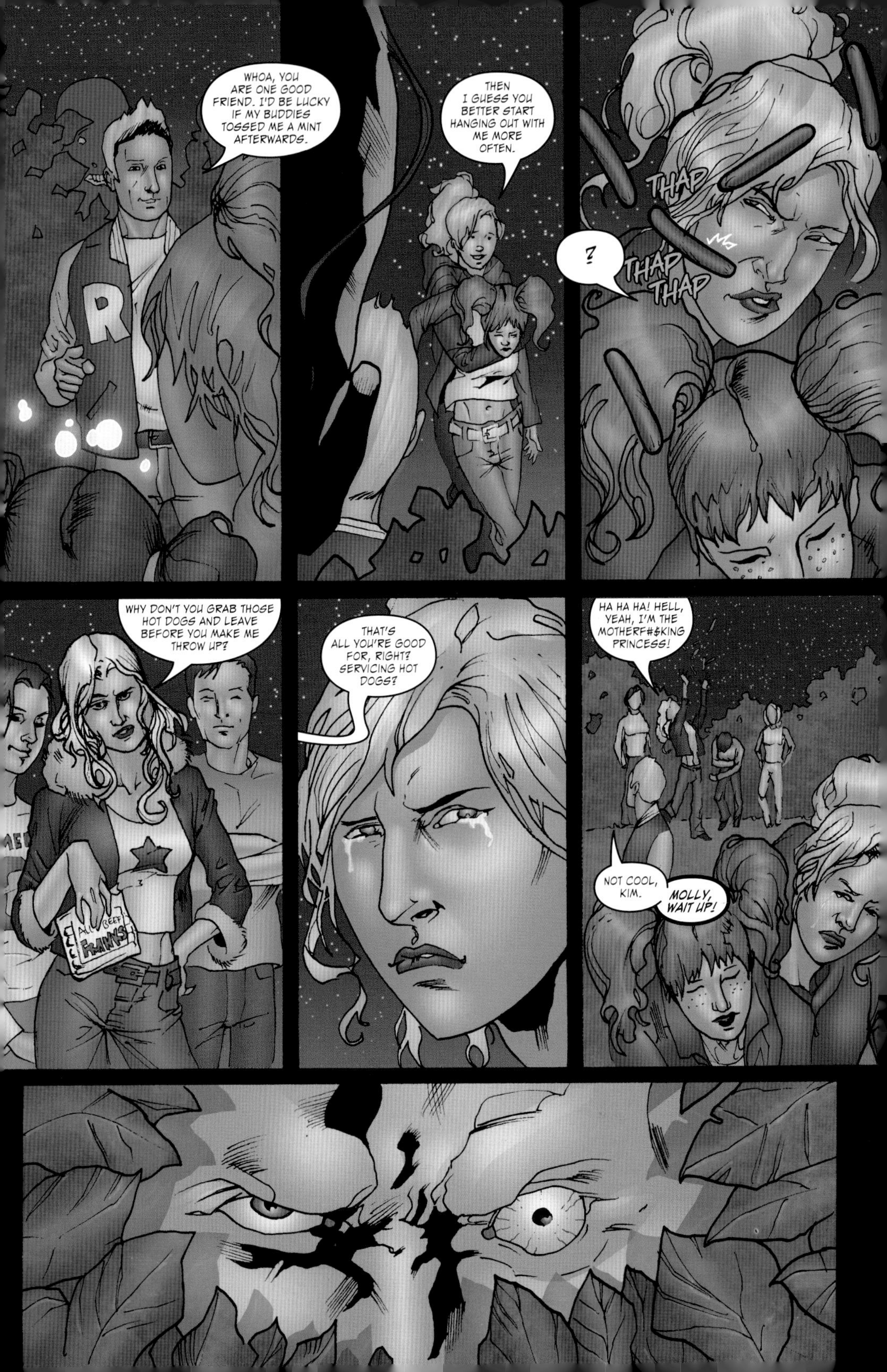
WHOA, YOU ARE ONE GOOD FRIEND. I'D BE LUCKY IF MY BUDDIES TOSSED ME A MINT AFTERWARDS.
THEN I GUESS YOU BETTER START HANGING OUT WITH ME MORE OFTEN.
THAP
?
THAP THAP
WHY DON'T YOU GRAB THOSE HOT DOGS AND LEAVE BEFORE YOU MAKE ME THROW UP?
ALL BEEF FRANKS
THAT'S ALL YOU'RE GOOD FOR, RIGHT? SERVICING HOT DOGS?
HA HA HA! HELL, YEAH, I'M THE MOTHERF#$KING PRINCESS!
NOT COOL, KIM.
MOLLY, WAIT UP!

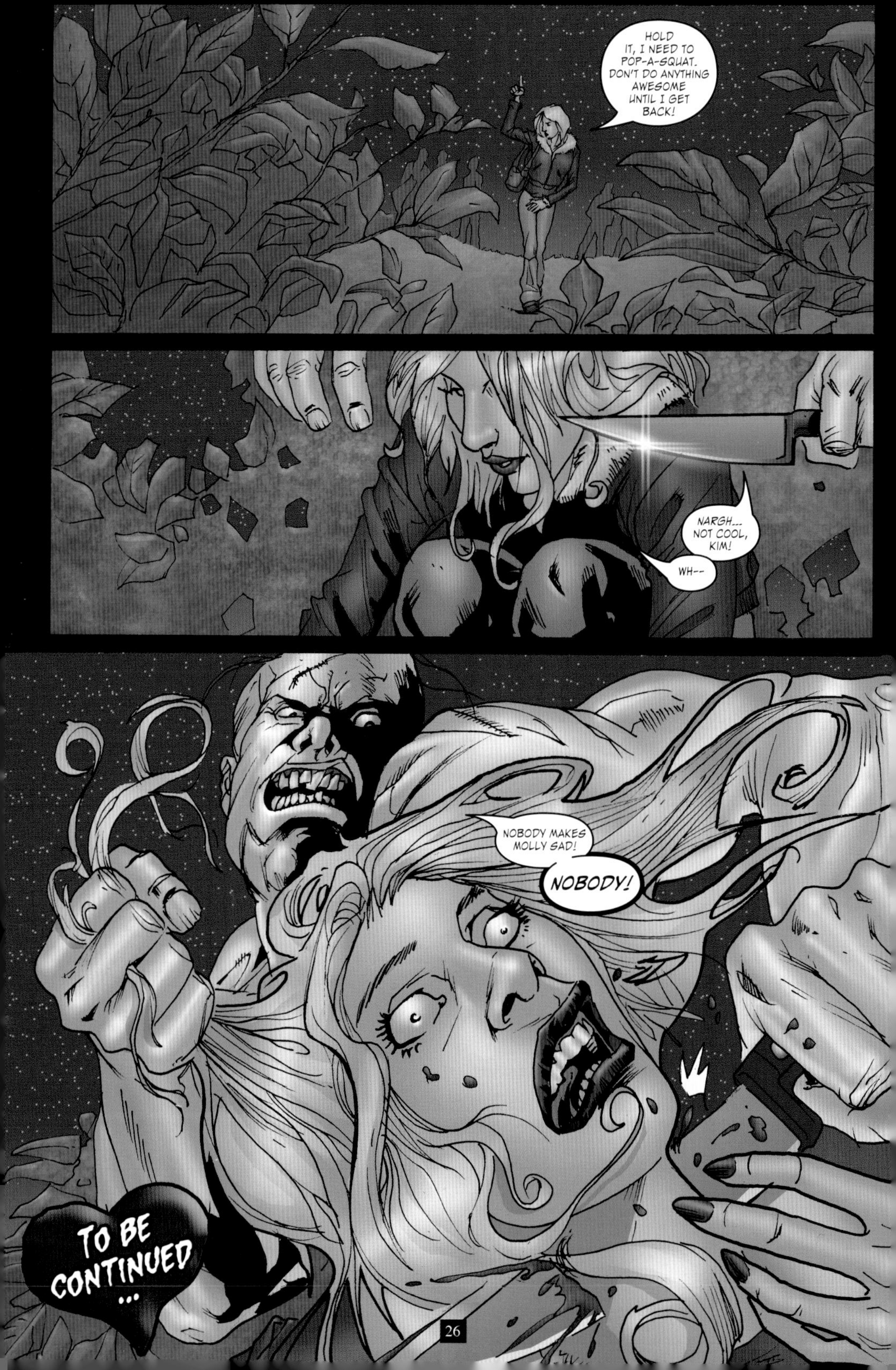
HOLD IT, I NEED TO POP-A-SQUAT. DON'T DO ANYTHING AWESOME UNTIL I GET BACK!
NARGH... NOT COOL, KIM!
WH--
NOBODY MAKES MOLLY SAD!
NOBODY!
TO BE CONTINUED ...

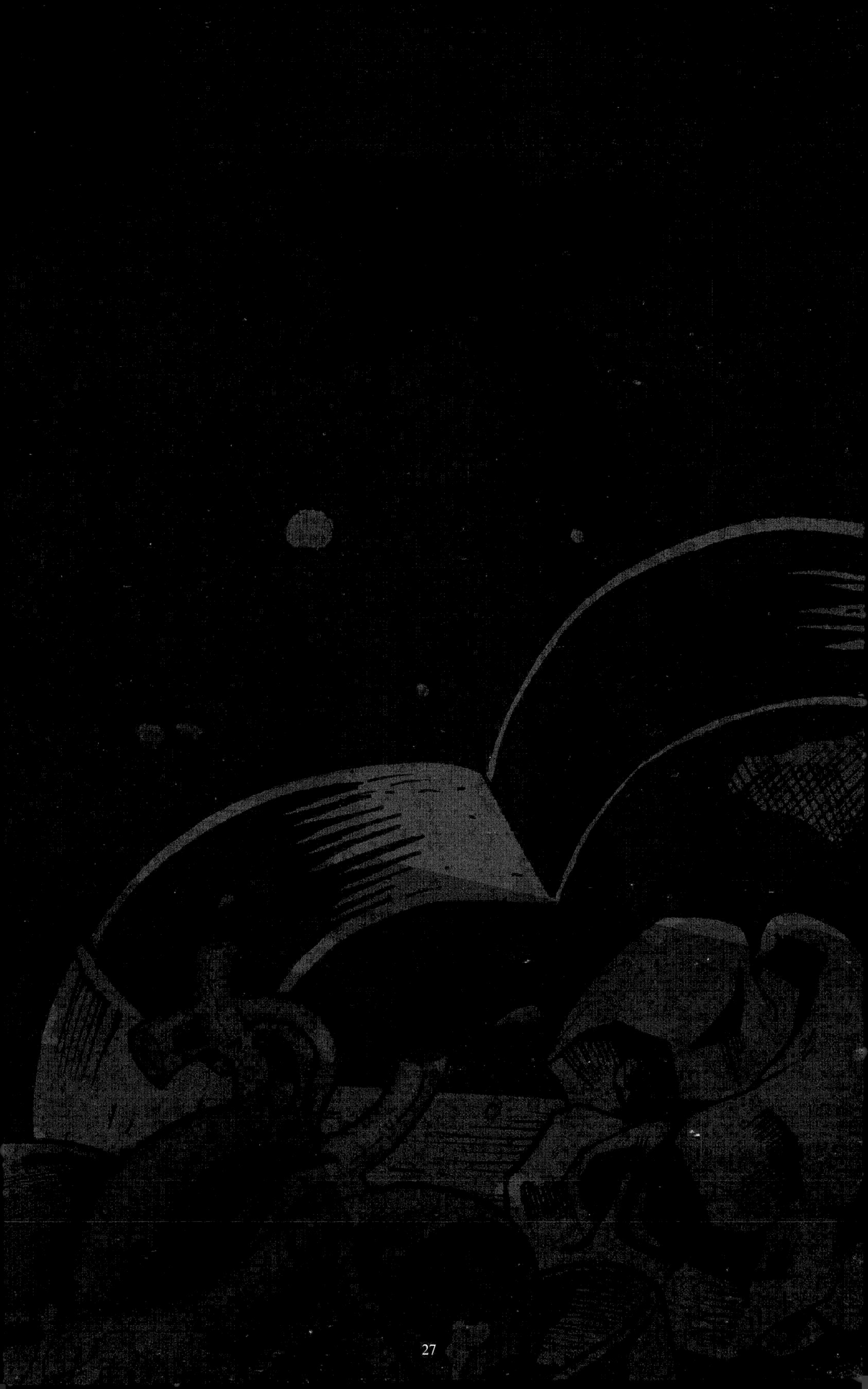

CHAPTER 2

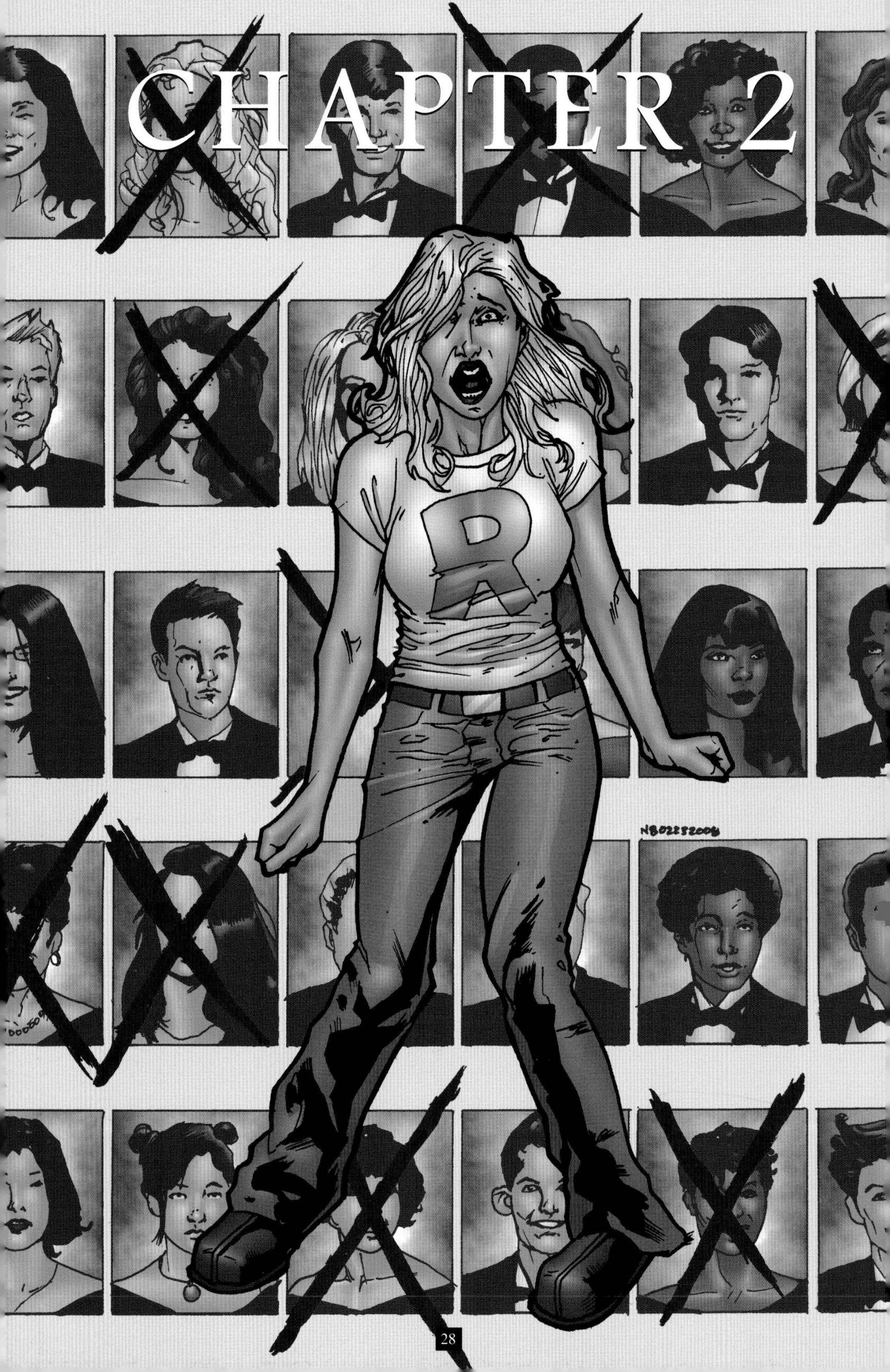

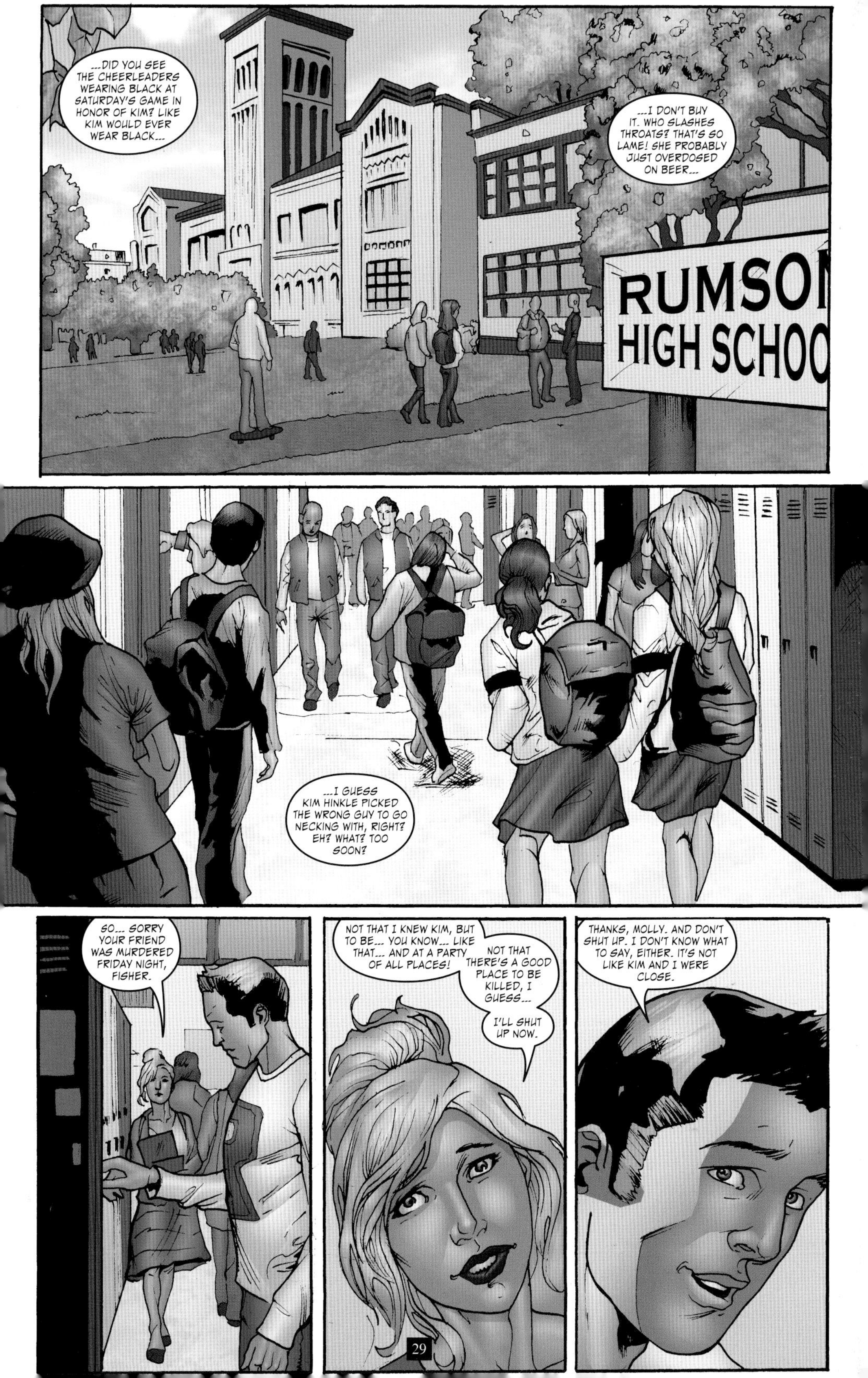
...DID YOU SEE THE CHEERLEADERS WEARING BLACK AT SATURDAY'S GAME IN HONOR OF KIM? LIKE KIM WOULD EVER WEAR BLACK...
...I DON'T BUY IT. WHO SLASHES THROATS? THAT'S SO LAME! SHE PROBABLY JUST OVERDOSED ON BEER...
RUMSON HIGH SCHOO
...I GUESS KIM HINKLE PICKED THE WRONG GUY TO GO NECKING WITH, RIGHT? EH? WHAT? TOO SOON?
SO... SORRY YOUR FRIEND WAS MURDERED FRIDAY NIGHT, FISHER.
NOT THAT I KNEW KIM, BUT TO BE... YOU KNOW... LIKE THAT... AND AT A PARTY OF ALL PLACES!
NOT THAT THERE'S A GOOD PLACE TO BE KILLED, I GUESS...
I'LL SHUT UP NOW.
THANKS, MOLLY. AND DON'T SHUT UP. I DON'T KNOW WHAT TO SAY, EITHER. IT'S NOT LIKE KIM AND I WERE CLOSE.

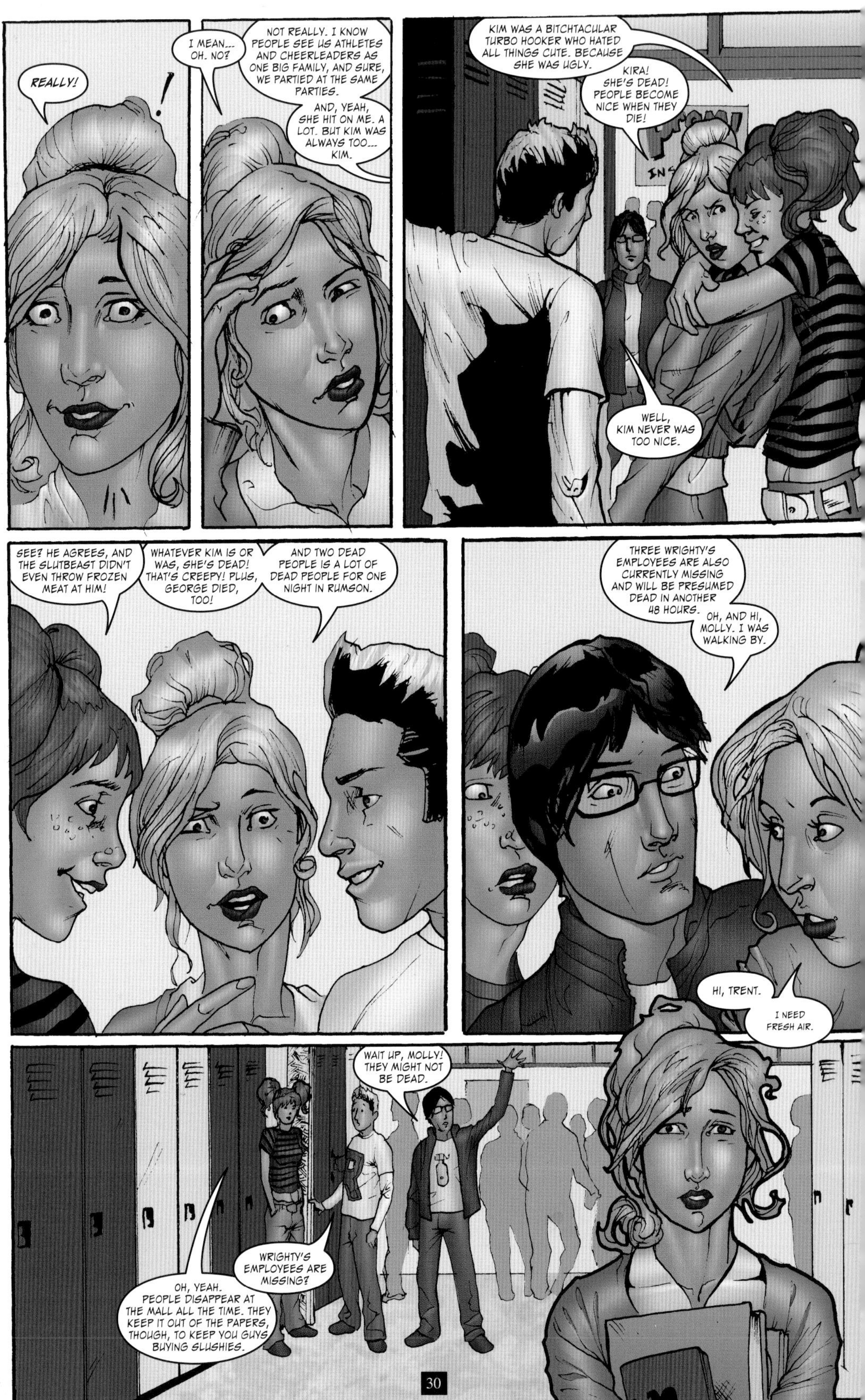
REALLY!
!
I MEAN... OH. NO?
NOT REALLY. I KNOW PEOPLE SEE US ATHLETES AND CHEERLEADERS AS ONE BIG FAMILY, AND SURE, WE PARTIED AT THE SAME PARTIES.
AND, YEAH, SHE HIT ON ME. A LOT. BUT KIM WAS ALWAYS TOO... KIM.
KIM WAS A BITCHTACULAR TURBO HOOKER WHO HATED ALL THINGS CUTE. BECAUSE SHE WAS UGLY.
KIRA! SHE'S DEAD! PEOPLE BECOME NICE WHEN THEY DIE!
WELL, KIM NEVER WAS TOO NICE.
SEE? HE AGREES, AND THE SLUTBEAST DIDN'T EVEN THROW FROZEN MEAT AT HIM!
WHATEVER KIM IS OR WAS, SHE'S DEAD! THAT'S CREEPY! PLUS, GEORGE DIED, TOO!
AND TWO DEAD PEOPLE IS A LOT OF DEAD PEOPLE FOR ONE NIGHT IN RUMSON.
THREE WRIGHTY'S EMPLOYEES ARE ALSO CURRENTLY MISSING AND WILL BE PRESUMED DEAD IN ANOTHER 48 HOURS.
OH, AND HI, MOLLY. I WAS WALKING BY.
HI, TRENT.
I NEED FRESH AIR.
WAIT UP, MOLLY! THEY MIGHT NOT BE DEAD.
WRIGHTY'S EMPLOYEES ARE MISSING?
OH, YEAH. PEOPLE DISAPPEAR AT THE MALL ALL THE TIME. THEY KEEP IT OUT OF THE PAPERS, THOUGH, TO KEEP YOU GUYS BUYING SLUSHIES.

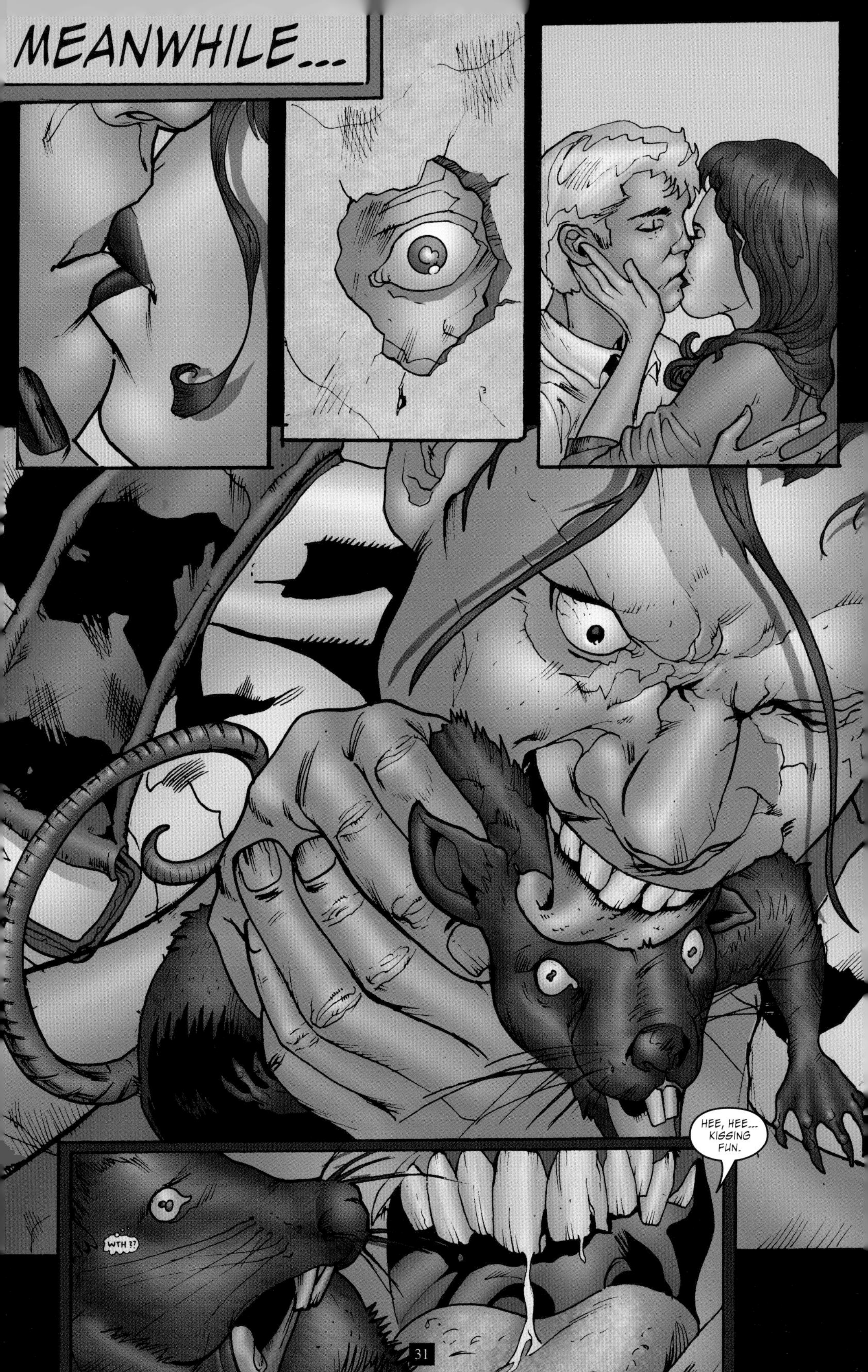
MEANWHILE...
HEE, HEE... KISSING FUN.
WTH ?!

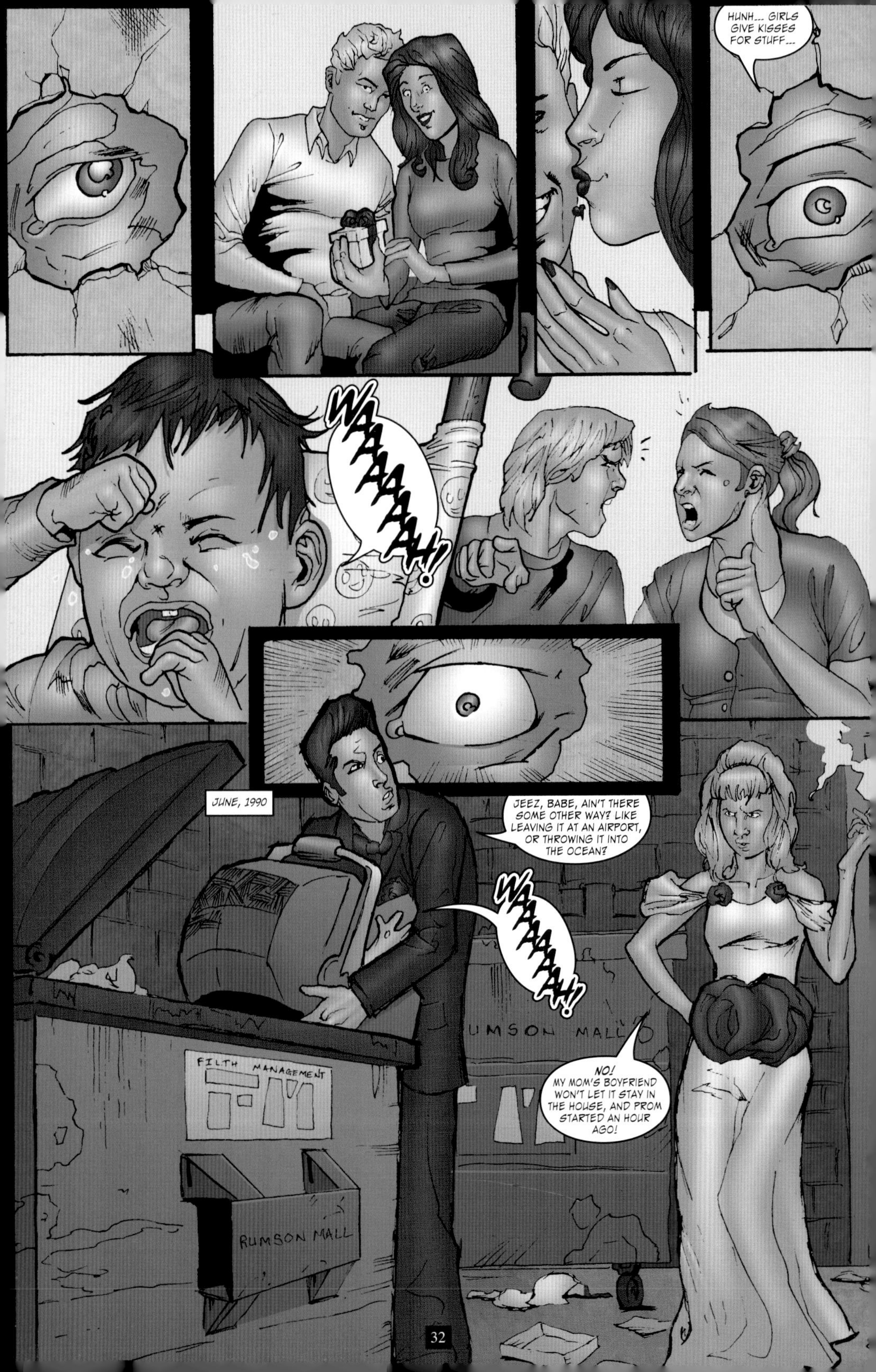
HUNH... GIRLS GIVE KISSES FOR STUFF...
WAAAAAAAAH!
JUNE, 1990
JEEZ, BABE, AIN'T THERE SOME OTHER WAY? LIKE LEAVING IT AT AN AIRPORT, OR THROWING IT INTO THE OCEAN?
WAAAAAAAH!
NO! MY MOM'S BOYFRIEND WON'T LET IT STAY IN THE HOUSE, AND PROM STARTED AN HOUR AGO!
FILTH MANAGEMENT
RUMSON MALL
RUMSON MALL

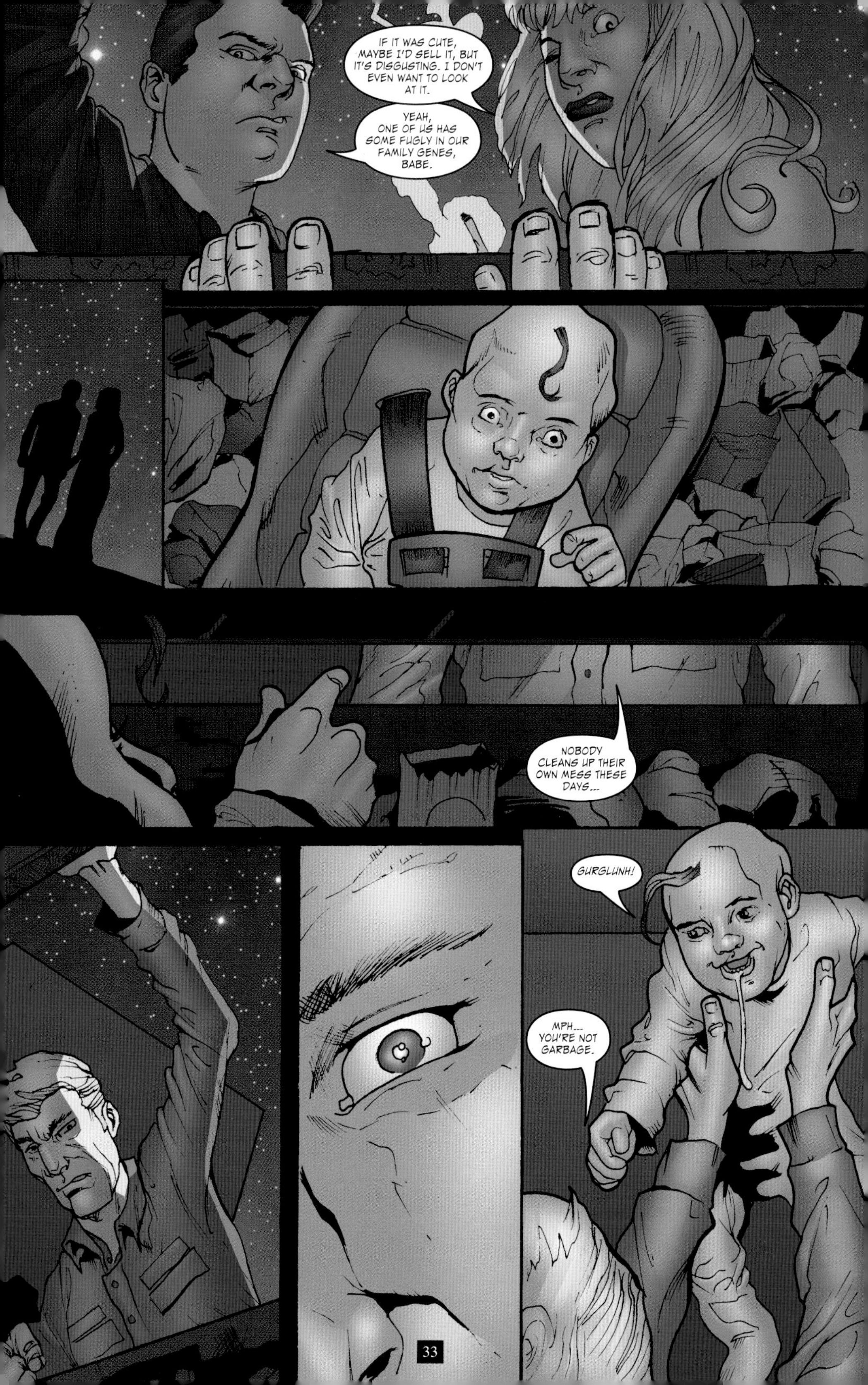
IF IT WAS CUTE, MAYBE I'D SELL IT, BUT IT'S DISGUSTING. I DON'T EVEN WANT TO LOOK AT IT.
YEAH, ONE OF US HAS SOME FUGLY IN OUR FAMILY GENES, BABE.
NOBODY CLEANS UP THEIR OWN MESS THESE DAYS...
GURGLUNH!
MPH... YOU'RE NOT GARBAGE.

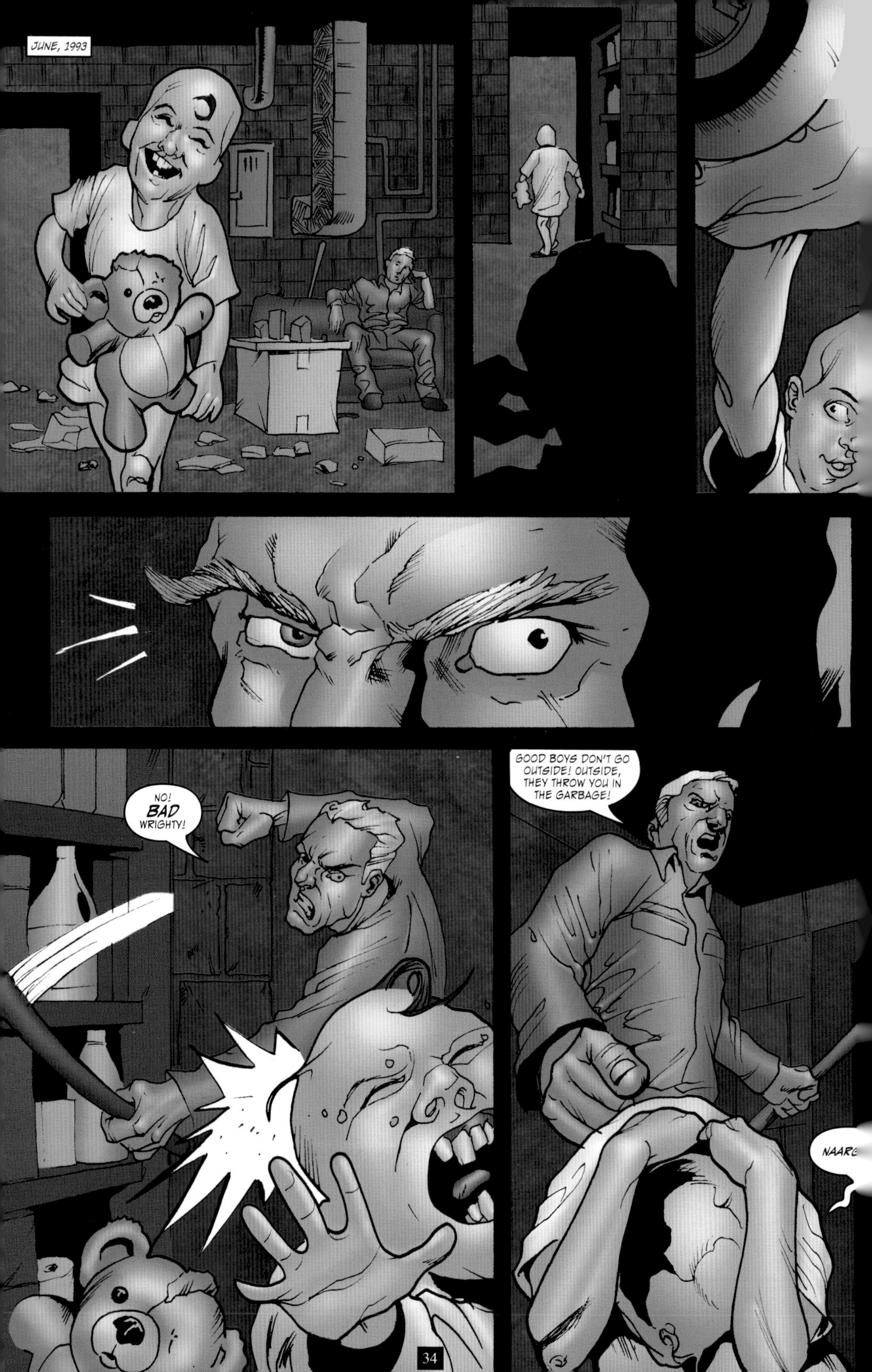
JUNE, 1993
NO! BAD WRIGHTY!
GOOD BOYS DON'T GO OUTSIDE! OUTSIDE, THEY THROW YOU IN THE GARBAGE!
NAARG

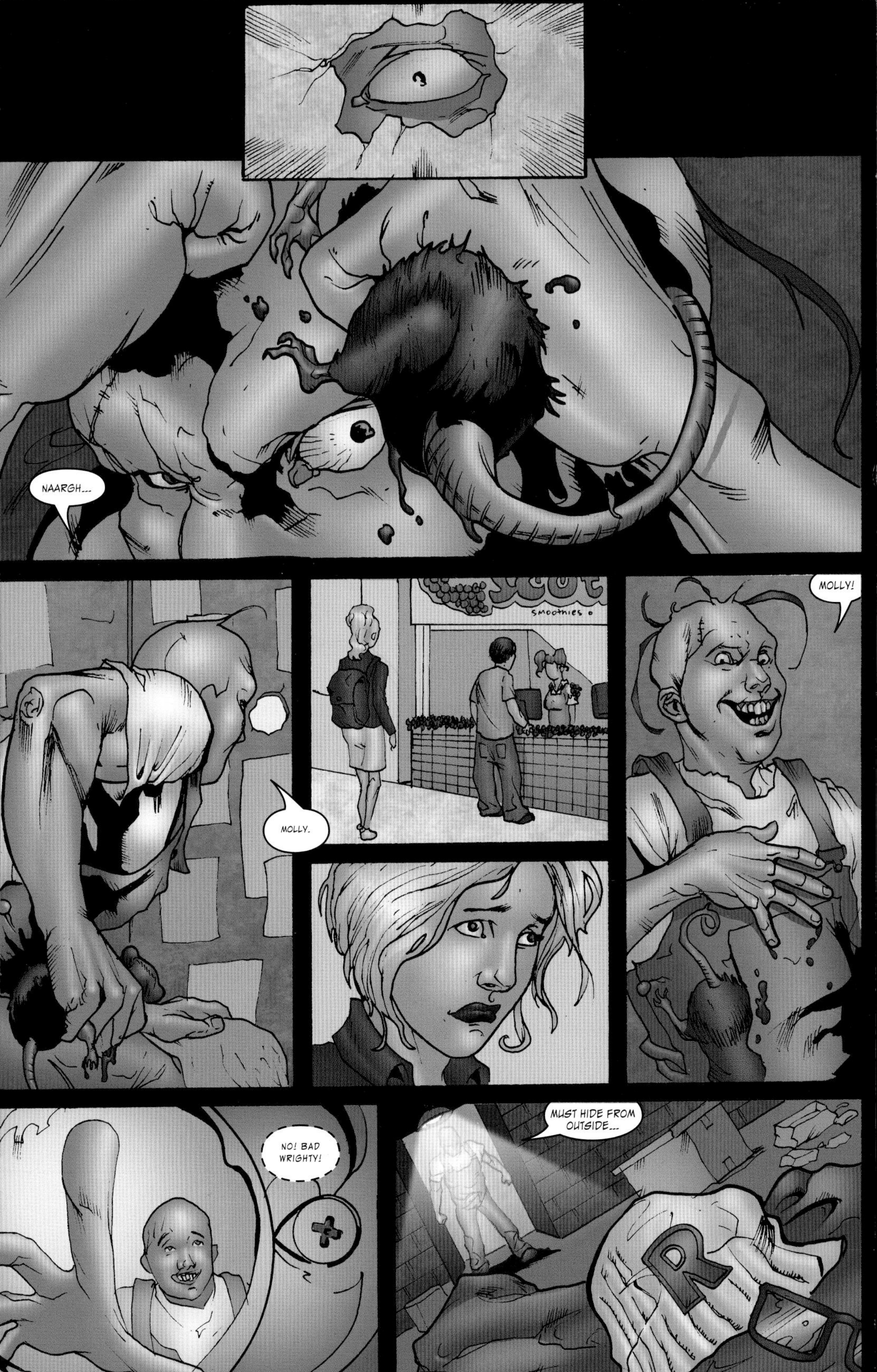
NAARGH...
MOLLY.
smoothies
MOLLY!
NO! BAD WRIGHTY!
MUST HIDE FROM OUTSIDE...

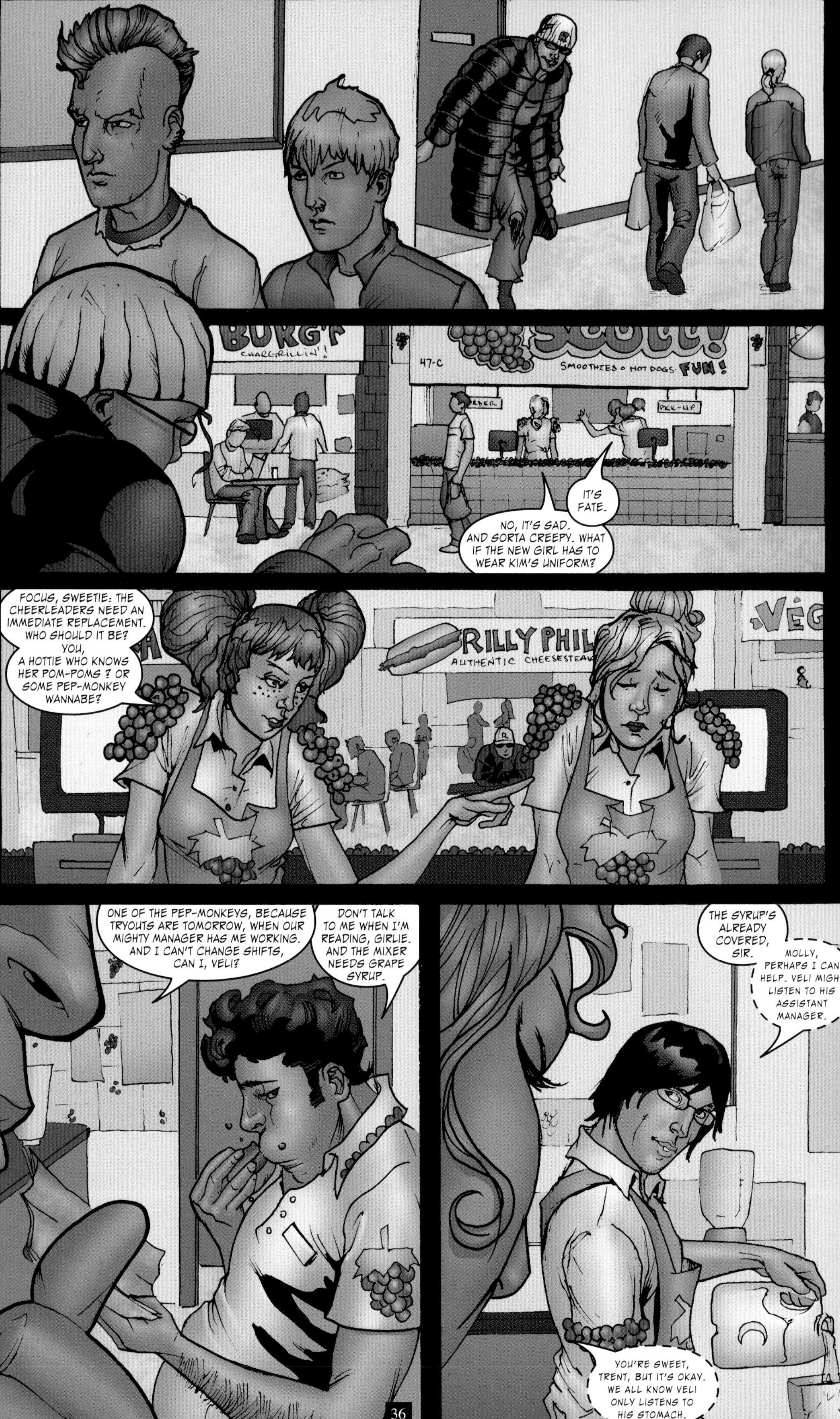
BURG'R
CHARGRILLIN'!
47-C
SMOOTHIES ○ HOT DOGS FUN!
IT'S FATE.
NO, IT'S SAD. AND SORTA CREEPY. WHAT IF THE NEW GIRL HAS TO WEAR KIM'S UNIFORM?
FOCUS, SWEETIE: THE CHEERLEADERS NEED AN IMMEDIATE REPLACEMENT. WHO SHOULD IT BE? YOU, A HOTTIE WHO KNOWS HER POM-POMS? OR SOME PEP-MONKEY WANNABE?
RILLY PHIL
AUTHENTIC CHEESESTEAK
ONE OF THE PEP-MONKEYS, BECAUSE TRYOUTS ARE TOMORROW, WHEN OUR MIGHTY MANAGER HAS ME WORKING. AND I CAN'T CHANGE SHIFTS, CAN I, VELI?
DON'T TALK TO ME WHEN I'M READING, GIRLIE. AND THE MIXER NEEDS GRAPE SYRUP.
THE SYRUP'S ALREADY COVERED, SIR.
MOLLY, PERHAPS I CAN HELP. VELI MIGHT LISTEN TO HIS ASSISTANT MANAGER.
YOU'RE SWEET, TRENT, BUT IT'S OKAY. WE ALL KNOW VELI ONLY LISTENS TO HIS STOMACH.

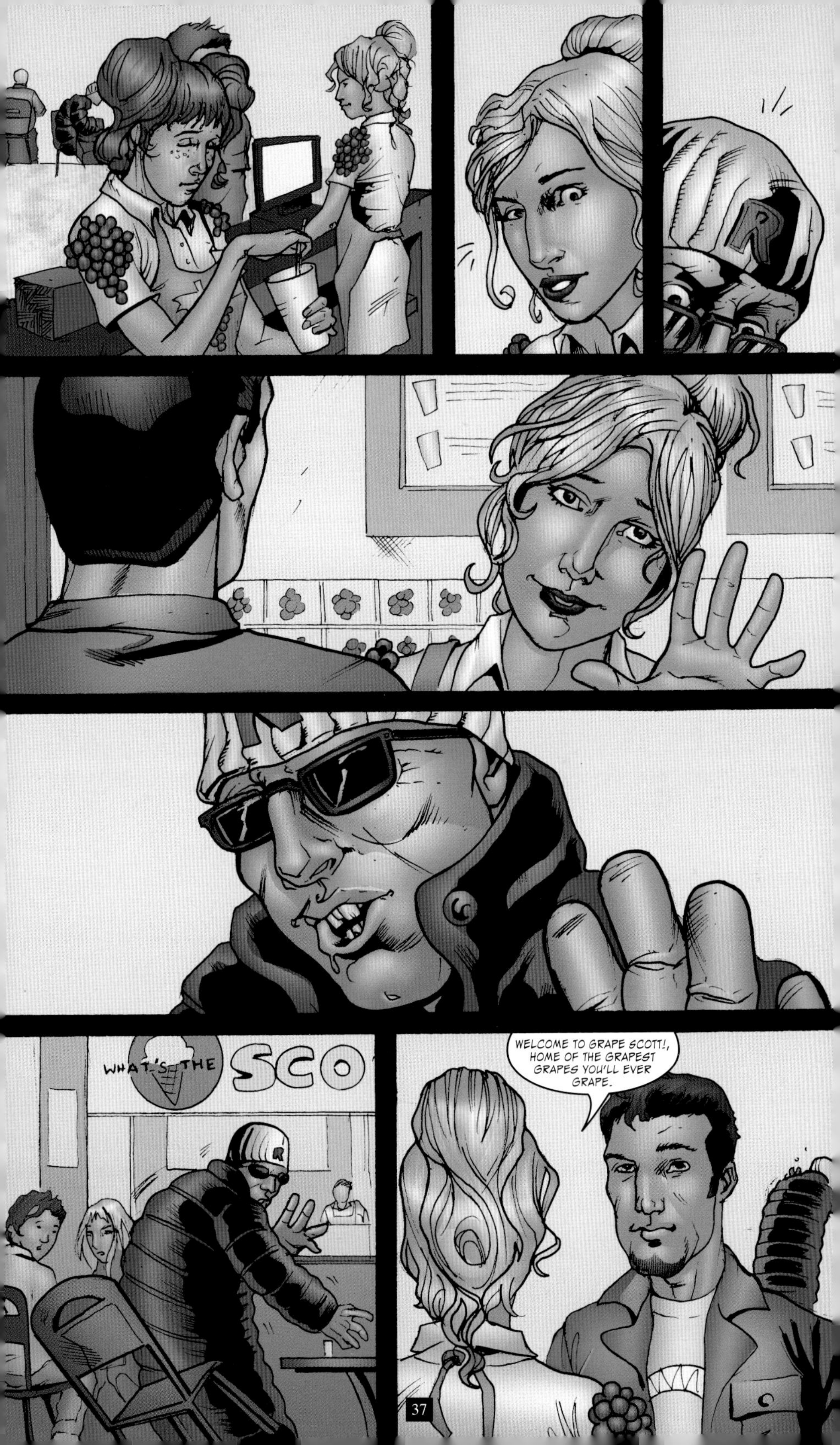
WHAT'S THE SCO
WELCOME TO GRAPE SCOTT!, HOME OF THE GRAPEST GRAPES YOU'LL EVER GRAPE.

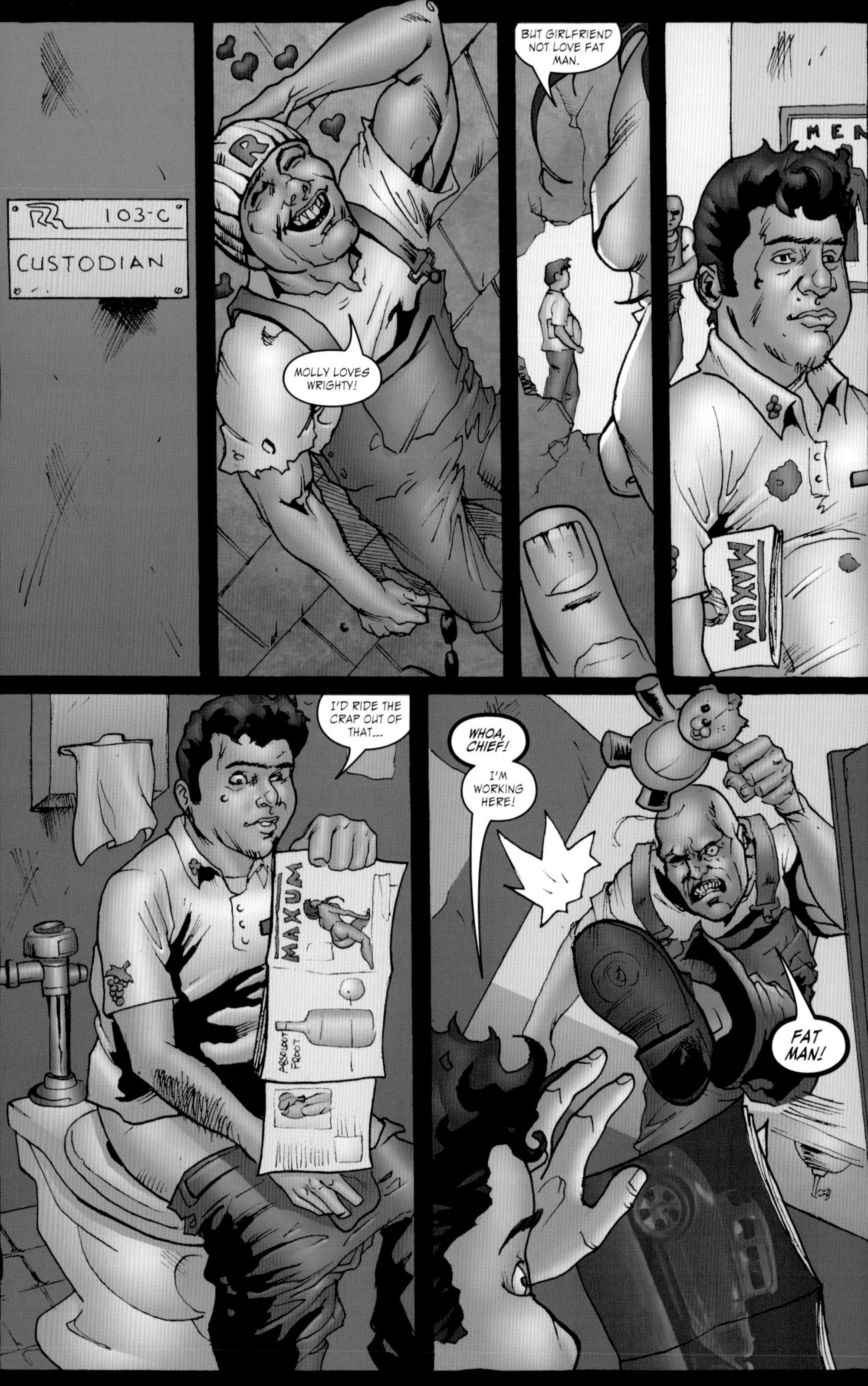
103-C
CUSTODIAN
MOLLY LOVES WRIGHTY!
BUT GIRLFRIEND NOT LOVE FAT MAN.
MEN
MAXUM
I'D RIDE THE CRAP OUT OF THAT...
MAXUM
ABSOLOOT FROOT
WHOA, CHIEF!
I'M WORKING HERE!
FAT MAN!

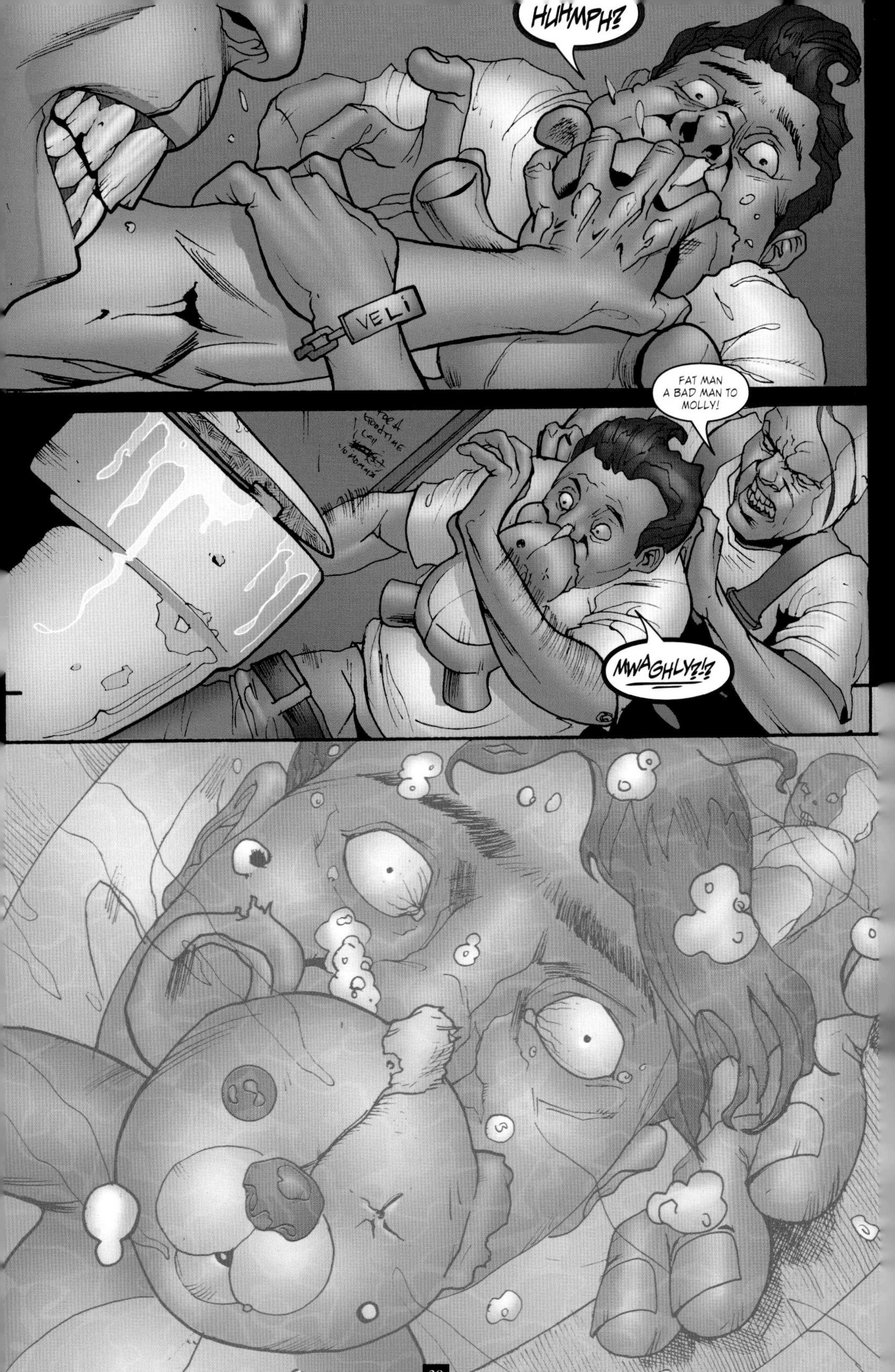
HUHMPH?
VELI
FAT MAN A BAD MAN TO MOLLY!
MWAGHLY?!?

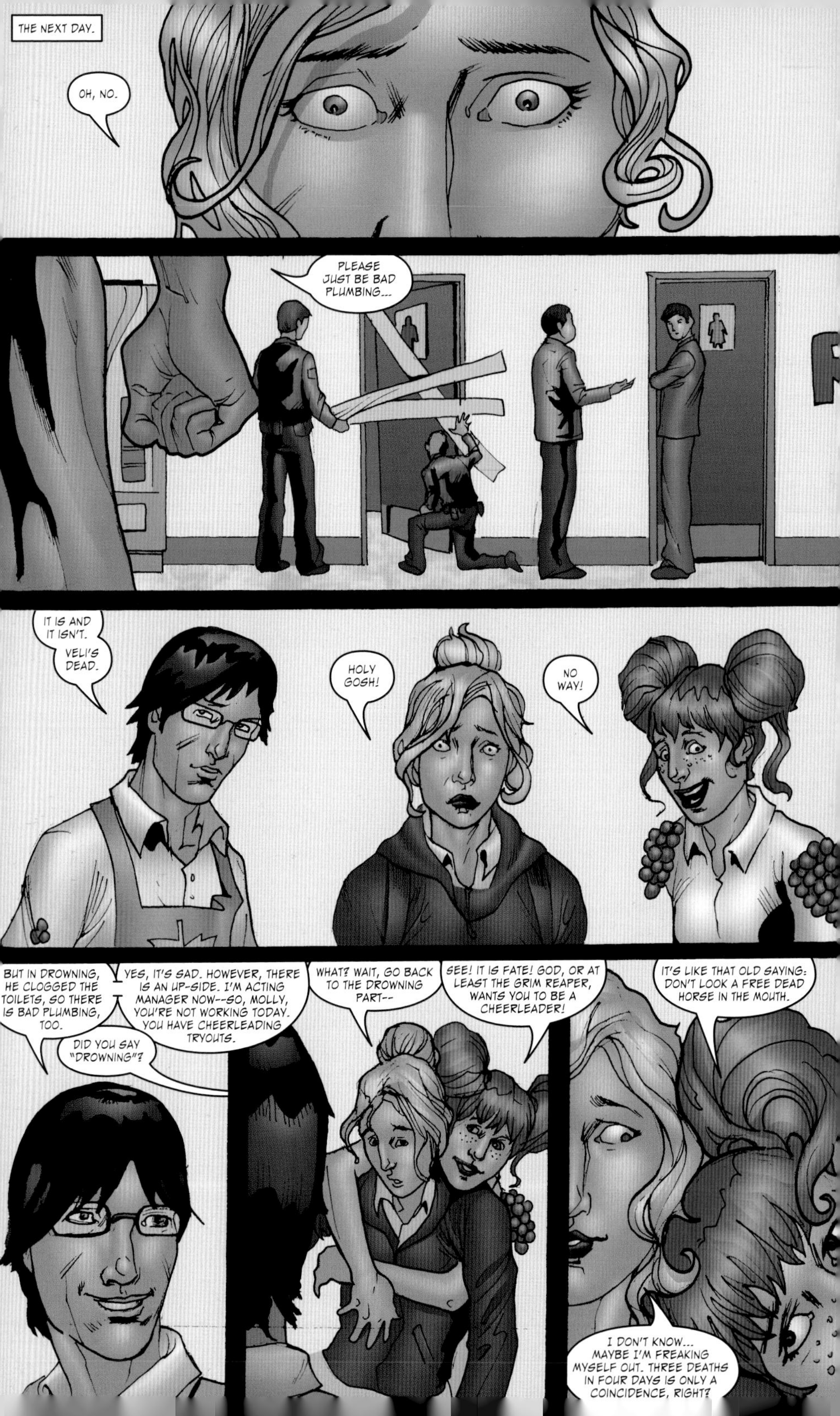
THE NEXT DAY.
OH, NO.
PLEASE JUST BE BAD PLUMBING...
IT IS AND IT ISN'T.
VELI'S DEAD.
HOLY GOSH!
NO WAY!
BUT IN DROWNING, HE CLOGGED THE TOILETS, SO THERE IS BAD PLUMBING, TOO.
YES, IT'S SAD. HOWEVER, THERE IS AN UP-SIDE. I'M ACTING MANAGER NOW--SO, MOLLY, YOU'RE NOT WORKING TODAY. YOU HAVE CHEERLEADING TRYOUTS.
DID YOU SAY "DROWNING"?
WHAT? WAIT, GO BACK TO THE DROWNING PART--
SEE! IT IS FATE! GOD, OR AT LEAST THE GRIM REAPER, WANTS YOU TO BE A CHEERLEADER!
IT'S LIKE THAT OLD SAYING: DON'T LOOK A FREE DEAD HORSE IN THE MOUTH.
I DON'T KNOW... MAYBE I'M FREAKING MYSELF OUT. THREE DEATHS IN FOUR DAYS IS ONLY A COINCIDENCE, RIGHT?

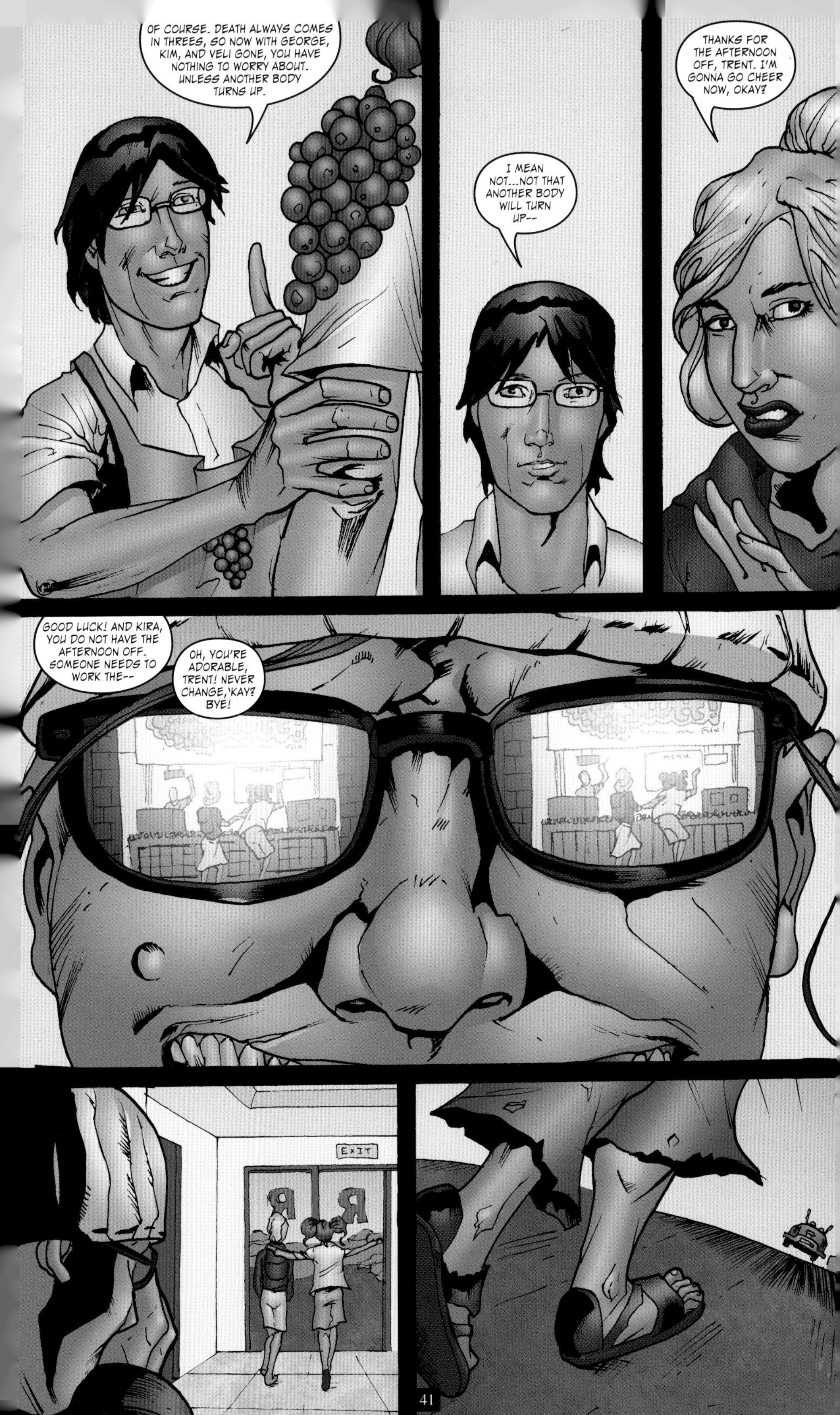
OF COURSE. DEATH ALWAYS COMES IN THREES, SO NOW WITH GEORGE, KIM, AND VELI GONE, YOU HAVE NOTHING TO WORRY ABOUT. UNLESS ANOTHER BODY TURNS UP.
I MEAN NOT...NOT THAT ANOTHER BODY WILL TURN UP--
THANKS FOR THE AFTERNOON OFF, TRENT. I'M GONNA GO CHEER NOW, OKAY?
GOOD LUCK! AND KIRA, YOU DO NOT HAVE THE AFTERNOON OFF. SOMEONE NEEDS TO WORK THE--
OH, YOU'RE ADORABLE, TRENT! NEVER CHANGE, 'KAY? BYE!
EXIT

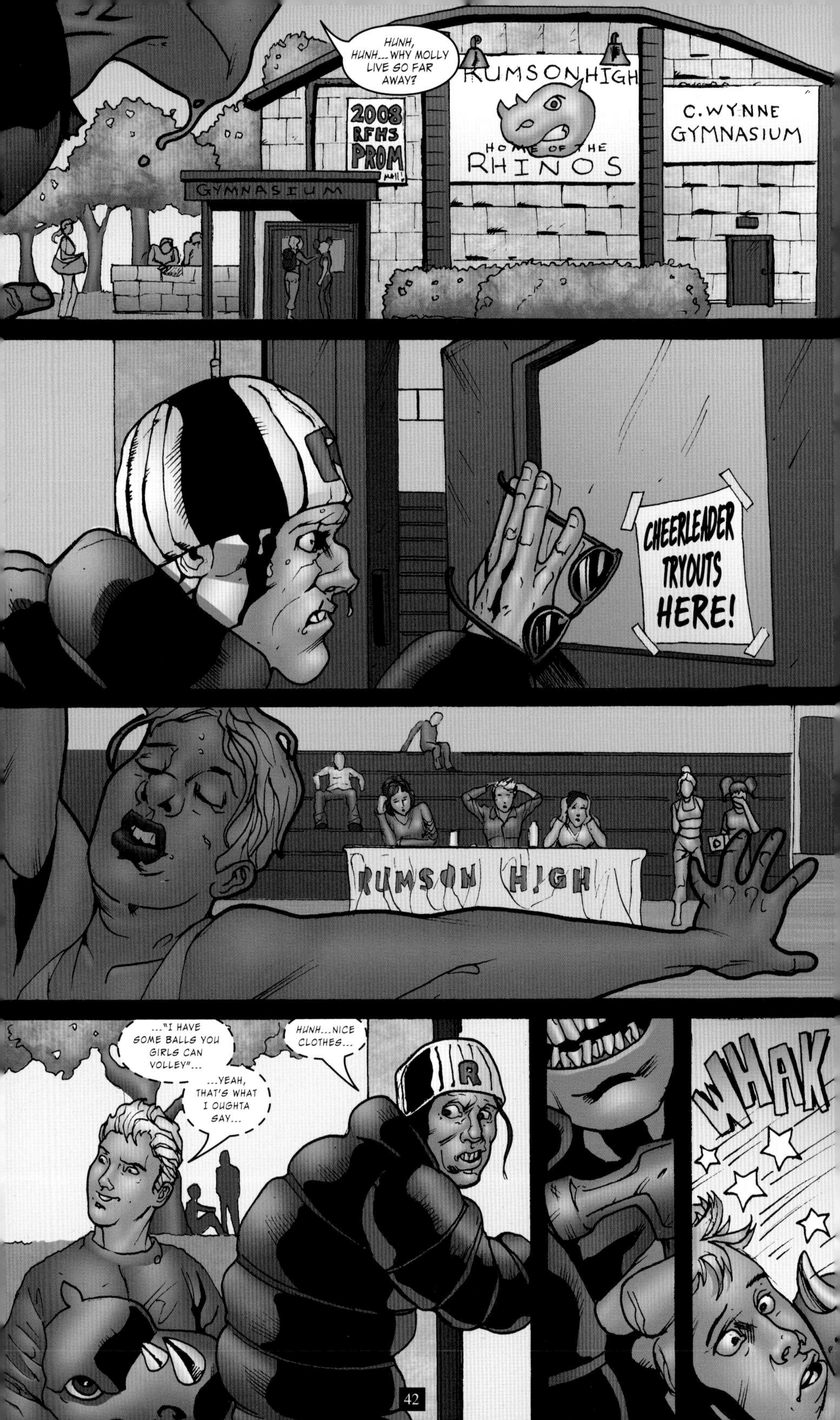
HUNH, HUNH... WHY MOLLY LIVE SO FAR AWAY?
2008 RFHS PROM
RUMSON HIGH
HOME OF THE RHINOS
C. WYNNE GYMNASIUM
GYMNASIUM
CHEERLEADER TRYOUTS HERE!
RUMSON HIGH
..."I HAVE SOME BALLS YOU GIRLS CAN VOLLEY"...
...YEAH, THAT'S WHAT I OUGHTA SAY...
HUNH...NICE CLOTHES...
WHAK

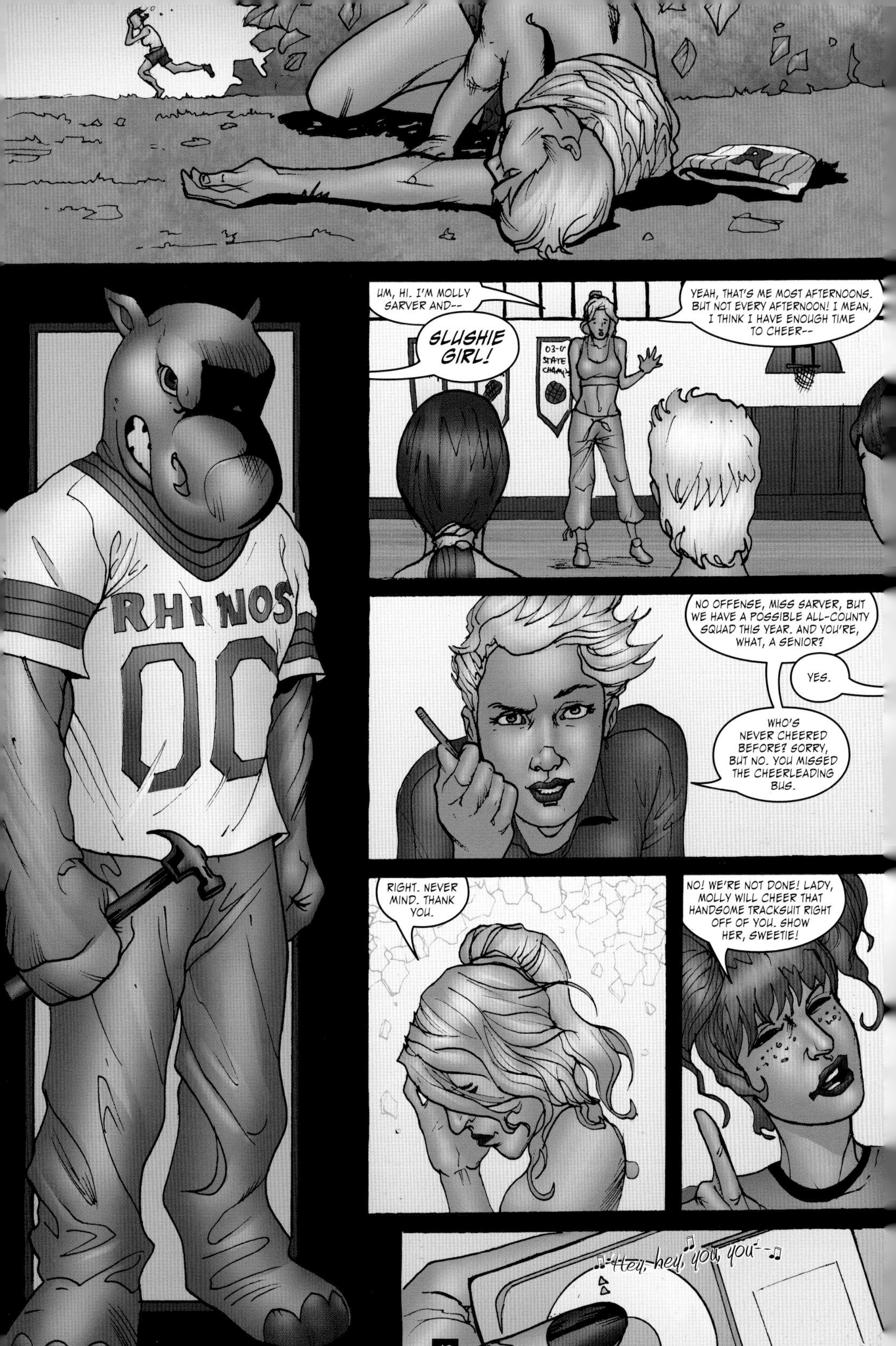
UM, HI. I'M MOLLY SARVER AND--
SLUSHIE GIRL!
YEAH, THAT'S ME MOST AFTERNOONS. BUT NOT EVERY AFTERNOON! I MEAN, I THINK I HAVE ENOUGH TIME TO CHEER--
03-04 STATE CHAMPS
RHINOS
00
NO OFFENSE, MISS SARVER, BUT WE HAVE A POSSIBLE ALL-COUNTY SQUAD THIS YEAR. AND YOU'RE, WHAT, A SENIOR?
YES.
WHO'S NEVER CHEERED BEFORE? SORRY, BUT NO. YOU MISSED THE CHEERLEADING BUS.
RIGHT. NEVER MIND. THANK YOU.
NO! WE'RE NOT DONE! LADY, MOLLY WILL CHEER THAT HANDSOME TRACKSUIT RIGHT OFF OF YOU. SHOW HER, SWEETIE!
♫Hey, hey, you, you--♫

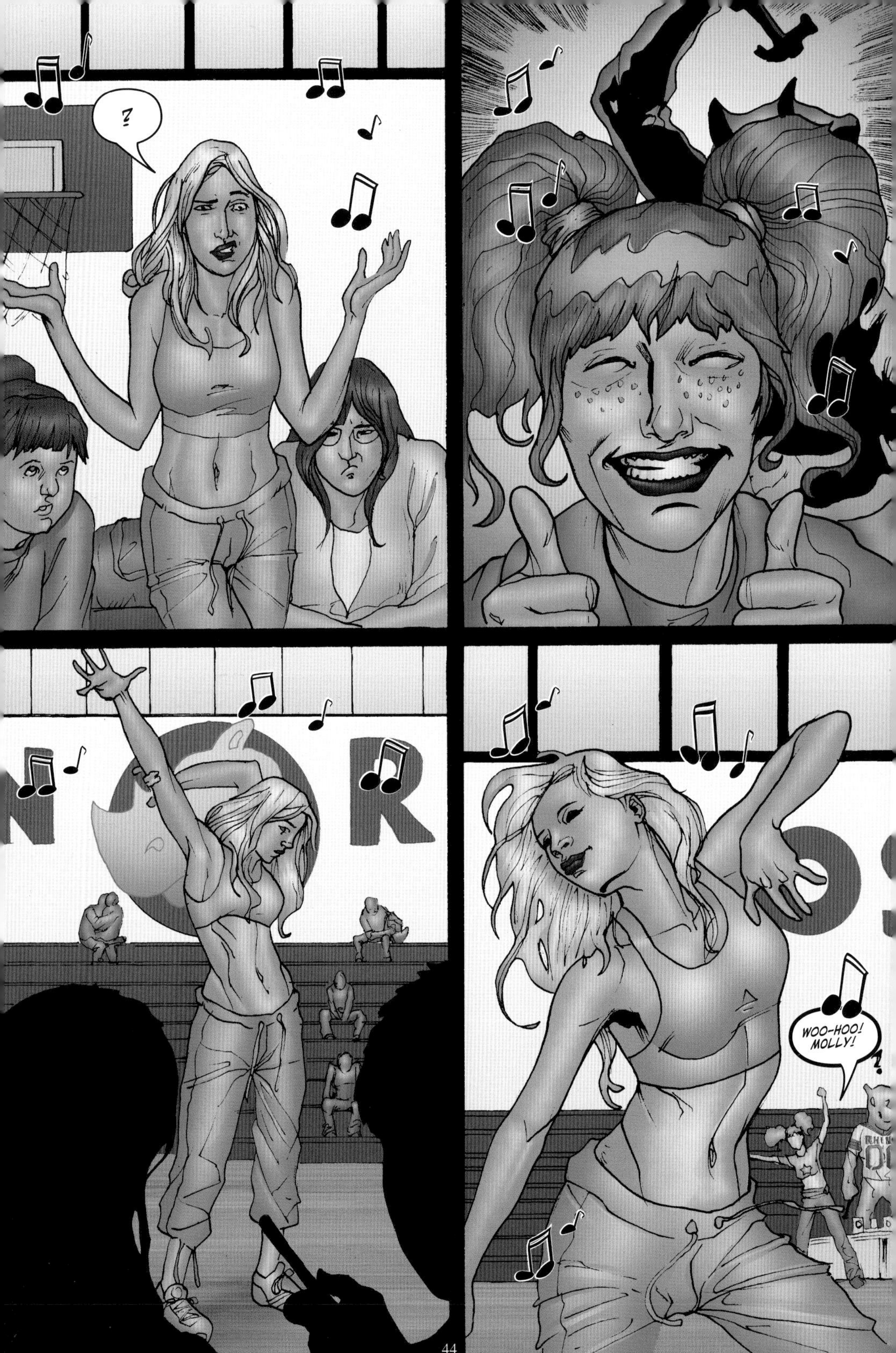
?
WOO-HOO! MOLLY!

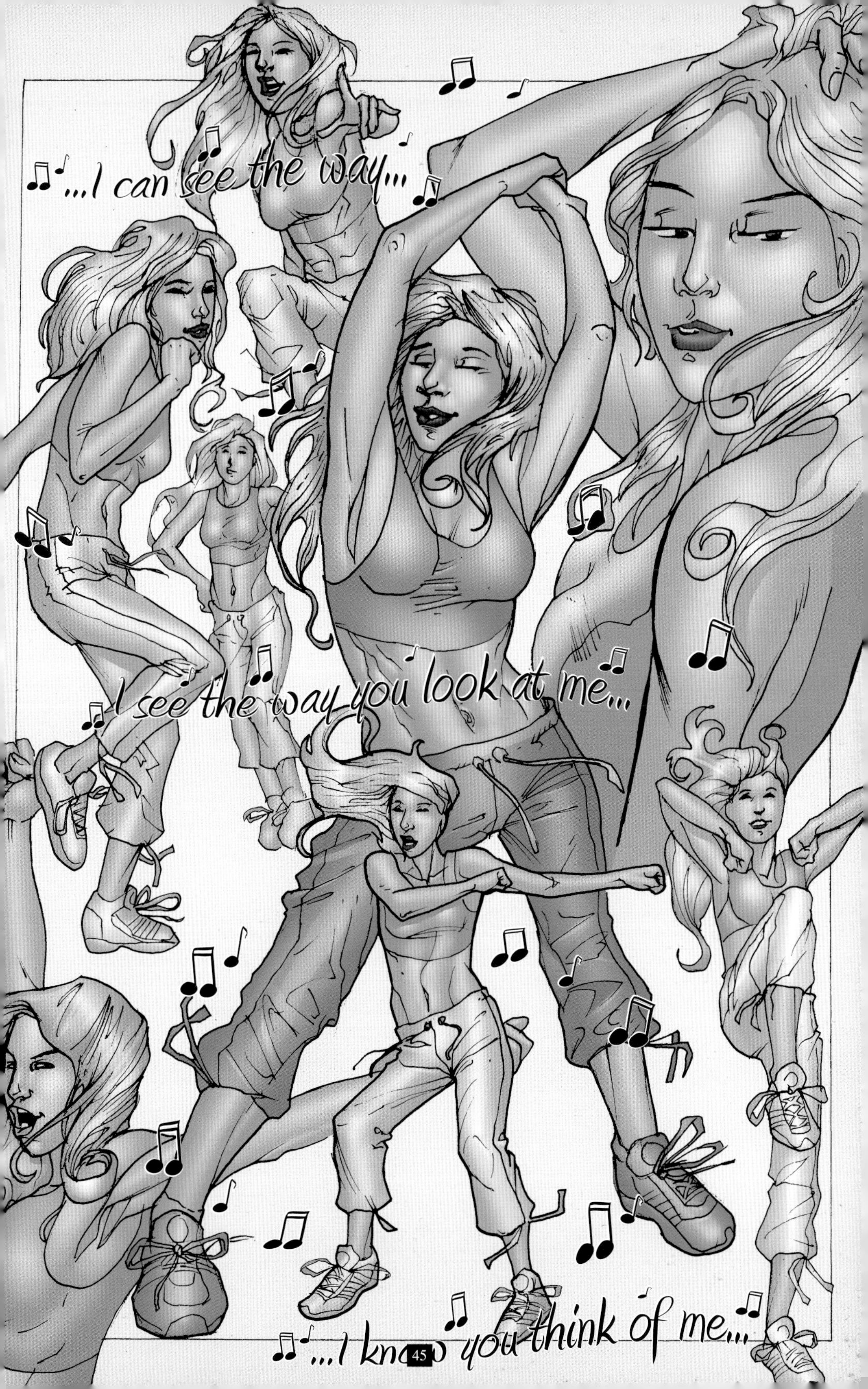
...I can see the way...
I see the way you look at me...
...I know you think of me...

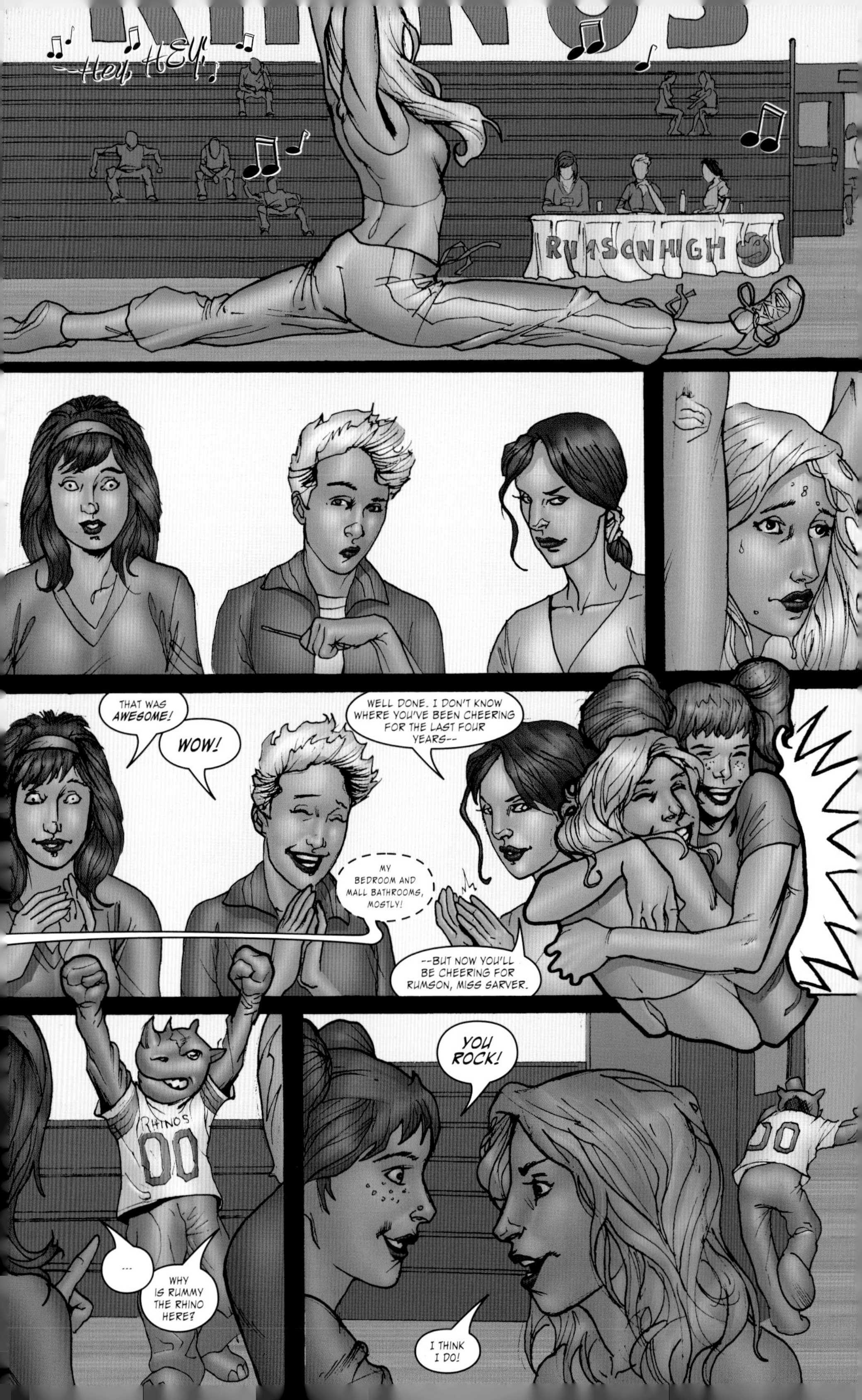
Hey, HEY!
THAT WAS AWESOME!
WOW!
WELL DONE. I DON'T KNOW WHERE YOU'VE BEEN CHEERING FOR THE LAST FOUR YEARS--
MY BEDROOM AND MALL BATHROOMS, MOSTLY!
--BUT NOW YOU'LL BE CHEERING FOR RUMSON, MISS SARVER.
YOU ROCK!
...
WHY IS RUMMY THE RHINO HERE?
I THINK I DO!

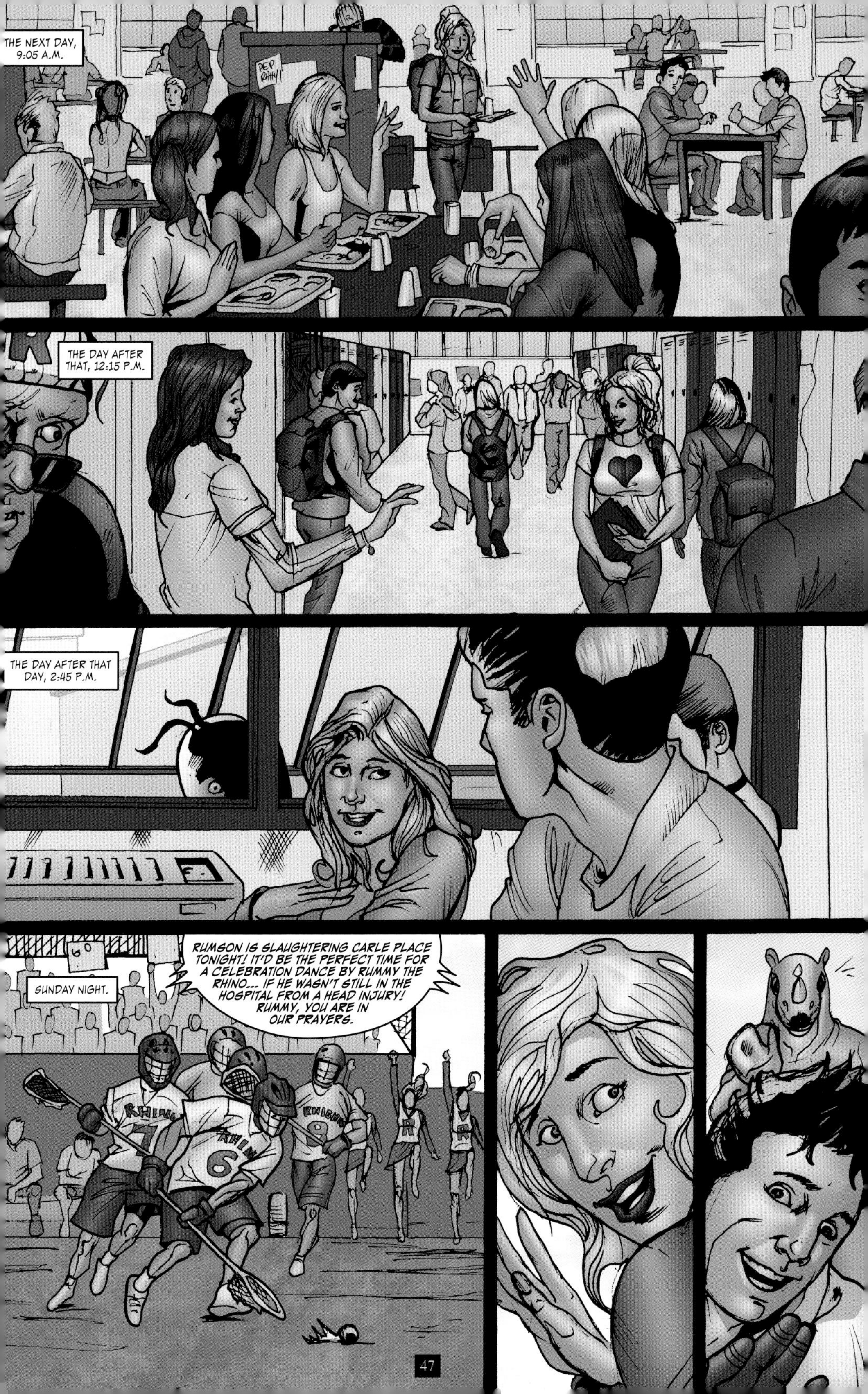
THE NEXT DAY, 9:05 A.M.
PEP RALLY!
THE DAY AFTER THAT, 12:15 P.M.
THE DAY AFTER THAT DAY, 2:45 P.M.
SUNDAY NIGHT.
RUMSON IS SLAUGHTERING CARLE PLACE TONIGHT! IT'D BE THE PERFECT TIME FOR A CELEBRATION DANCE BY RUMMY THE RHINO... IF HE WASN'T STILL IN THE HOSPITAL FROM A HEAD INJURY! RUMMY, YOU ARE IN OUR PRAYERS.
RHINO
KNIGHTS

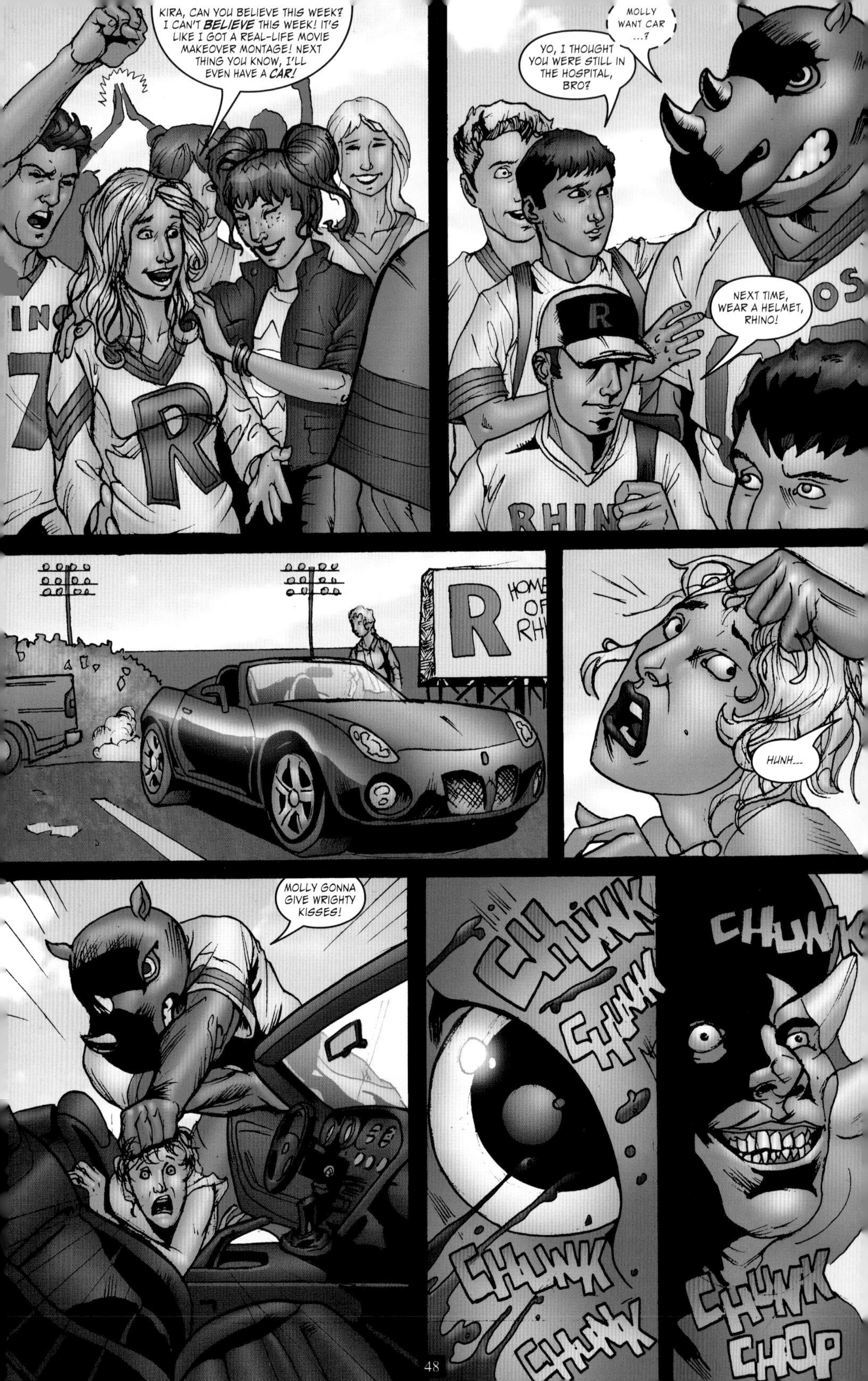

KIRA, CAN YOU BELIEVE THIS WEEK? I CAN'T **BELIEVE** THIS WEEK! IT'S LIKE I GOT A REAL-LIFE MOVIE MAKEOVER MONTAGE! NEXT THING YOU KNOW, I'LL EVEN HAVE A **CAR!**
MOLLY WANT CAR ...?
YO, I THOUGHT YOU WERE STILL IN THE HOSPITAL, BRO?
NEXT TIME, WEAR A HELMET, RHINO!
HUNH...
MOLLY GONNA GIVE WRIGHTY KISSES!
CHUNK
CHUNK
CHUNK
CHUNK
CHUNK
CHUNK
CHOP

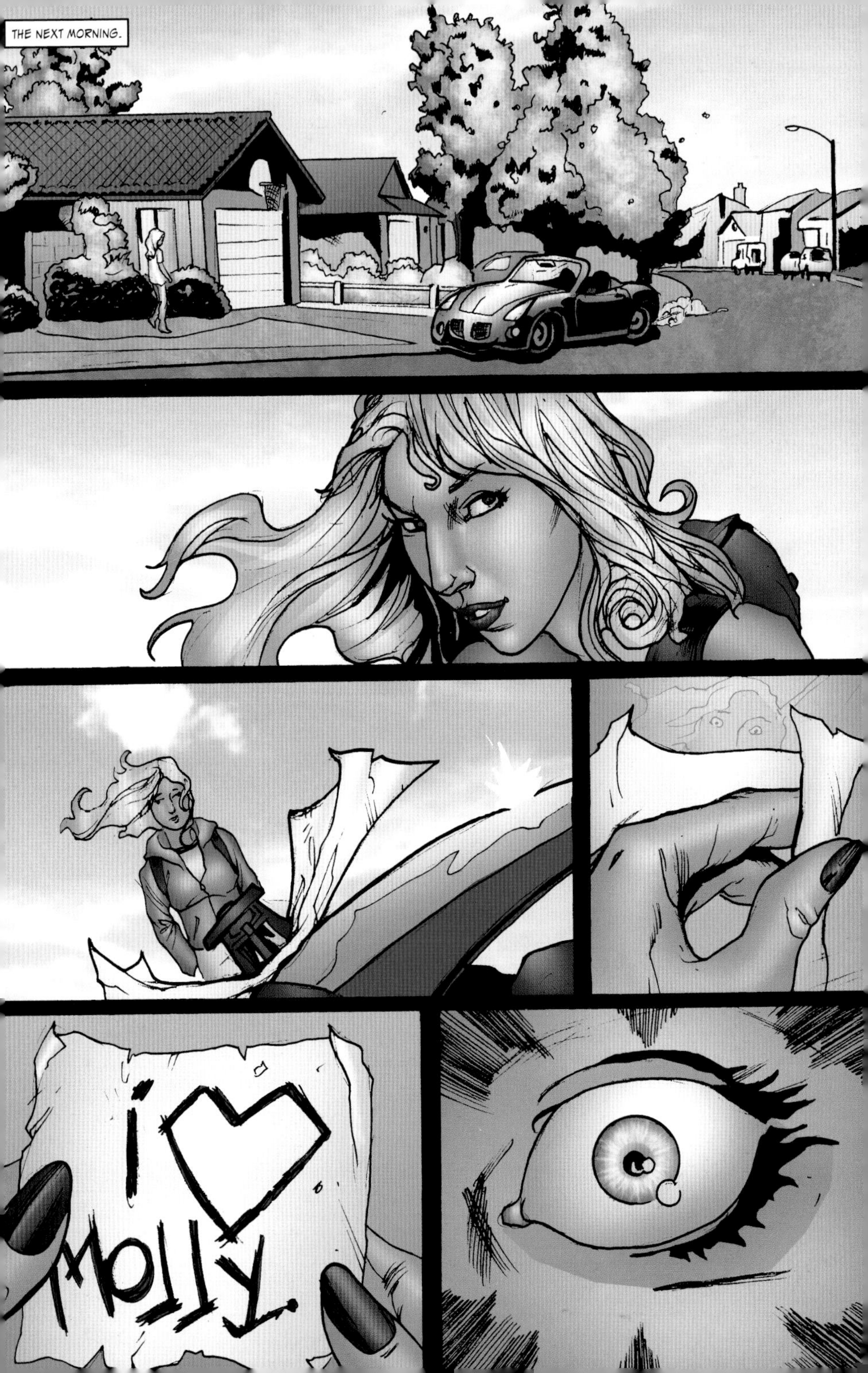
THE NEXT MORNING.
i ♥ MOLLY

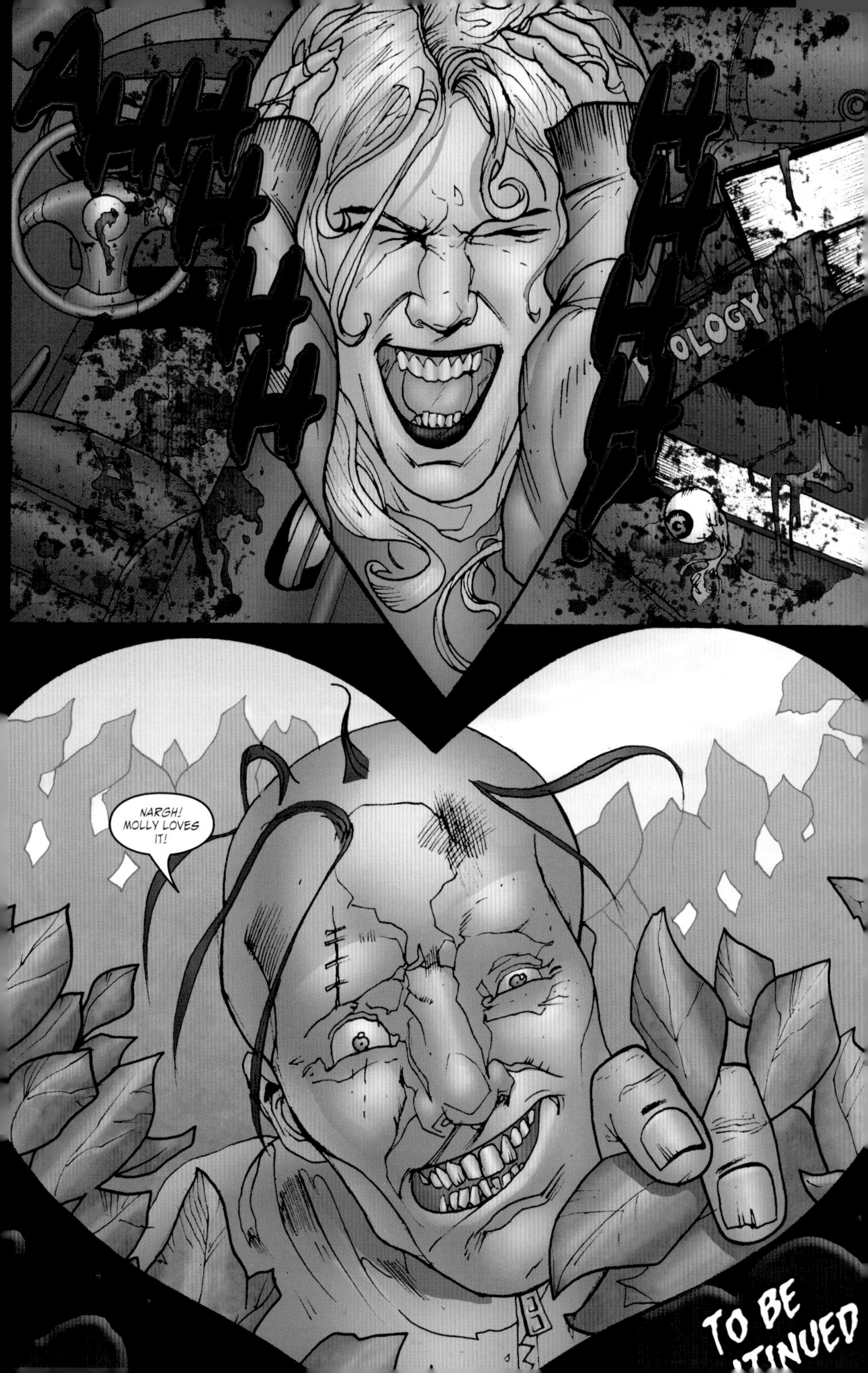
AHHHHHHHHHHHH!
OLOGY
NARGH! MOLLY LOVES IT!
TO BE
TINUED

CHAPTER 3

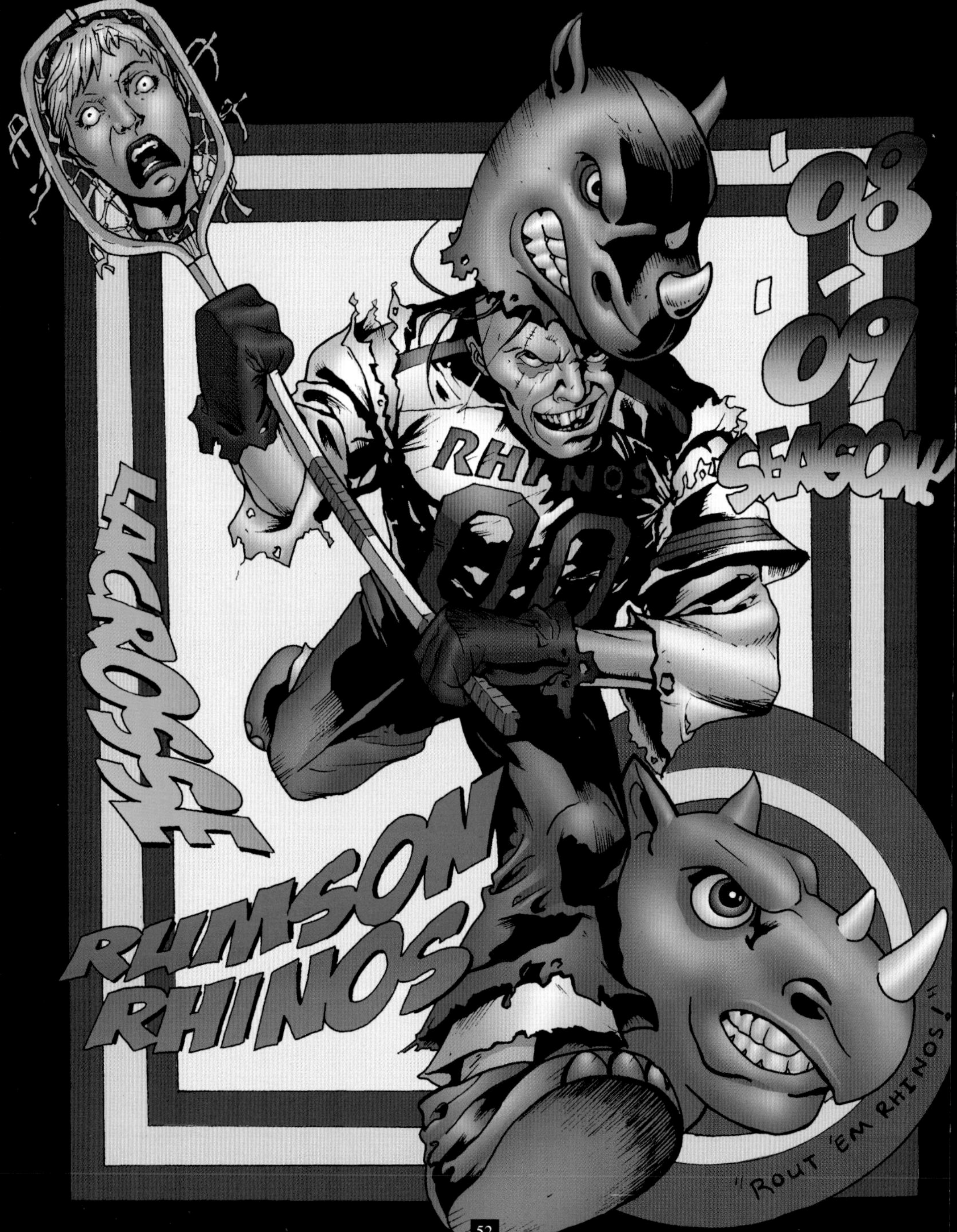

'08 - '09 SEASON!
RHINOS
LACROSSE
RUMSON RHINOS
"ROUT 'EM RHINOS!!"

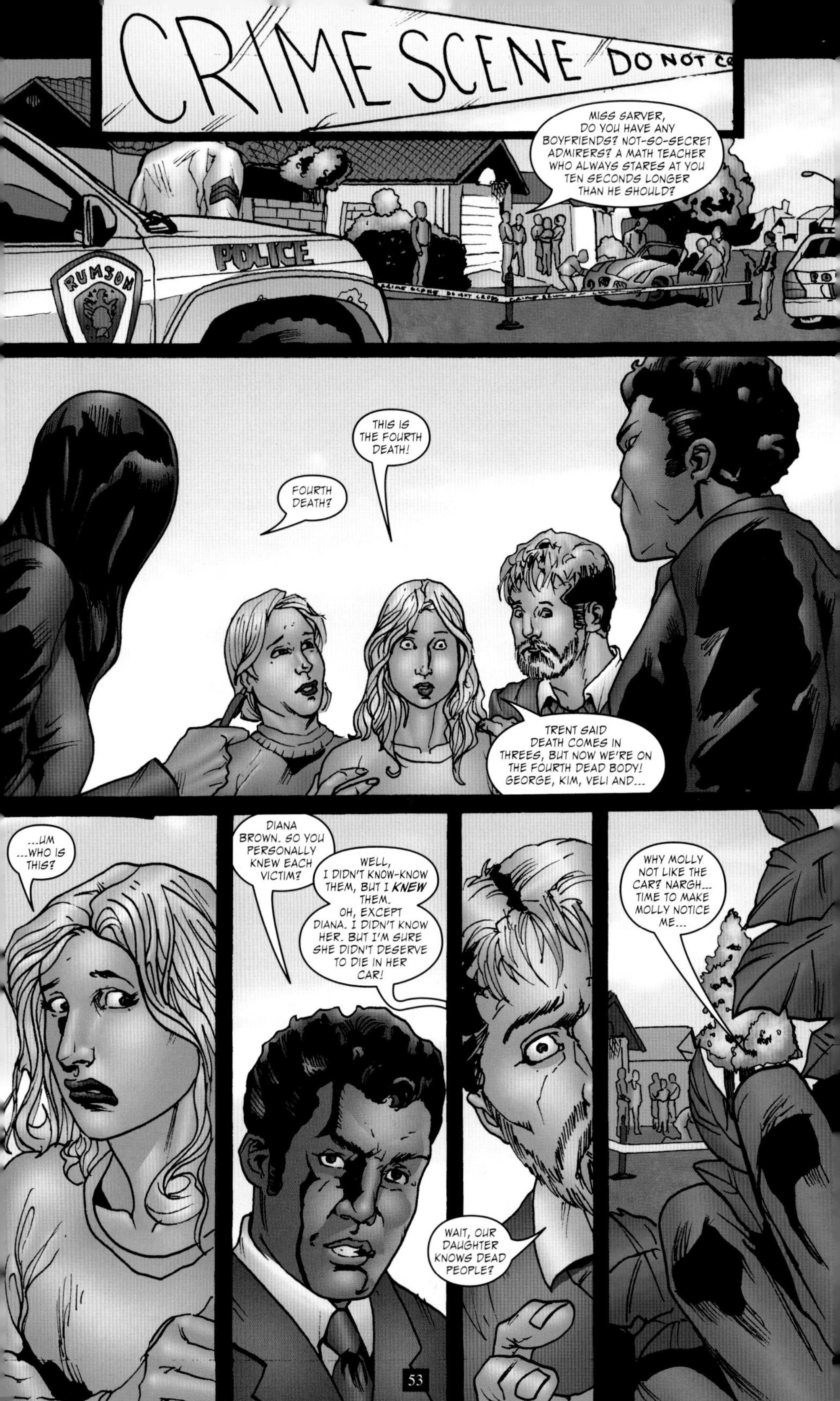
CRIME SCENE DO NOT CO
MISS SARVER, DO YOU HAVE ANY BOYFRIENDS? NOT-SO-SECRET ADMIRERS? A MATH TEACHER WHO ALWAYS STARES AT YOU TEN SECONDS LONGER THAN HE SHOULD?
RUMSON
POLICE
THIS IS THE FOURTH DEATH!
FOURTH DEATH?
TRENT SAID DEATH COMES IN THREES, BUT NOW WE'RE ON THE FOURTH DEAD BODY! GEORGE, KIM, VELI AND...
...UM ...WHO IS THIS?
DIANA BROWN. SO YOU PERSONALLY KNEW EACH VICTIM?
WELL, I DIDN'T KNOW-KNOW THEM, BUT I *KNEW* THEM. OH, EXCEPT DIANA. I DIDN'T KNOW HER. BUT I'M SURE SHE DIDN'T DESERVE TO DIE IN HER CAR!
WAIT, OUR DAUGHTER KNOWS DEAD PEOPLE?
WHY MOLLY NOT LIKE THE CAR? NARGH... TIME TO MAKE MOLLY NOTICE ME...

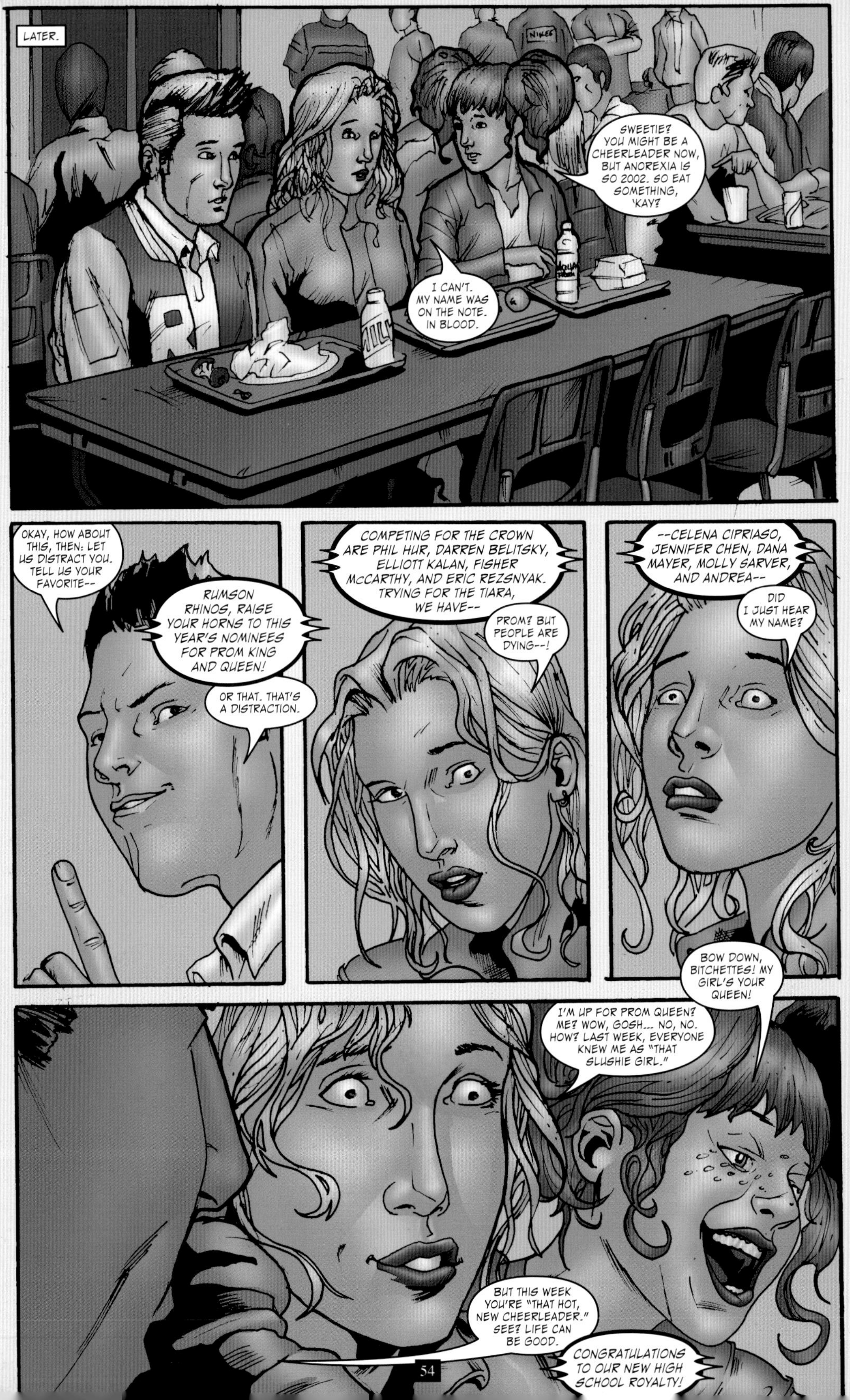
LATER.
SWEETIE? YOU MIGHT BE A CHEERLEADER NOW, BUT ANOREXIA IS SO 2002. SO EAT SOMETHING, 'KAY?
I CAN'T. MY NAME WAS ON THE NOTE. IN BLOOD.
OKAY, HOW ABOUT THIS, THEN: LET US DISTRACT YOU. TELL US YOUR FAVORITE--
RUMSON RHINOS, RAISE YOUR HORNS TO THIS YEAR'S NOMINEES FOR PROM KING AND QUEEN!
OR THAT. THAT'S A DISTRACTION.
COMPETING FOR THE CROWN ARE PHIL HUR, DARREN BELITSKY, ELLIOTT KALAN, FISHER McCARTHY, AND ERIC REZSNYAK. TRYING FOR THE TIARA, WE HAVE--
PROM? BUT PEOPLE ARE DYING--!
--CELENA CIPRIASO, JENNIFER CHEN, DANA MAYER, MOLLY SARVER, AND ANDREA--
DID I JUST HEAR MY NAME?
BOW DOWN, BITCHETTES! MY GIRL'S YOUR QUEEN!
I'M UP FOR PROM QUEEN? ME? WOW, GOSH... NO, NO. HOW? LAST WEEK, EVERYONE KNEW ME AS "THAT SLUSHIE GIRL."
BUT THIS WEEK YOU'RE "THAT HOT, NEW CHEERLEADER." SEE? LIFE CAN BE GOOD.
CONGRATULATIONS TO OUR NEW HIGH SCHOOL ROYALTY!

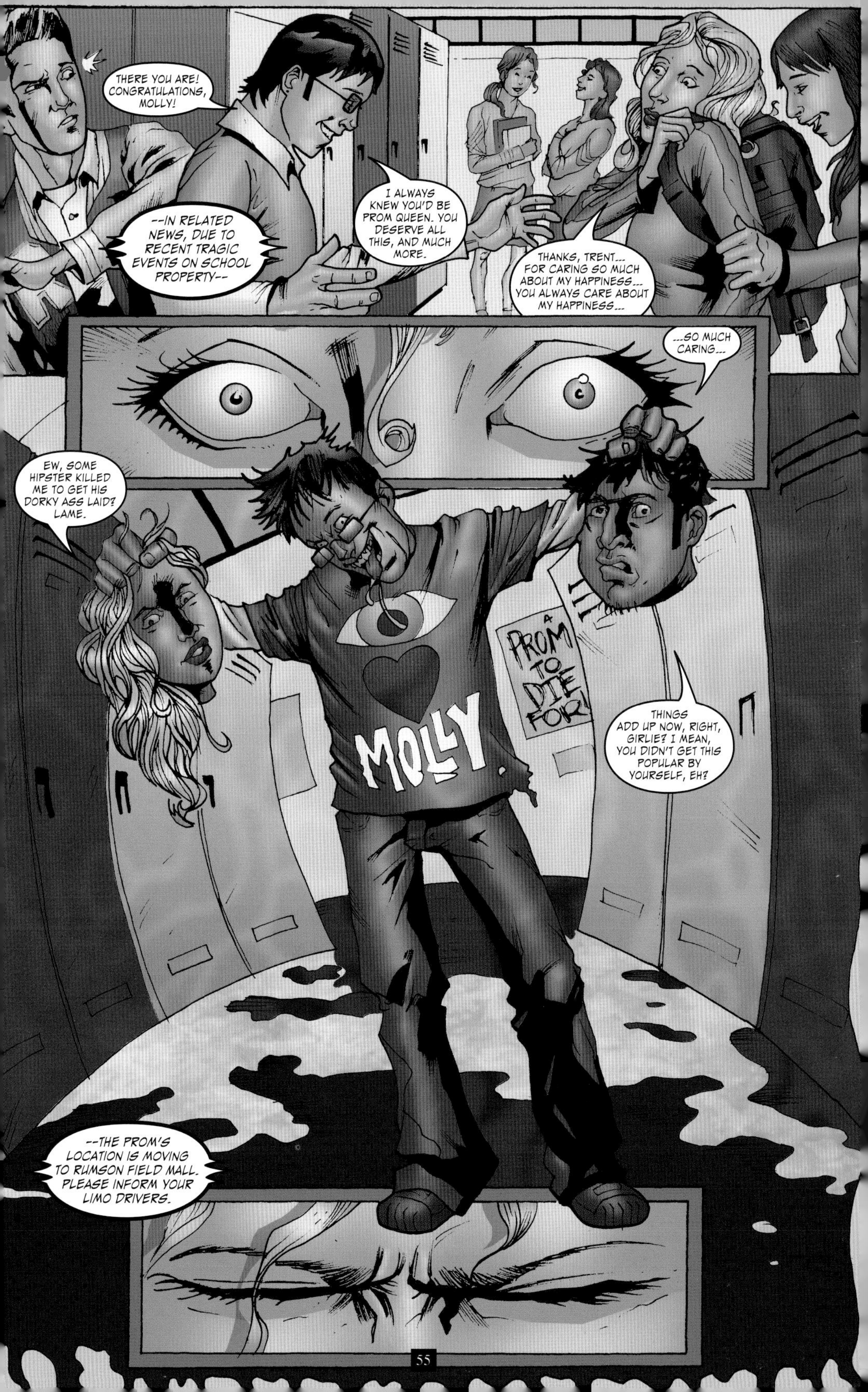
THERE YOU ARE! CONGRATULATIONS, MOLLY!
--IN RELATED NEWS, DUE TO RECENT TRAGIC EVENTS ON SCHOOL PROPERTY--
I ALWAYS KNEW YOU'D BE PROM QUEEN. YOU DESERVE ALL THIS, AND MUCH MORE.
THANKS, TRENT... FOR CARING SO MUCH ABOUT MY HAPPINESS... YOU ALWAYS CARE ABOUT MY HAPPINESS...
...SO MUCH CARING...
EW, SOME HIPSTER KILLED ME TO GET HIS DORKY ASS LAID? LAME.
A PROM TO DIE FOR!
MOLLY
THINGS ADD UP NOW, RIGHT, GIRLIE? I MEAN, YOU DIDN'T GET THIS POPULAR BY YOURSELF, EH?
--THE PROM'S LOCATION IS MOVING TO RUMSON FIELD MALL. PLEASE INFORM YOUR LIMO DRIVERS.

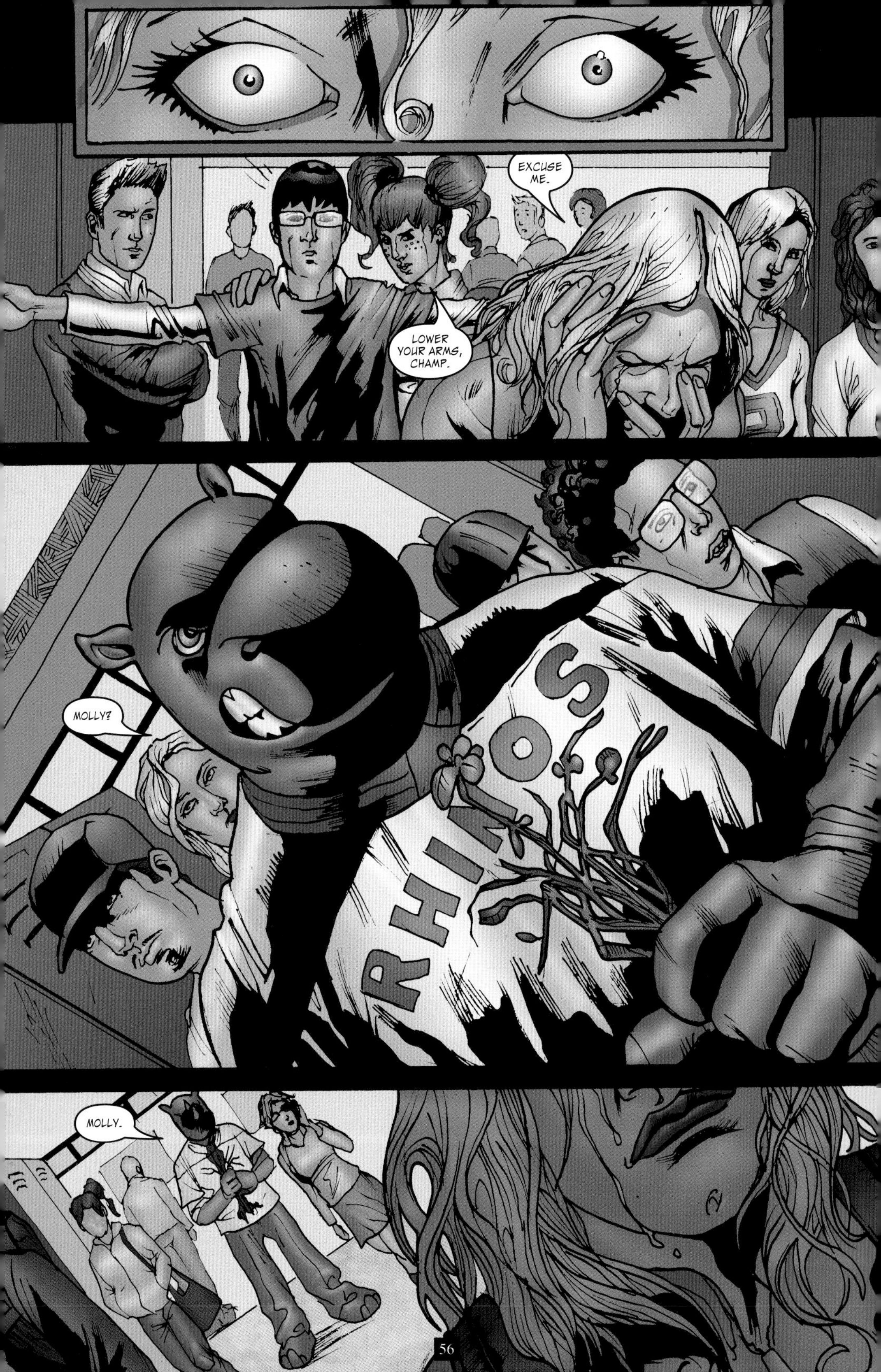
EXCUSE ME.
LOWER YOUR ARMS, CHAMP.
RHINOS
MOLLY?
MOLLY.

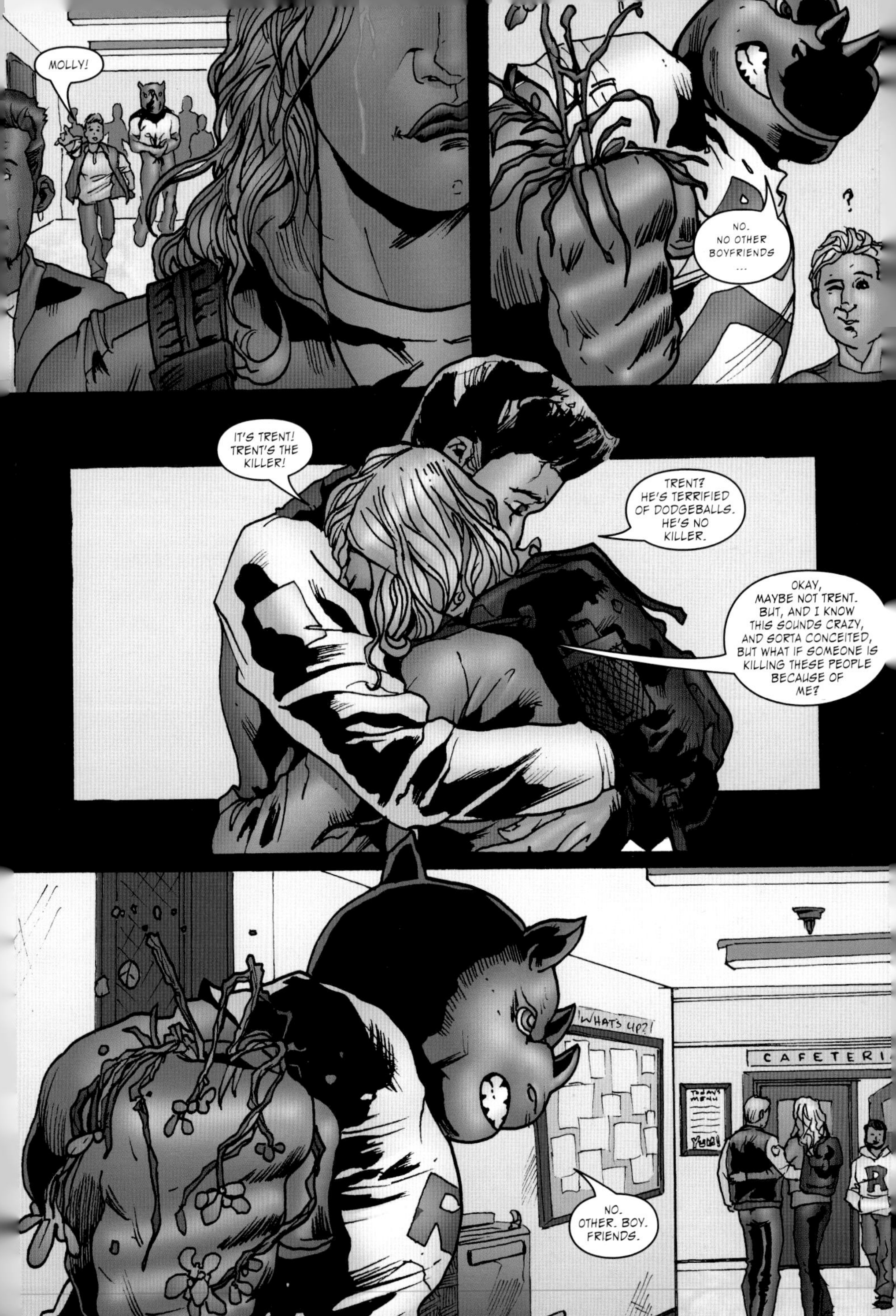
MOLLY!
NO.
NO OTHER
BOYFRIENDS
...
?
IT'S TRENT!
TRENT'S THE
KILLER!
TRENT?
HE'S TERRIFIED
OF DODGEBALLS.
HE'S NO
KILLER.
OKAY,
MAYBE NOT TRENT.
BUT, AND I KNOW
THIS SOUNDS CRAZY,
AND SORTA CONCEITED,
BUT WHAT IF SOMEONE IS
KILLING THESE PEOPLE
BECAUSE OF
ME?
'WHAT'S UP?!
CAFETERI
NO.
OTHER. BOY.
FRIENDS.

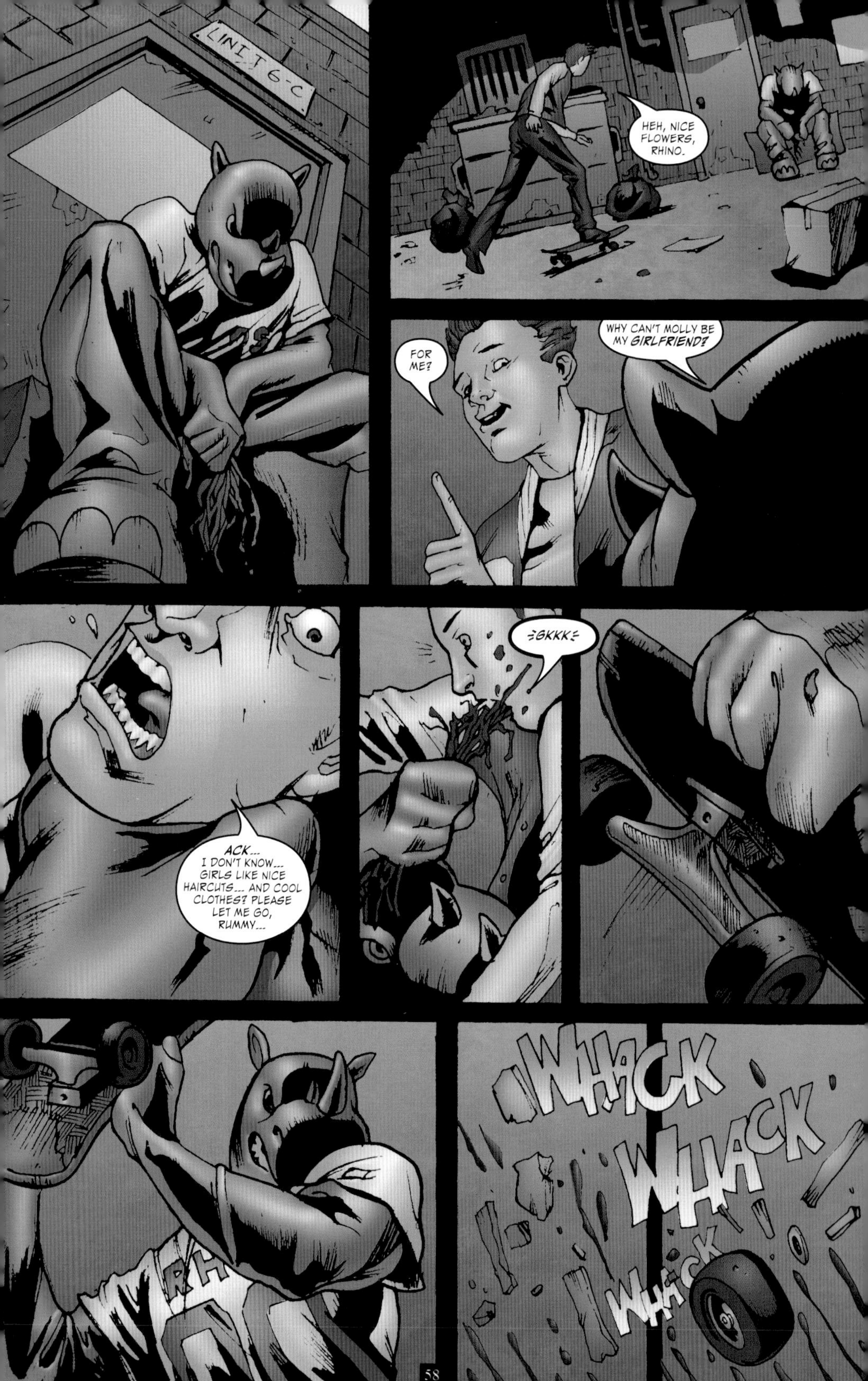
UNIT 6-C
HEH, NICE FLOWERS, RHINO.
FOR ME?
WHY CAN'T MOLLY BE MY GIRLFRIEND?
ACK... I DON'T KNOW... GIRLS LIKE NICE HAIRCUTS... AND COOL CLOTHES? PLEASE LET ME GO, RUMMY...
GKKK
WHACK
WHACK
WHACK

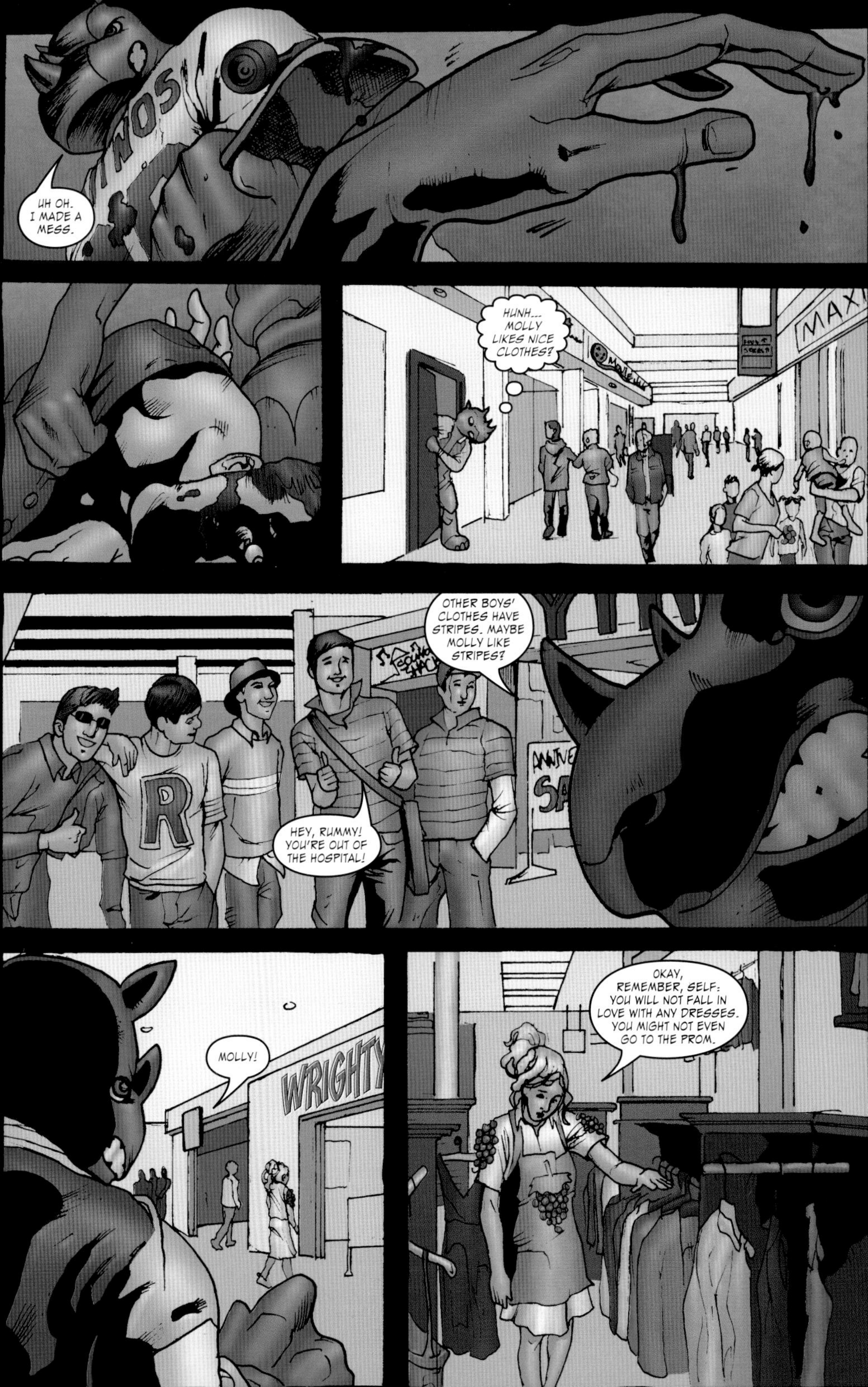
UH OH.
I MADE A MESS.
HUNH... MOLLY LIKES NICE CLOTHES?
OTHER BOYS' CLOTHES HAVE STRIPES. MAYBE MOLLY LIKE STRIPES?
HEY, RUMMY! YOU'RE OUT OF THE HOSPITAL!
MOLLY!
WRIGHTY
OKAY, REMEMBER, SELF: YOU WILL NOT FALL IN LOVE WITH ANY DRESSES. YOU MIGHT NOT EVEN GO TO THE PROM.

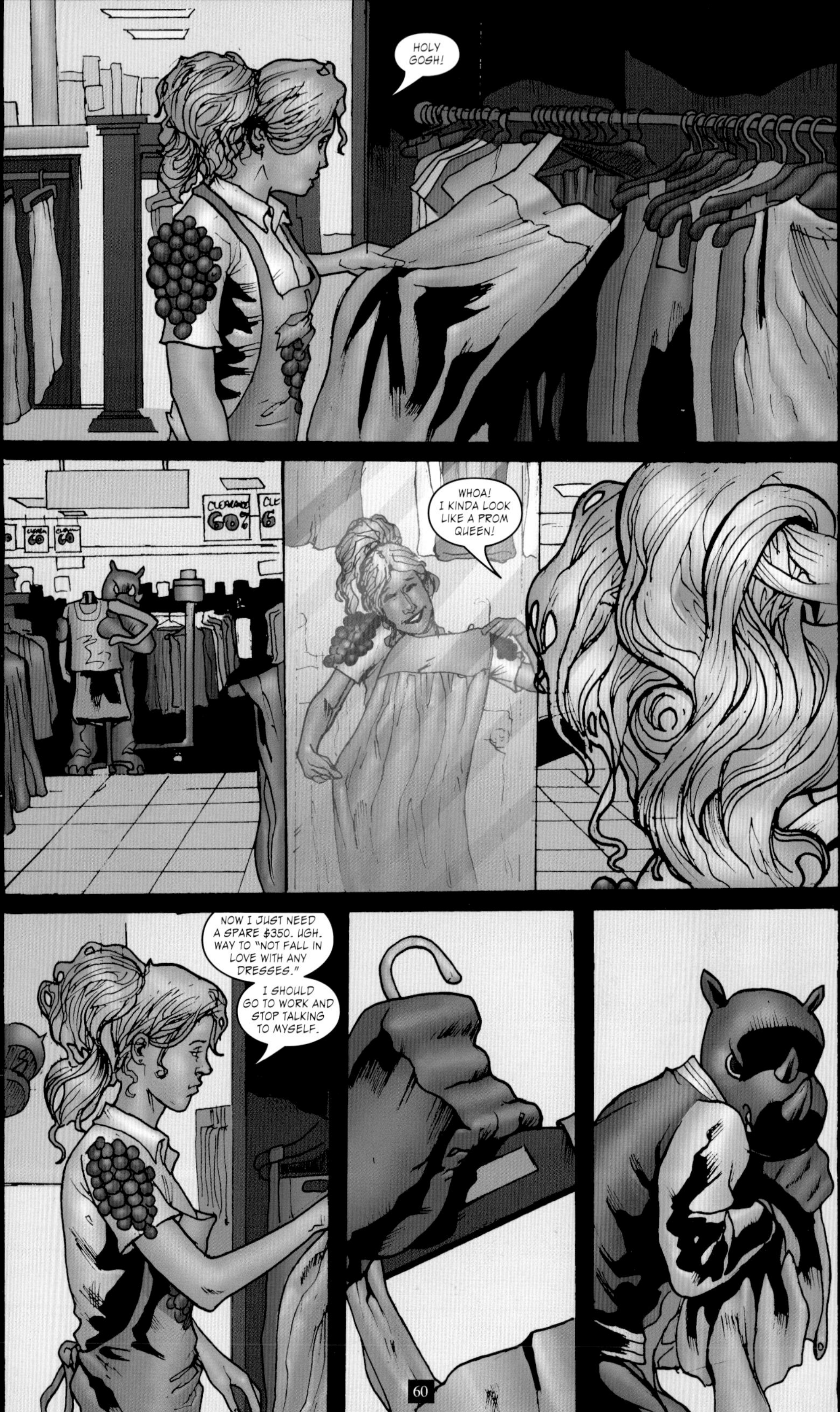
HOLY GOSH!
CLEARANCE 60%
WHOA! I KINDA LOOK LIKE A PROM QUEEN!
NOW I JUST NEED A SPARE $350. UGH. WAY TO "NOT FALL IN LOVE WITH ANY DRESSES."
I SHOULD GO TO WORK AND STOP TALKING TO MYSELF.

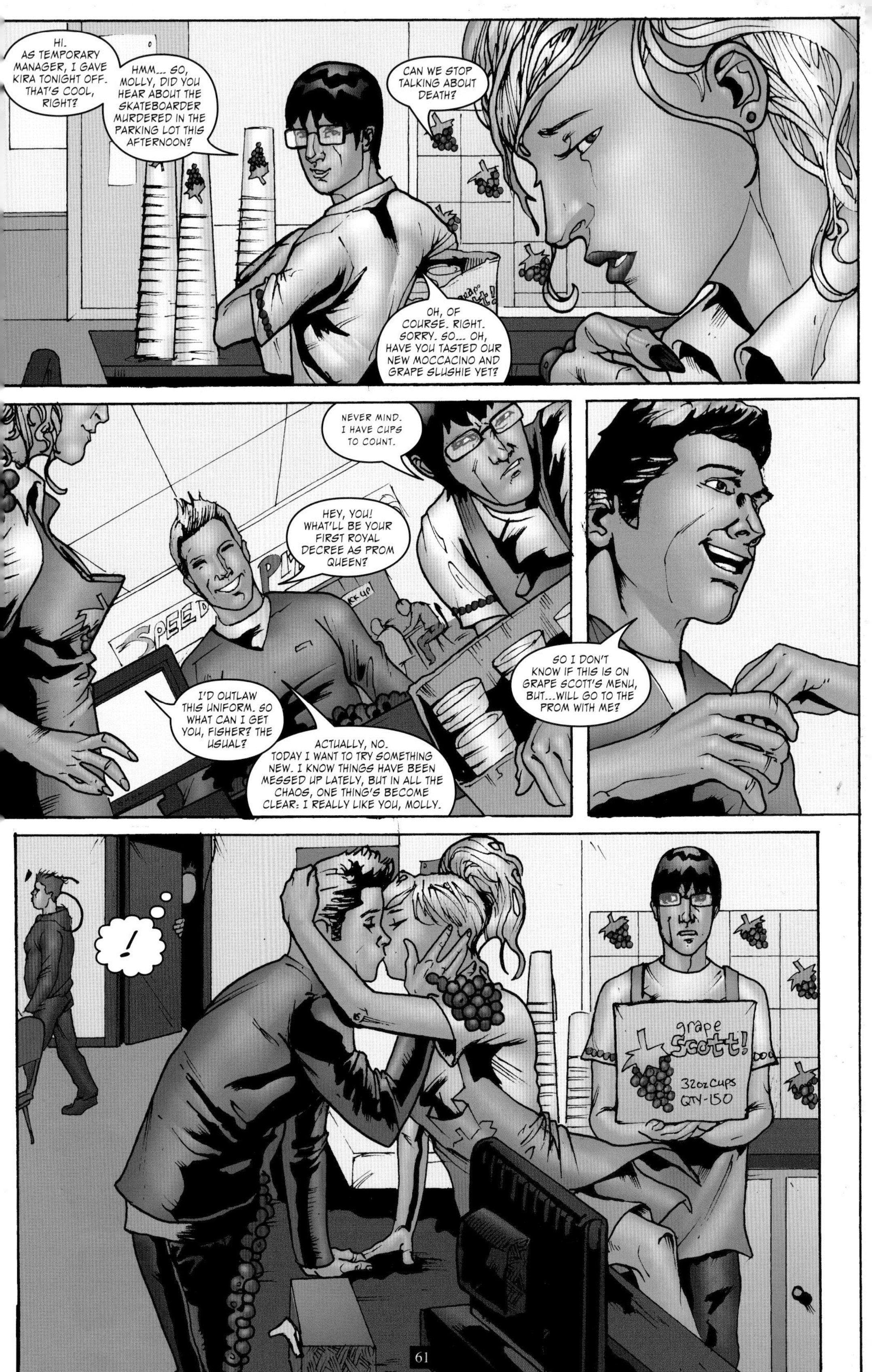
HI. AS TEMPORARY MANAGER, I GAVE KIRA TONIGHT OFF. THAT'S COOL, RIGHT?
HMM... SO, MOLLY, DID YOU HEAR ABOUT THE SKATEBOARDER MURDERED IN THE PARKING LOT THIS AFTERNOON?
CAN WE STOP TALKING ABOUT DEATH?
OH, OF COURSE. RIGHT. SORRY. SO... OH, HAVE YOU TASTED OUR NEW MOCCACINO AND GRAPE SLUSHIE YET?
NEVER MIND. I HAVE CUPS TO COUNT.
HEY, YOU! WHAT'LL BE YOUR FIRST ROYAL DECREE AS PROM QUEEN?
I'D OUTLAW THIS UNIFORM. SO WHAT CAN I GET YOU, FISHER? THE USUAL?
ACTUALLY, NO. TODAY I WANT TO TRY SOMETHING NEW. I KNOW THINGS HAVE BEEN MESSED UP LATELY, BUT IN ALL THE CHAOS, ONE THING'S BECOME CLEAR: I REALLY LIKE YOU, MOLLY.
SO I DON'T KNOW IF THIS IS ON GRAPE SCOTT'S MENU, BUT...WILL GO TO THE PROM WITH ME?
!
grape Scott!
32oz CUPS QTY-150

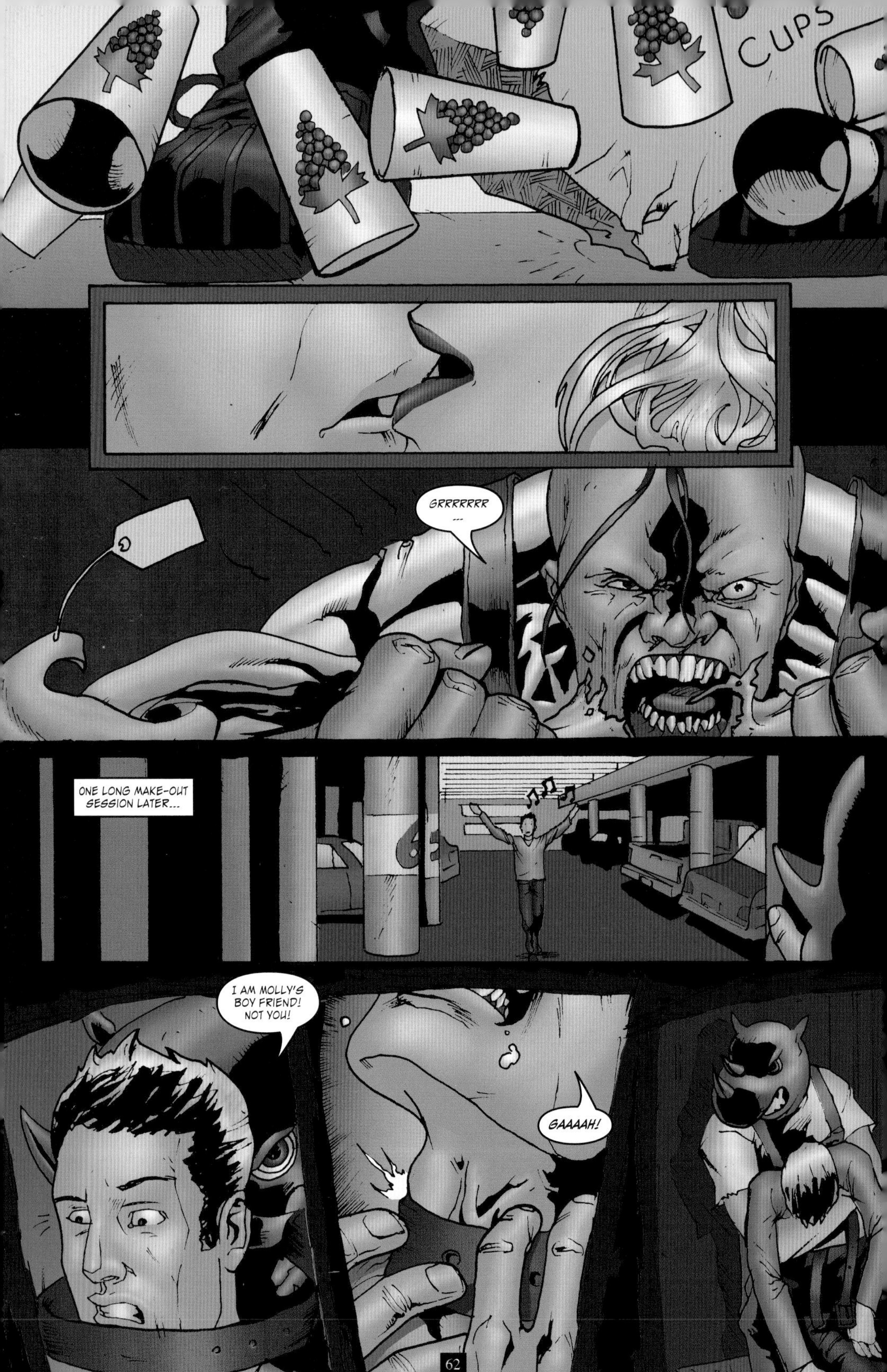
CUPS
GRRRRRR---
ONE LONG MAKE-OUT SESSION LATER...
I AM MOLLY'S BOY FRIEND! NOT YOU!
GAAAAH!

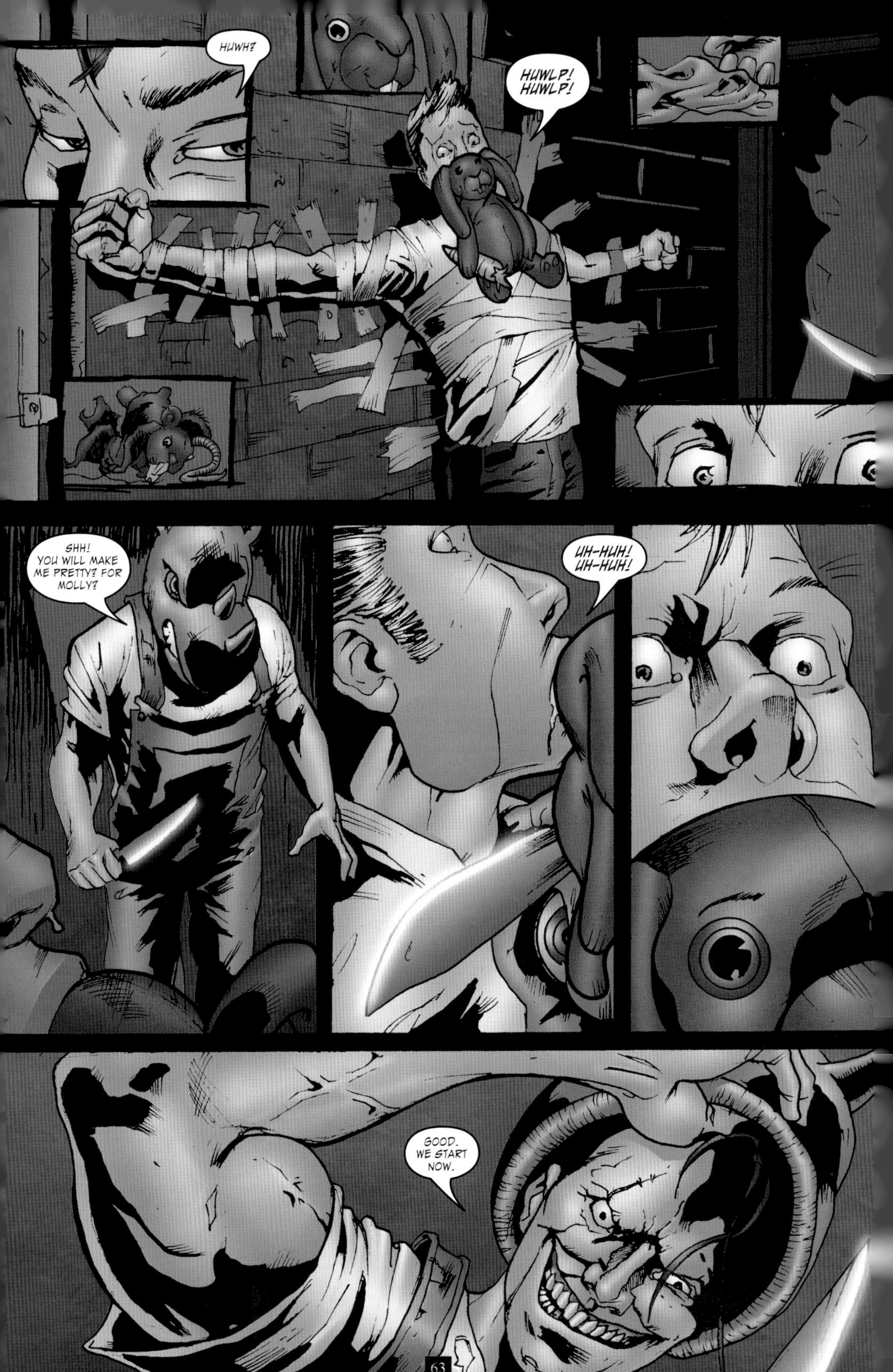
HUWH?
HUWLP! HUWLP!
SHH! YOU WILL MAKE ME PRETTY? FOR MOLLY?
UH-HUH! UH-HUH!
GOOD. WE START NOW.

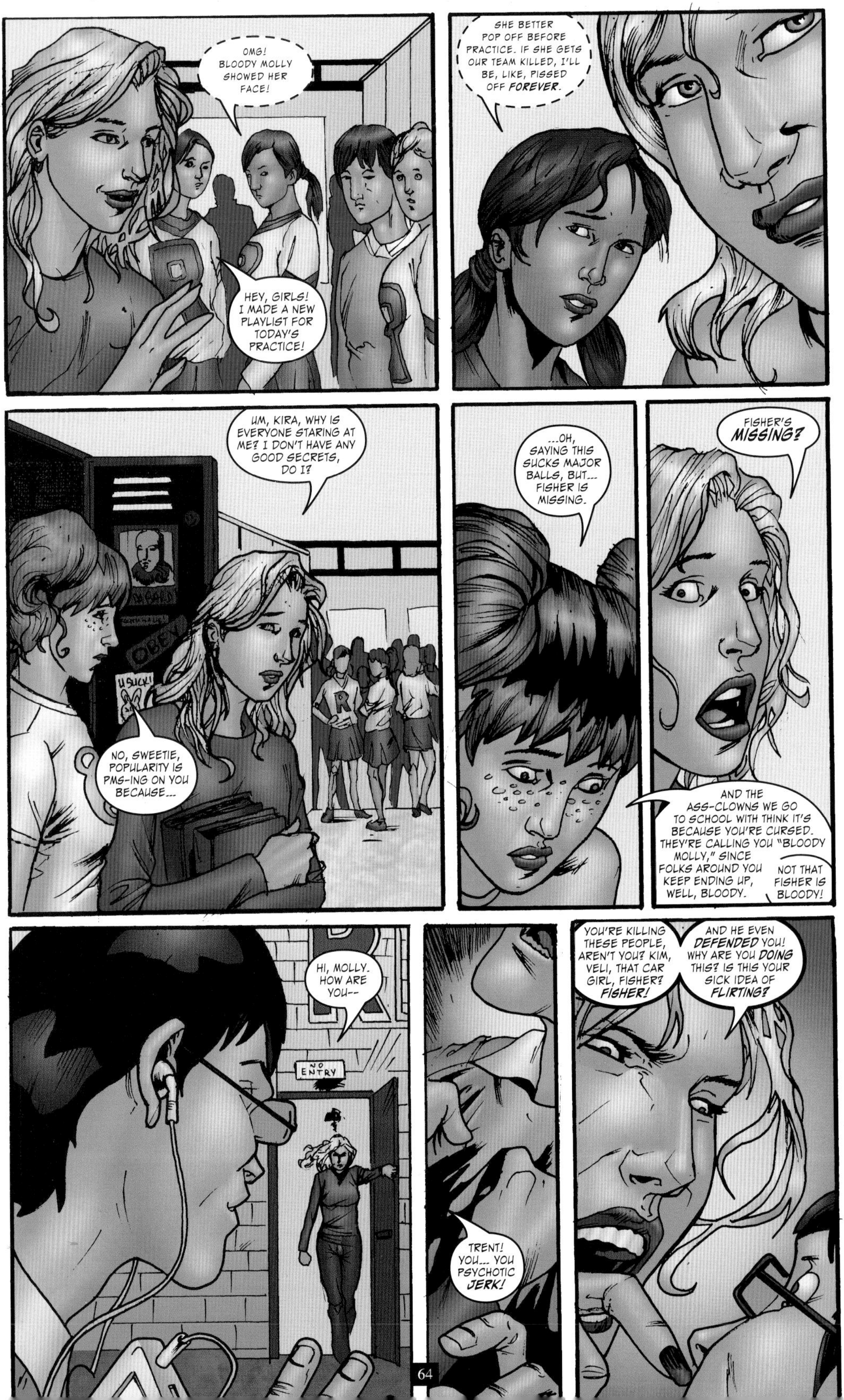
OMG! BLOODY MOLLY SHOWED HER FACE!
HEY, GIRLS! I MADE A NEW PLAYLIST FOR TODAY'S PRACTICE!
SHE BETTER POP OFF BEFORE PRACTICE. IF SHE GETS OUR TEAM KILLED, I'LL BE, LIKE, PISSED OFF FOREVER.
UM, KIRA, WHY IS EVERYONE STARING AT ME? I DON'T HAVE ANY GOOD SECRETS, DO I?
OBEY
NO, SWEETIE, POPULARITY IS PMS-ING ON YOU BECAUSE...
...OH, SAYING THIS SUCKS MAJOR BALLS, BUT... FISHER IS MISSING.
FISHER'S MISSING?
AND THE ASS-CLOWNS WE GO TO SCHOOL WITH THINK IT'S BECAUSE YOU'RE CURSED. THEY'RE CALLING YOU "BLOODY MOLLY," SINCE FOLKS AROUND YOU KEEP ENDING UP, WELL, BLOODY.
NOT THAT FISHER IS BLOODY!
HI, MOLLY. HOW ARE YOU--
NO ENTRY
TRENT! YOU... YOU PSYCHOTIC JERK!
YOU'RE KILLING THESE PEOPLE, AREN'T YOU? KIM, VELI, THAT CAR GIRL, FISHER? FISHER!
AND HE EVEN DEFENDED YOU! WHY ARE YOU DOING THIS? IS THIS YOUR SICK IDEA OF FLIRTING?

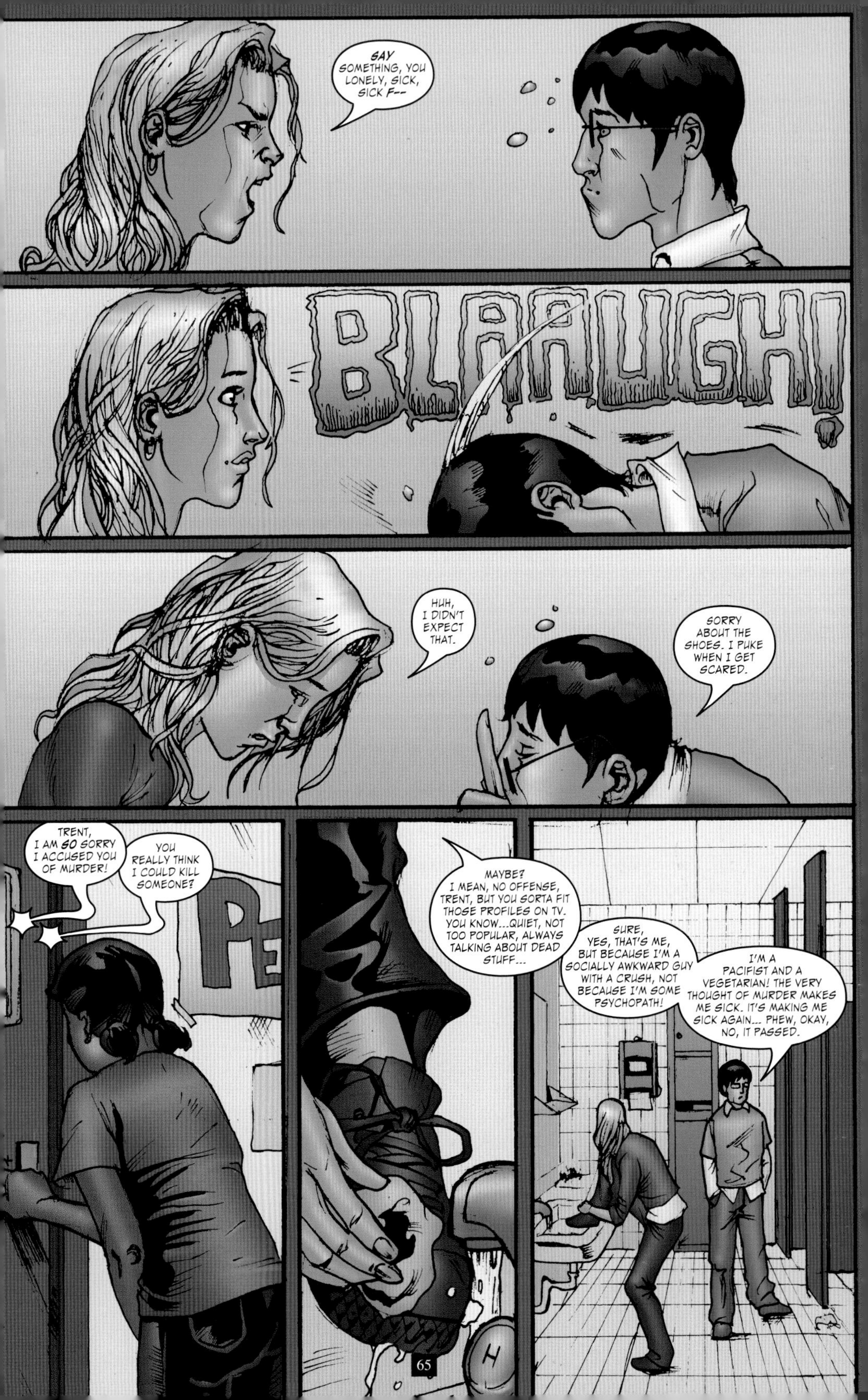
SAY SOMETHING, YOU LONELY, SICK, SICK F--
BLAAUGH!
HUH, I DIDN'T EXPECT THAT.
SORRY ABOUT THE SHOES. I PUKE WHEN I GET SCARED.
TRENT, I AM SO SORRY I ACCUSED YOU OF MURDER!
YOU REALLY THINK I COULD KILL SOMEONE?
MAYBE? I MEAN, NO OFFENSE, TRENT, BUT YOU SORTA FIT THOSE PROFILES ON TV. YOU KNOW...QUIET, NOT TOO POPULAR, ALWAYS TALKING ABOUT DEAD STUFF...
SURE, YES, THAT'S ME, BUT BECAUSE I'M A SOCIALLY AWKWARD GUY WITH A CRUSH, NOT BECAUSE I'M SOME PSYCHOPATH!
I'M A PACIFIST AND A VEGETARIAN! THE VERY THOUGHT OF MURDER MAKES ME SICK. IT'S MAKING ME SICK AGAIN... PHEW, OKAY, NO, IT PASSED.

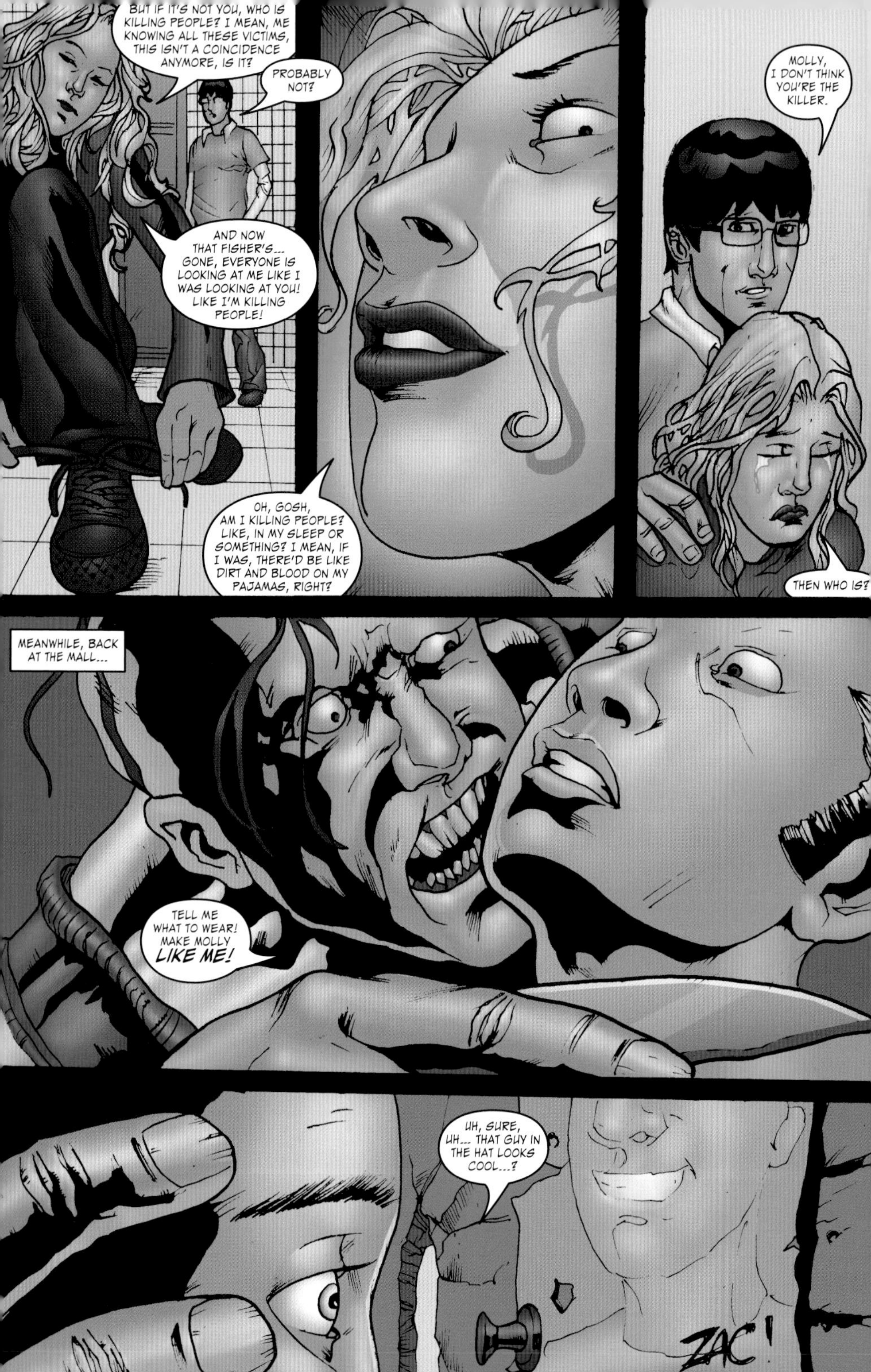

BUT IF IT'S NOT YOU, WHO IS KILLING PEOPLE? I MEAN, ME KNOWING ALL THESE VICTIMS, THIS ISN'T A COINCIDENCE ANYMORE, IS IT?
PROBABLY NOT?
AND NOW THAT FISHER'S... GONE, EVERYONE IS LOOKING AT ME LIKE I WAS LOOKING AT YOU! LIKE I'M KILLING PEOPLE!
OH, GOSH, AM I KILLING PEOPLE? LIKE, IN MY SLEEP OR SOMETHING? I MEAN, IF I WAS, THERE'D BE LIKE DIRT AND BLOOD ON MY PAJAMAS, RIGHT?
MOLLY, I DON'T THINK YOU'RE THE KILLER.
THEN WHO IS?
MEANWHILE, BACK AT THE MALL...
TELL ME WHAT TO WEAR! MAKE MOLLY LIKE ME!
UH, SURE, UH... THAT GUY IN THE HAT LOOKS COOL...?
ZAC!

HUNH... GIRLS DO LIKE HIM...

POINT TO STORES WITH THAT BOY'S CLOTHES! NOW! I NEED TO SHOP!

SURE, SURE, UH, GO TO "HOT MESS."

AND IF IT COMES UP, YOUR SIZE IS A XXL, OKAY?

MOLLY LIKE THIS?

CHECK IT: WE GOT A PLUSHIE!

FOR MOLLY

look WHAT!

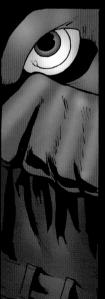

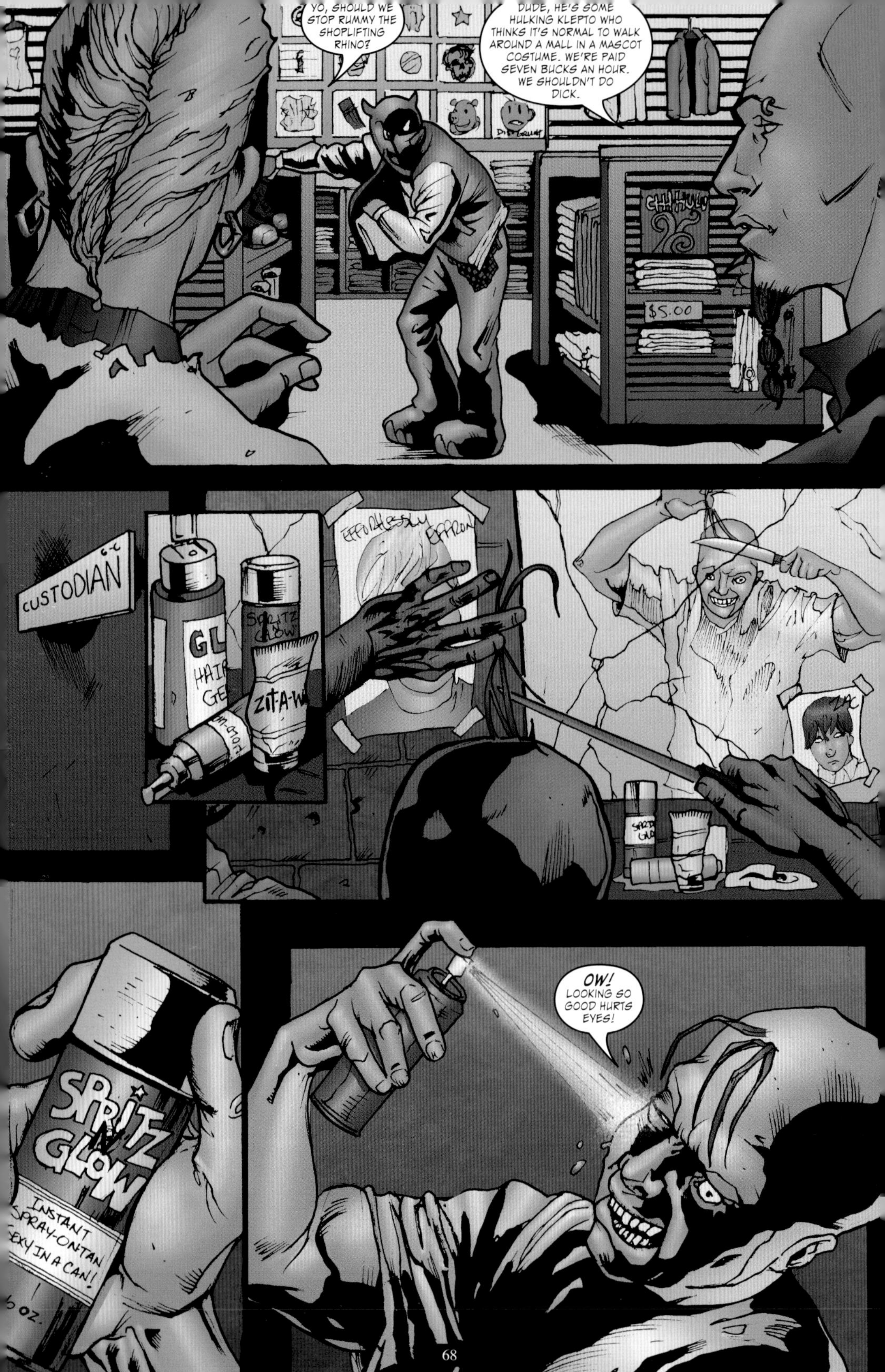

YO, SHOULD WE STOP RUMMY THE SHOPLIFTING RHINO?
DUDE, HE'S SOME HULKING KLEPTO WHO THINKS IT'S NORMAL TO WALK AROUND A MALL IN A MASCOT COSTUME. WE'RE PAID SEVEN BUCKS AN HOUR. WE SHOULDN'T DO DICK.
$5.00
CUSTODIAN
HAIR GEL
ZIT-A-W
SPRITZ N' GLOW
OW! LOOKING SO GOOD HURTS EYES!
SPRITZ N GLOW
INSTANT SPRAY-ON-TAN SEXY IN A CAN!

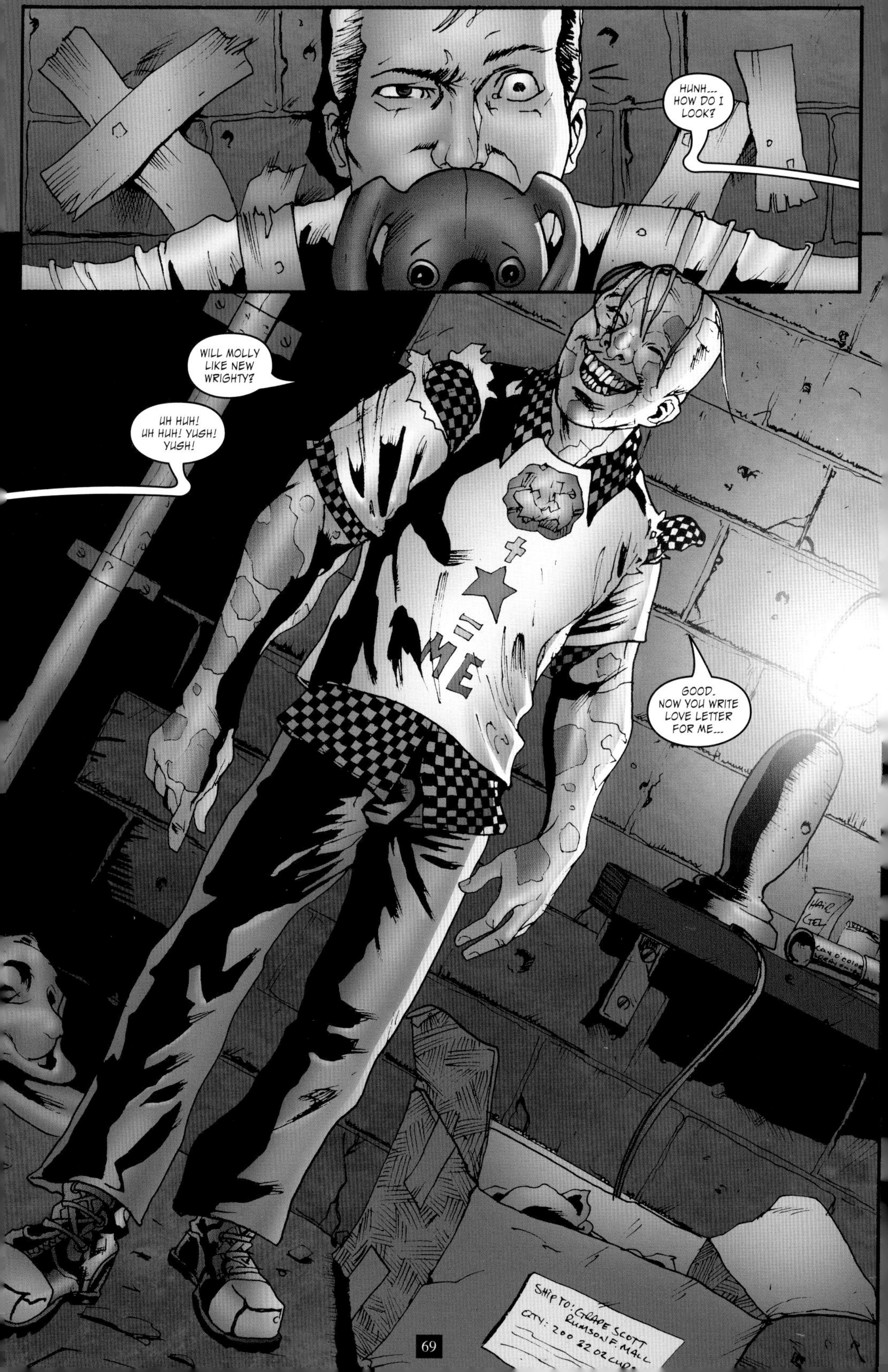
HUNH... HOW DO I LOOK?
WILL MOLLY LIKE NEW WRIGHTY?
UH HUH! UH HUH! YUSH! YUSH!
GOOD. NOW YOU WRITE LOVE LETTER FOR ME...
HAIR GEL

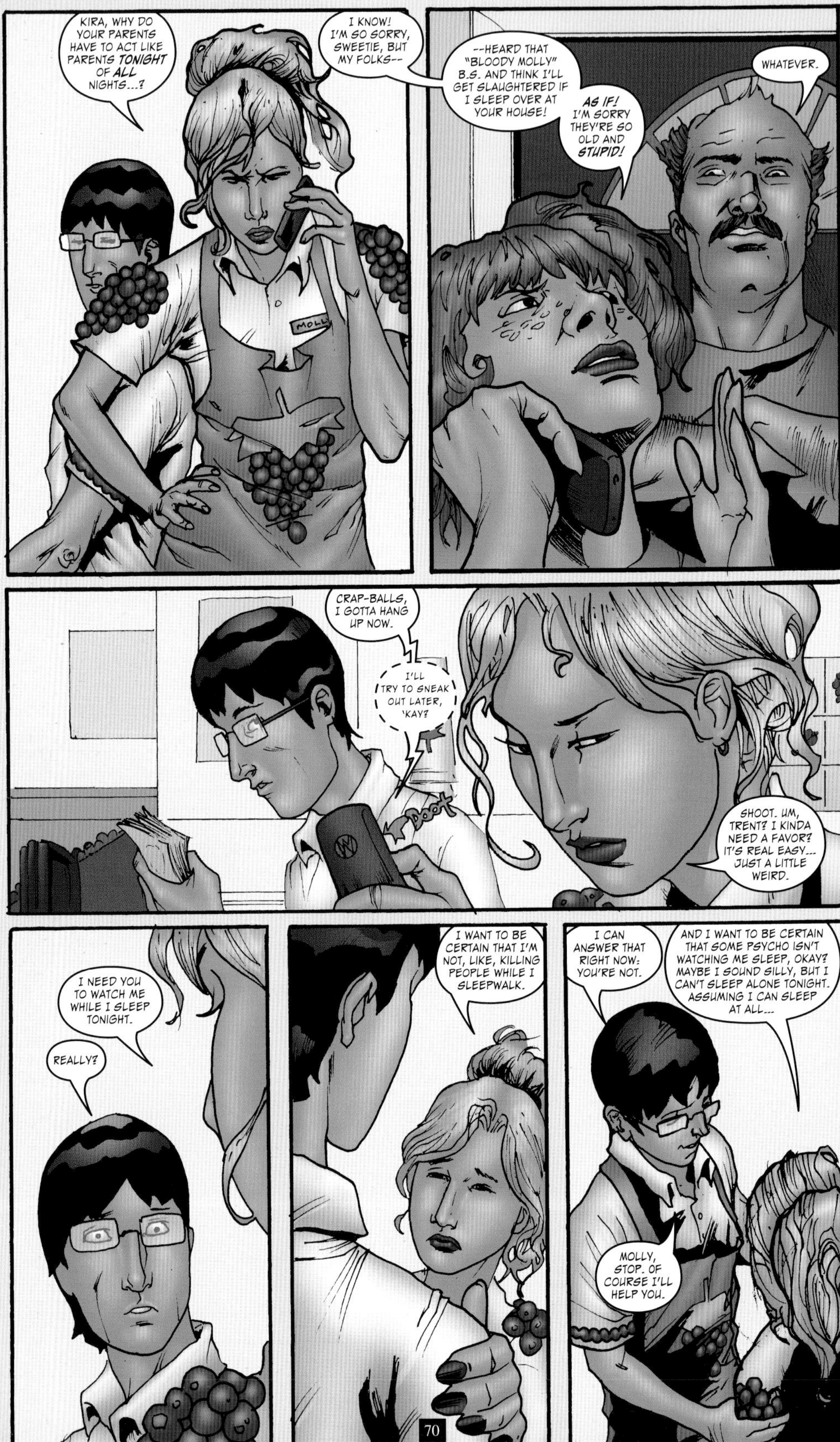
KIRA, WHY DO YOUR PARENTS HAVE TO ACT LIKE PARENTS TONIGHT OF ALL NIGHTS...?
I KNOW! I'M SO SORRY, SWEETIE, BUT MY FOLKS--
--HEARD THAT "BLOODY MOLLY" B.S. AND THINK I'LL GET SLAUGHTERED IF I SLEEP OVER AT YOUR HOUSE!
AS IF! I'M SORRY THEY'RE SO OLD AND STUPID!
WHATEVER.
MOLL
CRAP-BALLS, I GOTTA HANG UP NOW.
I'LL TRY TO SNEAK OUT LATER, 'KAY?
BOOP
SHOOT. UM, TRENT? I KINDA NEED A FAVOR? IT'S REAL EASY... JUST A LITTLE WEIRD.
I NEED YOU TO WATCH ME WHILE I SLEEP TONIGHT.
REALLY?
I WANT TO BE CERTAIN THAT I'M NOT, LIKE, KILLING PEOPLE WHILE I SLEEPWALK.
I CAN ANSWER THAT RIGHT NOW: YOU'RE NOT.
AND I WANT TO BE CERTAIN THAT SOME PSYCHO ISN'T WATCHING ME SLEEP, OKAY? MAYBE I SOUND SILLY, BUT I CAN'T SLEEP ALONE TONIGHT. ASSUMING I CAN SLEEP AT ALL...
MOLLY, STOP. OF COURSE I'LL HELP YOU.

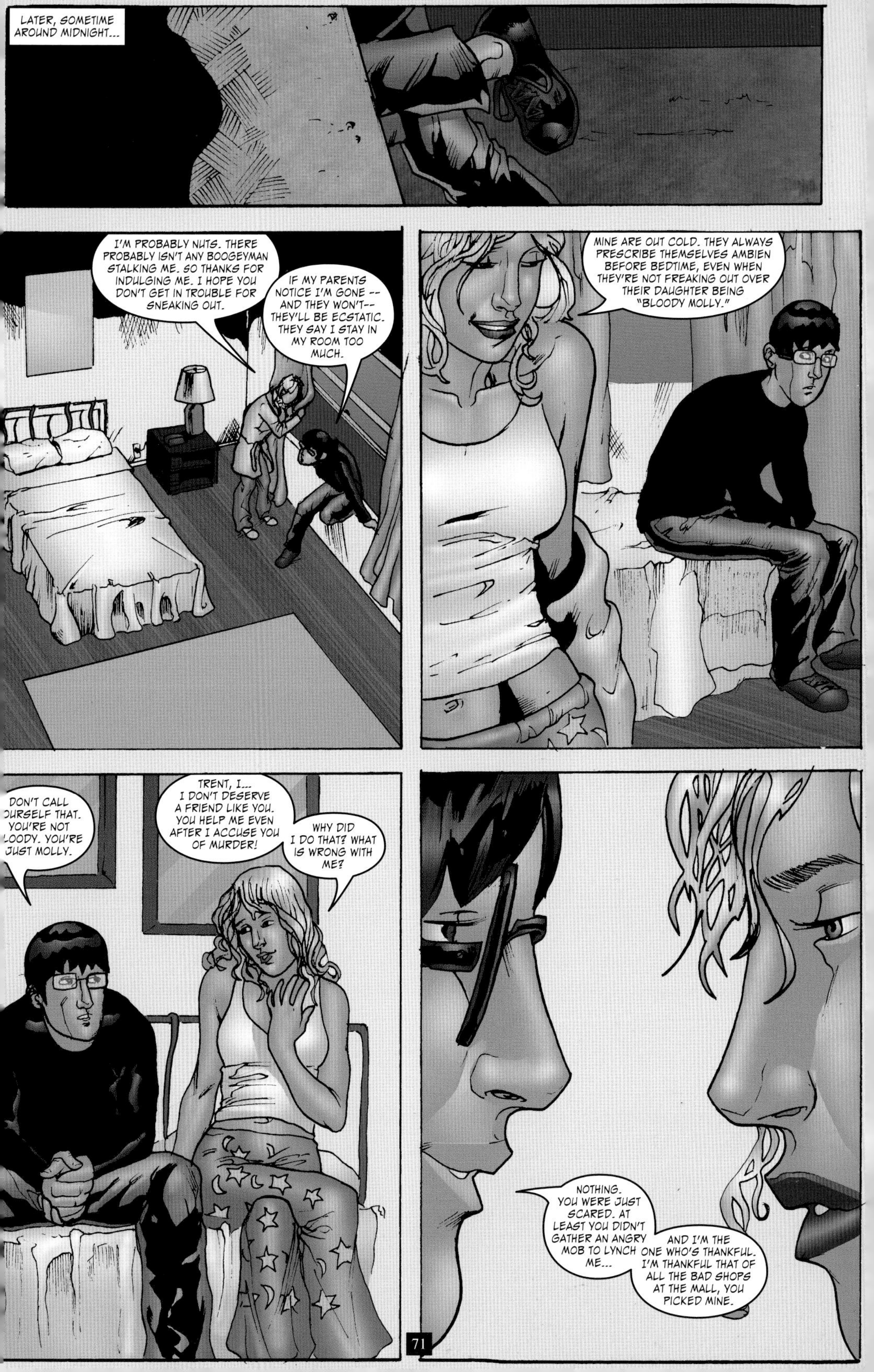
LATER, SOMETIME AROUND MIDNIGHT...
I'M PROBABLY NUTS. THERE PROBABLY ISN'T ANY BOOGEYMAN STALKING ME. SO THANKS FOR INDULGING ME. I HOPE YOU DON'T GET IN TROUBLE FOR SNEAKING OUT.
IF MY PARENTS NOTICE I'M GONE -- AND THEY WON'T-- THEY'LL BE ECSTATIC. THEY SAY I STAY IN MY ROOM TOO MUCH.
MINE ARE OUT COLD. THEY ALWAYS PRESCRIBE THEMSELVES AMBIEN BEFORE BEDTIME, EVEN WHEN THEY'RE NOT FREAKING OUT OVER THEIR DAUGHTER BEING "BLOODY MOLLY."
DON'T CALL OURSELF THAT. YOU'RE NOT LOODY. YOU'RE JUST MOLLY.
TRENT, I... I DON'T DESERVE A FRIEND LIKE YOU. YOU HELP ME EVEN AFTER I ACCUSE YOU OF MURDER!
WHY DID I DO THAT? WHAT IS WRONG WITH ME?
NOTHING. YOU WERE JUST SCARED. AT LEAST YOU DIDN'T GATHER AN ANGRY MOB TO LYNCH ME...
AND I'M THE ONE WHO'S THANKFUL. I'M THANKFUL THAT OF ALL THE BAD SHOPS AT THE MALL, YOU PICKED MINE.

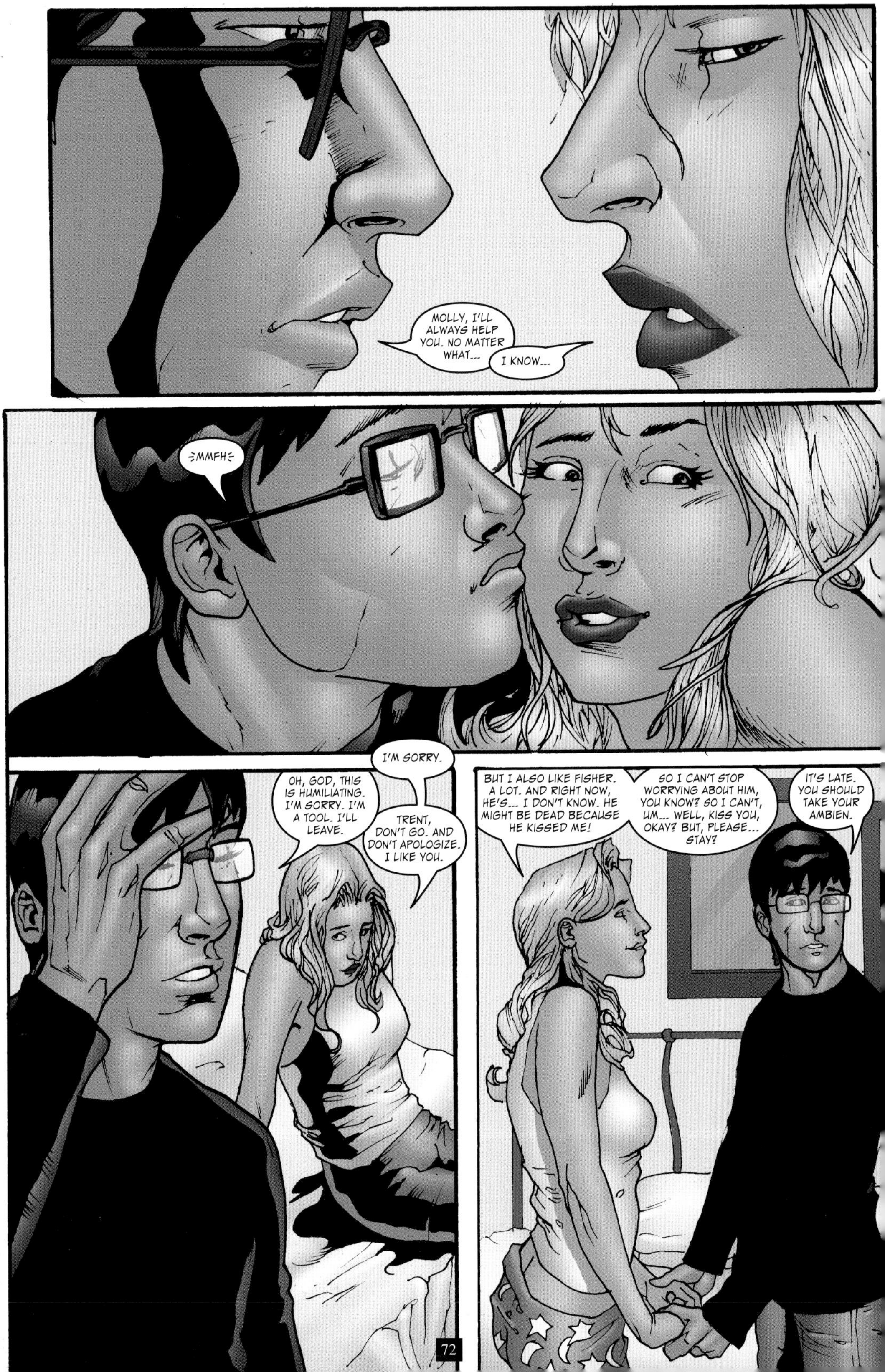
MOLLY, I'LL ALWAYS HELP YOU. NO MATTER WHAT...
I KNOW...
MMFH
OH, GOD, THIS IS HUMILIATING. I'M SORRY. I'M A TOOL. I'LL LEAVE.
I'M SORRY.
TRENT, DON'T GO. AND DON'T APOLOGIZE. I LIKE YOU.
BUT I ALSO LIKE FISHER. A LOT. AND RIGHT NOW, HE'S... I DON'T KNOW. HE MIGHT BE DEAD BECAUSE HE KISSED ME!
SO I CAN'T STOP WORRYING ABOUT HIM, YOU KNOW? SO I CAN'T, UM... WELL, KISS YOU, OKAY? BUT, PLEASE... STAY?
IT'S LATE. YOU SHOULD TAKE YOUR AMBIEN.

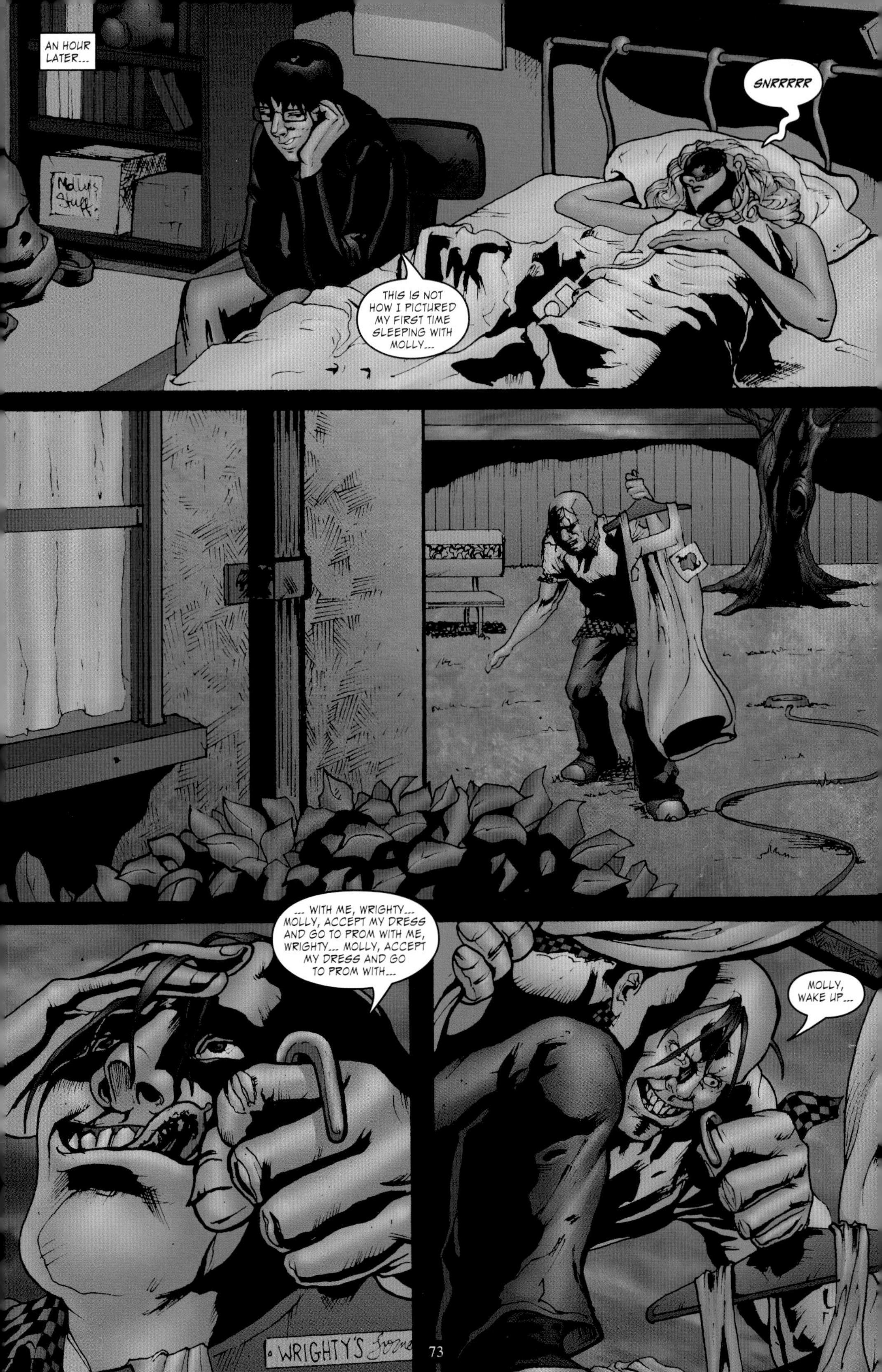
AN HOUR LATER...
SNRRRRR
THIS IS NOT HOW I PICTURED MY FIRST TIME SLEEPING WITH MOLLY...
Molly's Stuff!
... WITH ME, WRIGHTY... MOLLY, ACCEPT MY DRESS AND GO TO PROM WITH ME, WRIGHTY... MOLLY, ACCEPT MY DRESS AND GO TO PROM WITH...
MOLLY, WAKE UP...
WRIGHTY'S

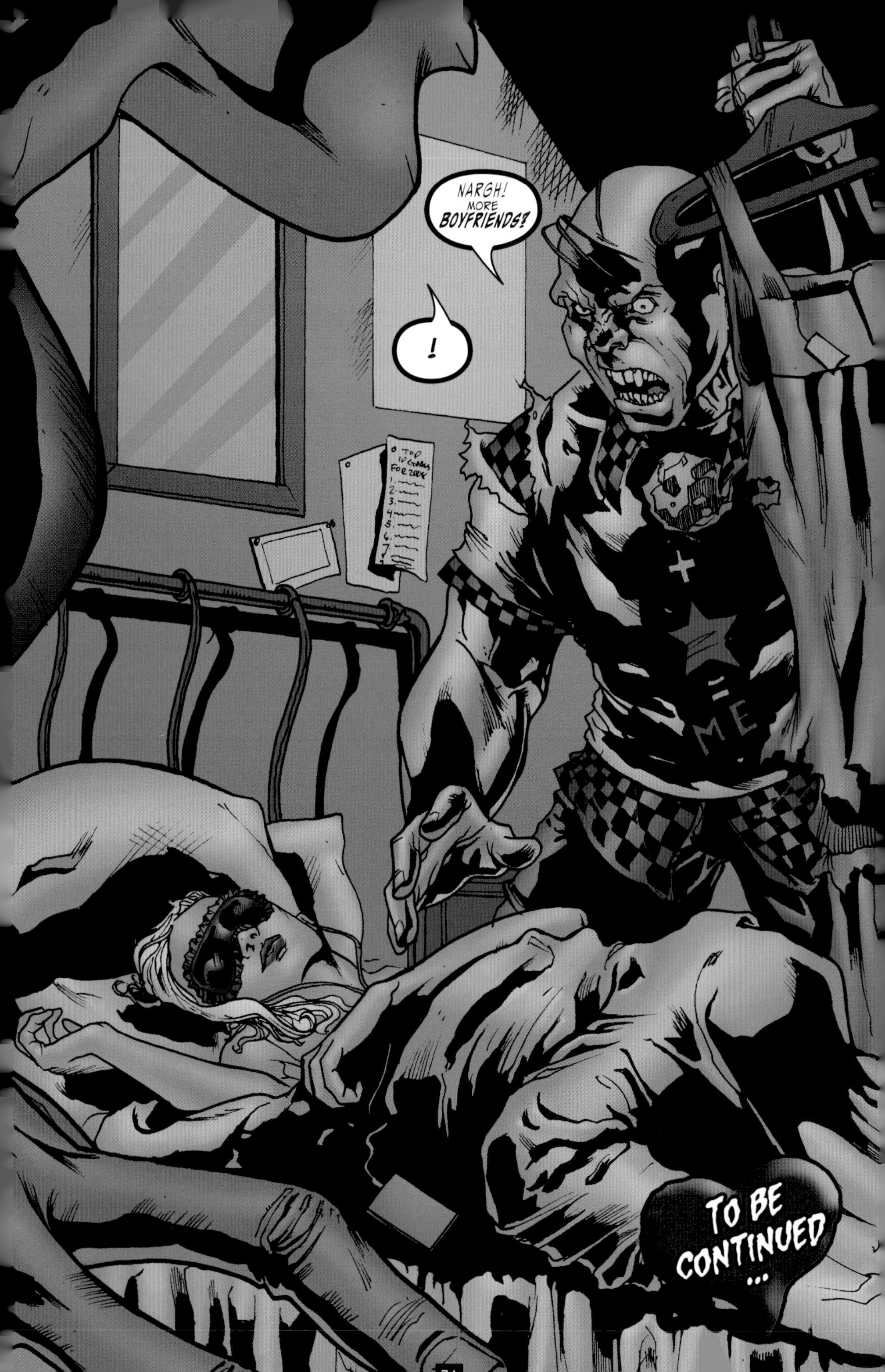
NARGH! MORE BOYFRIENDS?
!
TO BE CONTINUED ...

CHAPTER 4

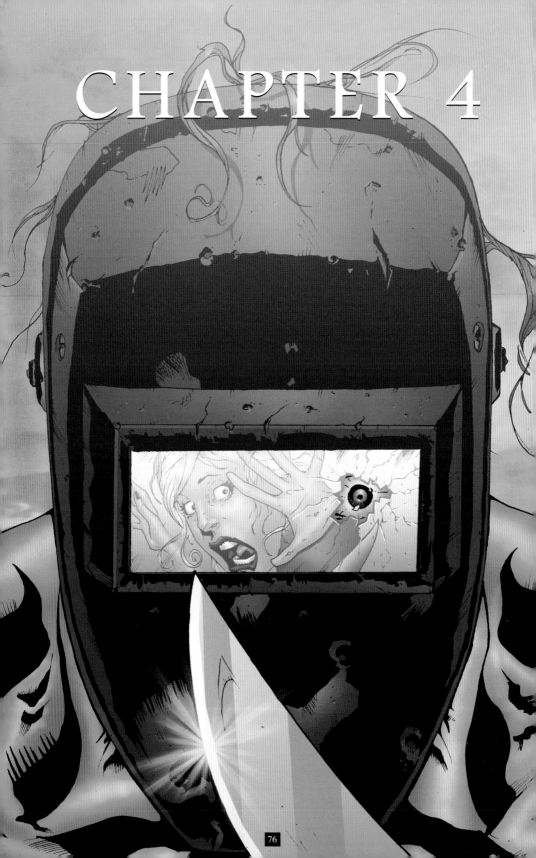

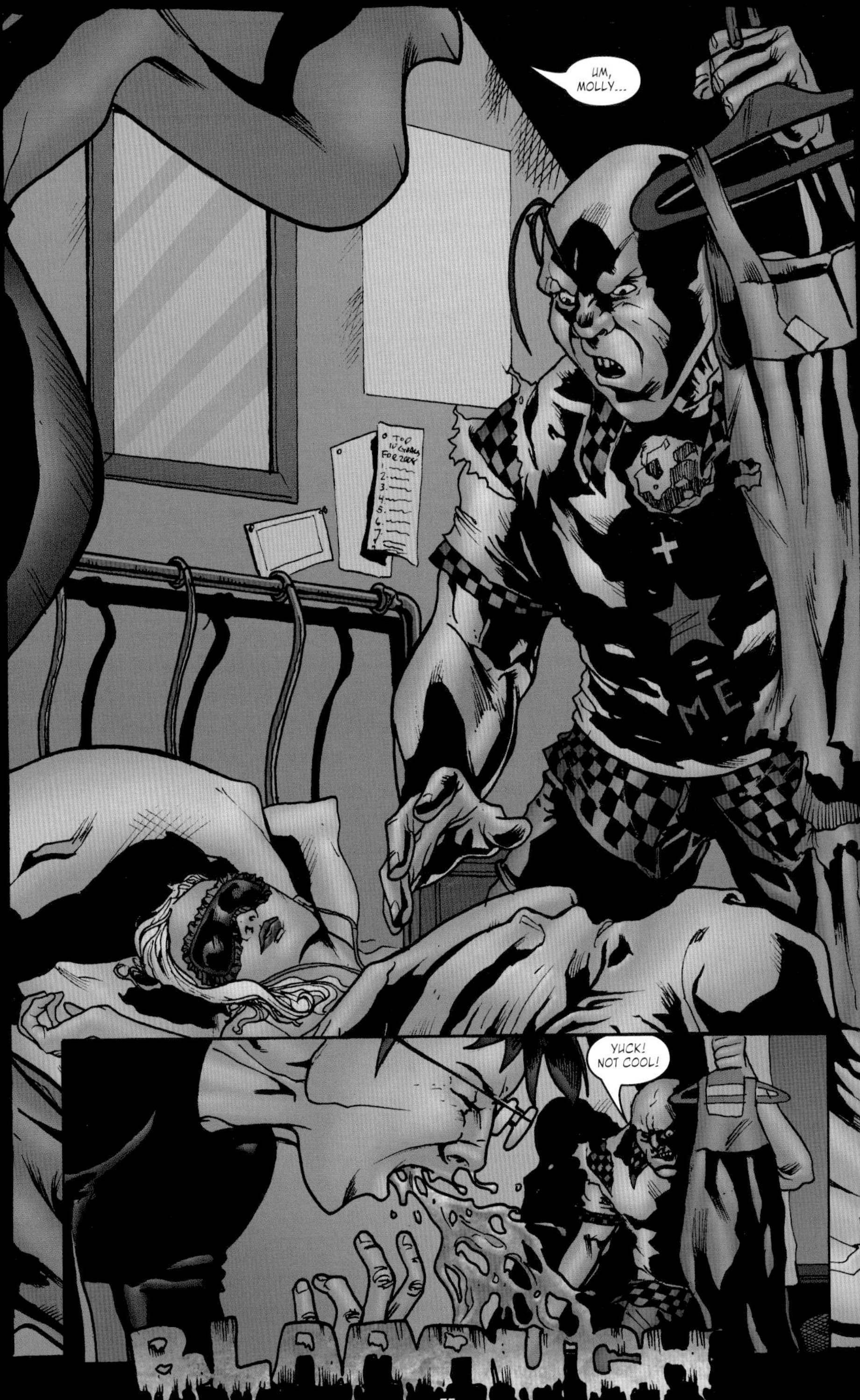
UM,
MOLLY...
YUCK!
NOT COOL!

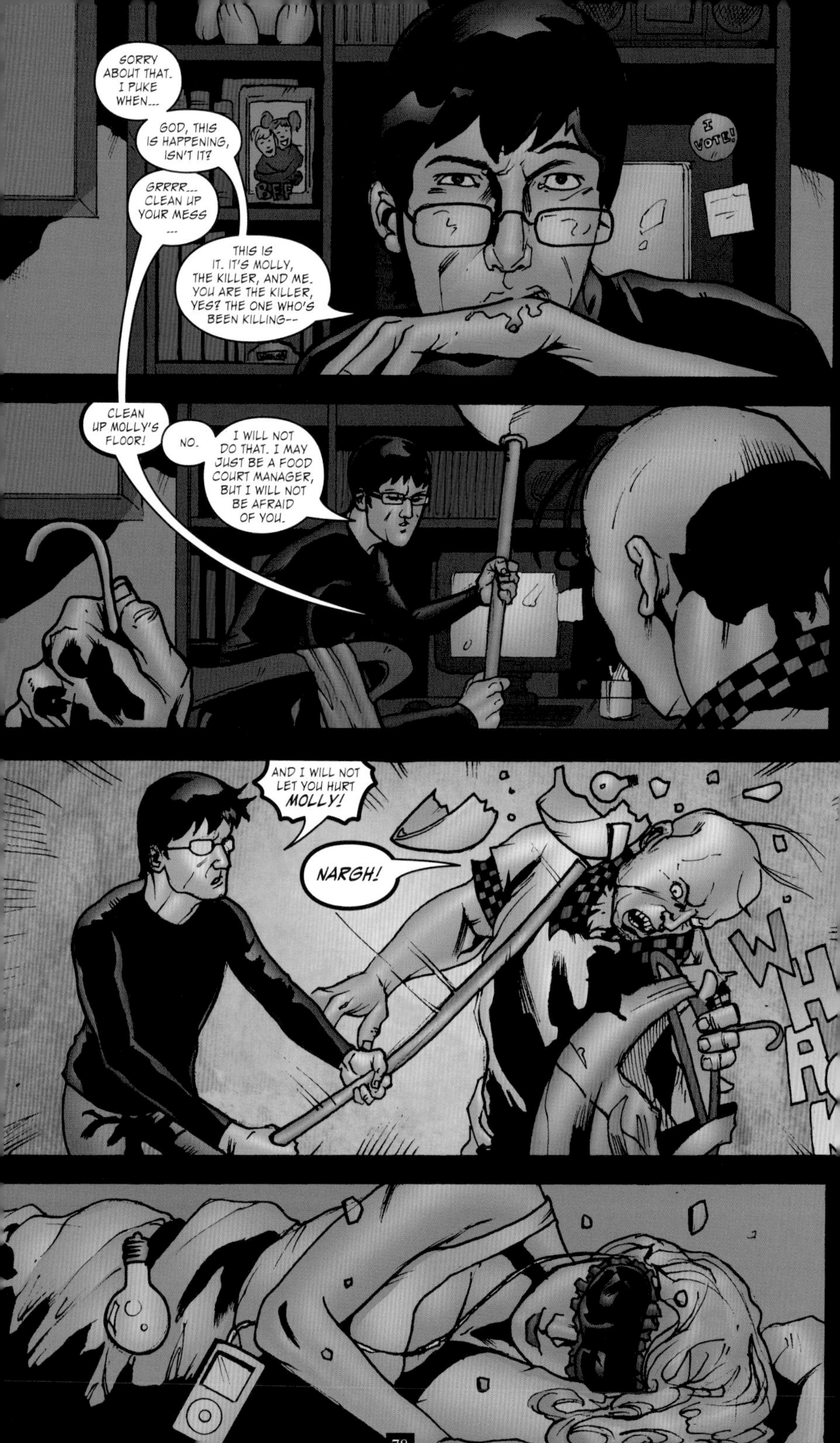

SORRY ABOUT THAT. I PUKE WHEN...
GOD, THIS IS HAPPENING, ISN'T IT?
GRRRR... CLEAN UP YOUR MESS ...
THIS IS IT. IT'S MOLLY, THE KILLER, AND ME. YOU ARE THE KILLER, YES? THE ONE WHO'S BEEN KILLING--
I VOTE!
BFF
CLEAN UP MOLLY'S FLOOR!
NO.
I WILL NOT DO THAT. I MAY JUST BE A FOOD COURT MANAGER, BUT I WILL NOT BE AFRAID OF YOU.
AND I WILL NOT LET YOU HURT MOLLY!
NARGH!

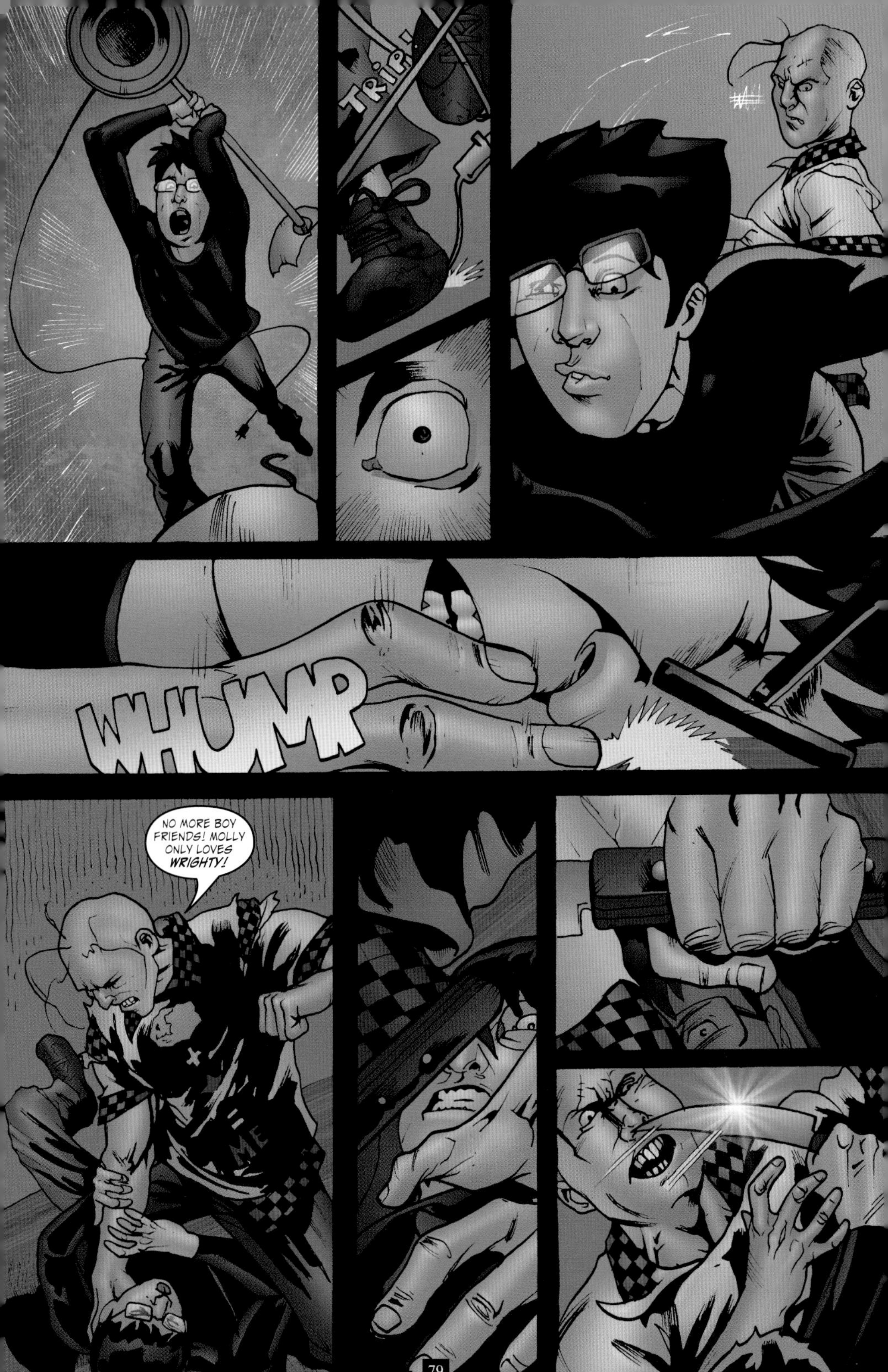
TRIP!
WHUMP
NO MORE BOY FRIENDS! MOLLY ONLY LOVES *WRIGHTY!*

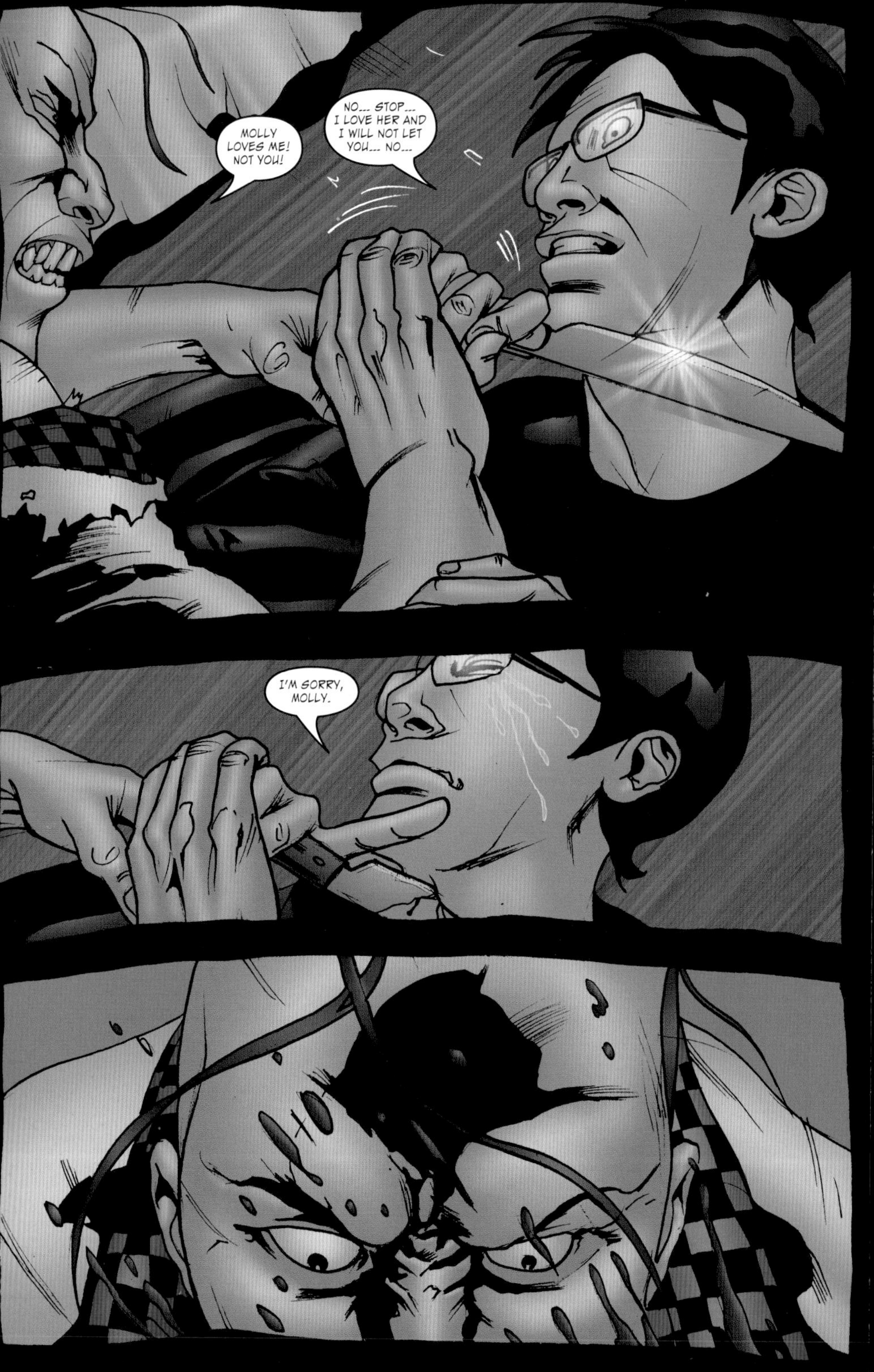
MOLLY LOVES ME! NOT YOU!
NO... STOP... I LOVE HER AND I WILL NOT LET YOU... NO...
I'M SORRY, MOLLY.

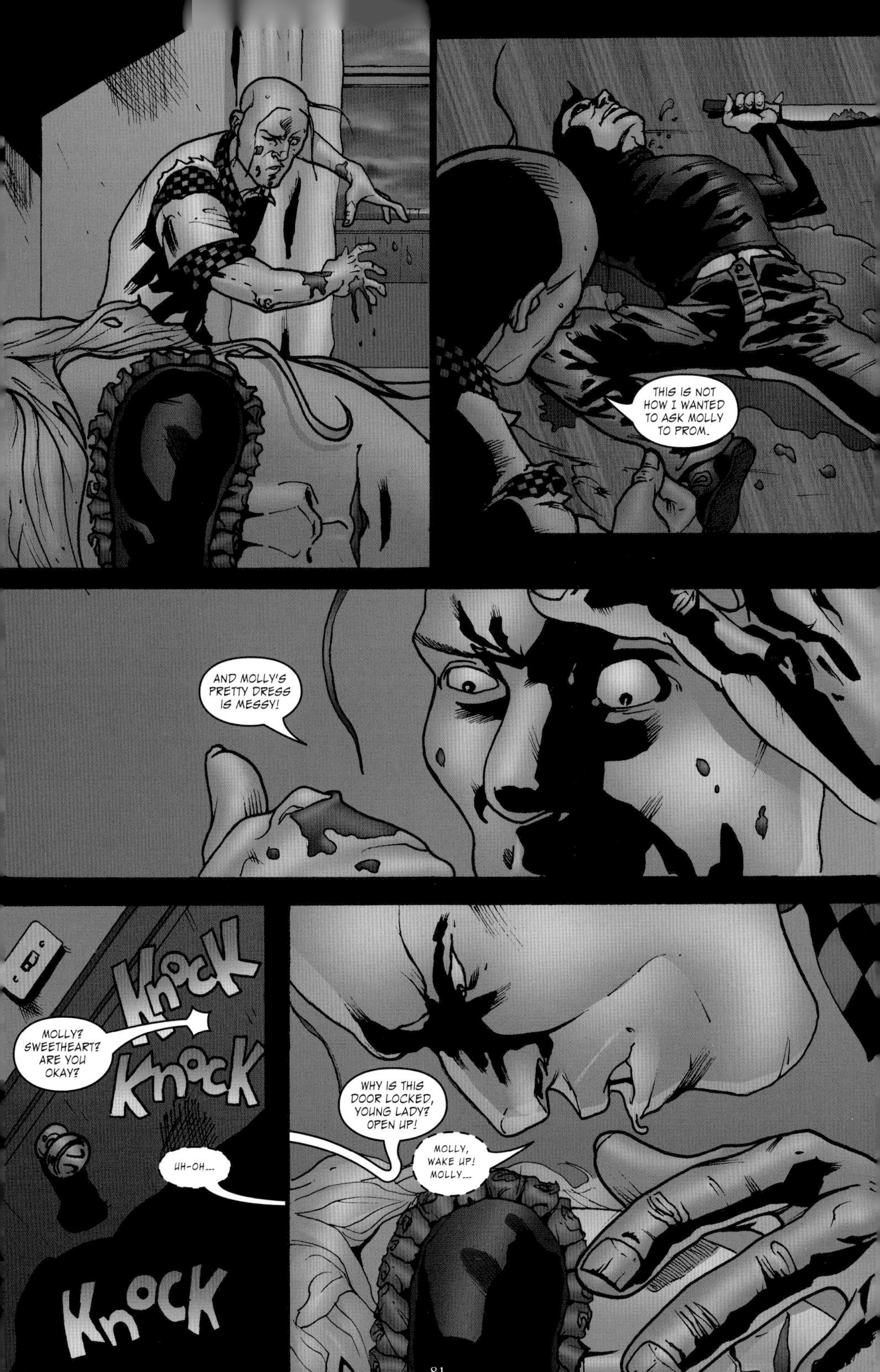
THIS IS NOT HOW I WANTED TO ASK MOLLY TO PROM.
AND MOLLY'S PRETTY DRESS IS MESSY!
KNOCK KNOCK
MOLLY? SWEETHEART? ARE YOU OKAY?
KNOCK
UH-OH...
WHY IS THIS DOOR LOCKED, YOUNG LADY? OPEN UP!
MOLLY, WAKE UP! MOLLY...

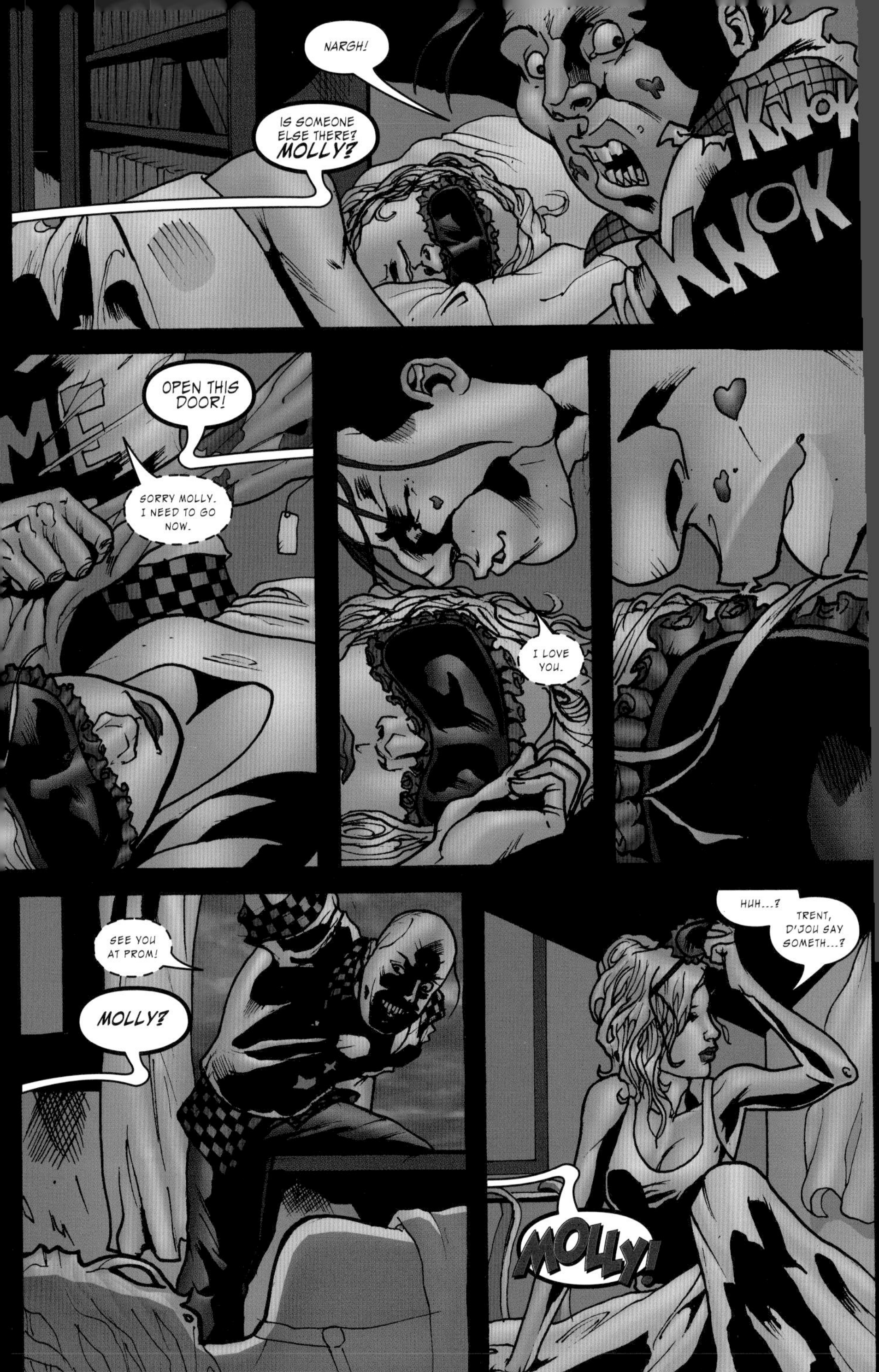
NARGH!
IS SOMEONE ELSE THERE? MOLLY?
KNOK KNOK
OPEN THIS DOOR!
SORRY MOLLY. I NEED TO GO NOW.
I LOVE YOU.
SEE YOU AT PROM!
MOLLY?
HUH...?
TRENT, D'JOU SAY SOMETH...?
MOLLY!

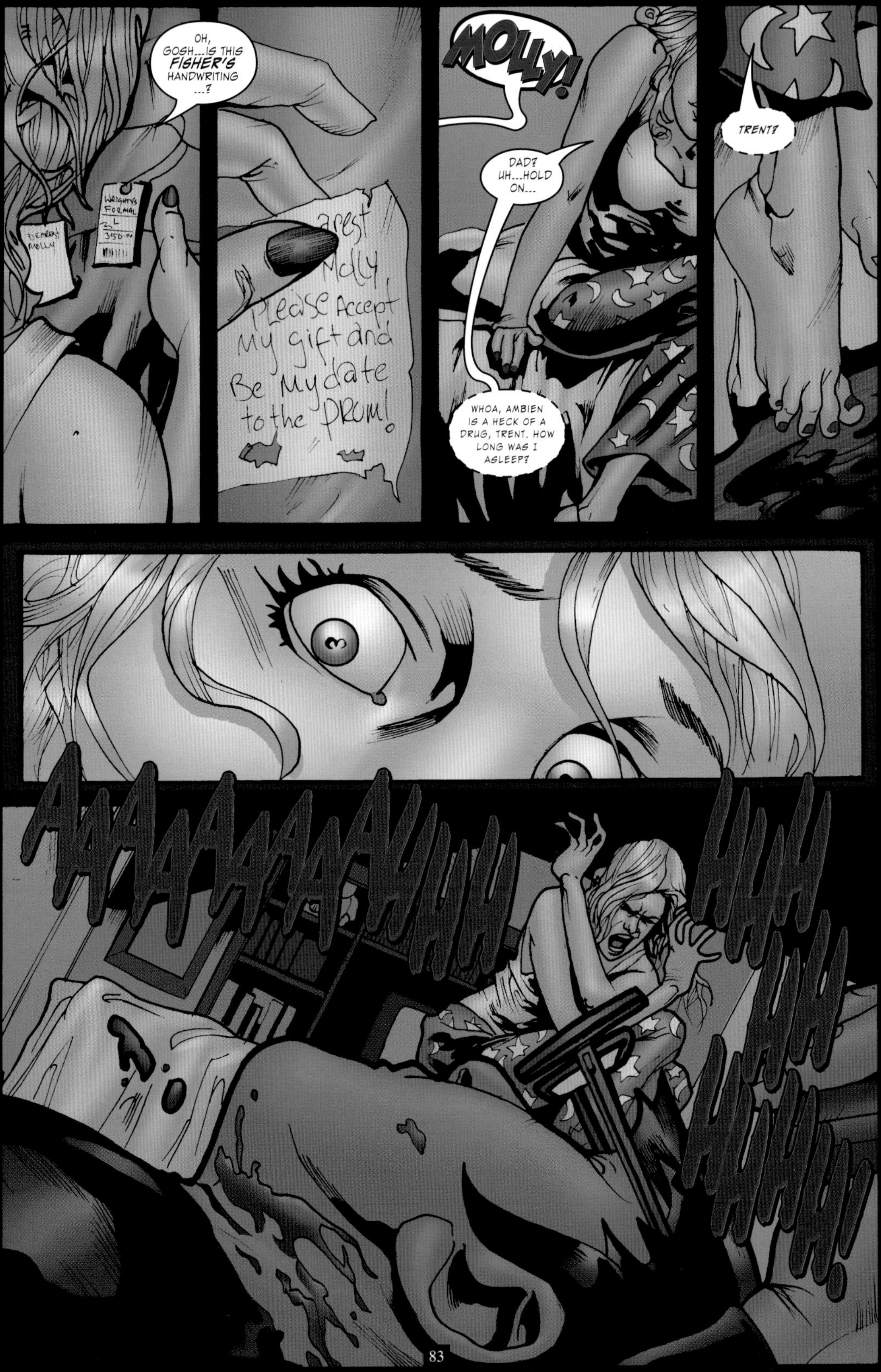
OH, GOSH...IS THIS FISHER'S HANDWRITING ...?
WRIGHTY'S FORMAL
DEAREST MOLLY
...arest Molly, Please Accept My gift and Be My date to the PROM!
MOLLY!
DAD? UH...HOLD ON...
WHOA, AMBIEN IS A HECK OF A DRUG, TRENT. HOW LONG WAS I ASLEEP?
TRENT?
AAAAAAAAAAHHH
HUH HUH HUH HUH!

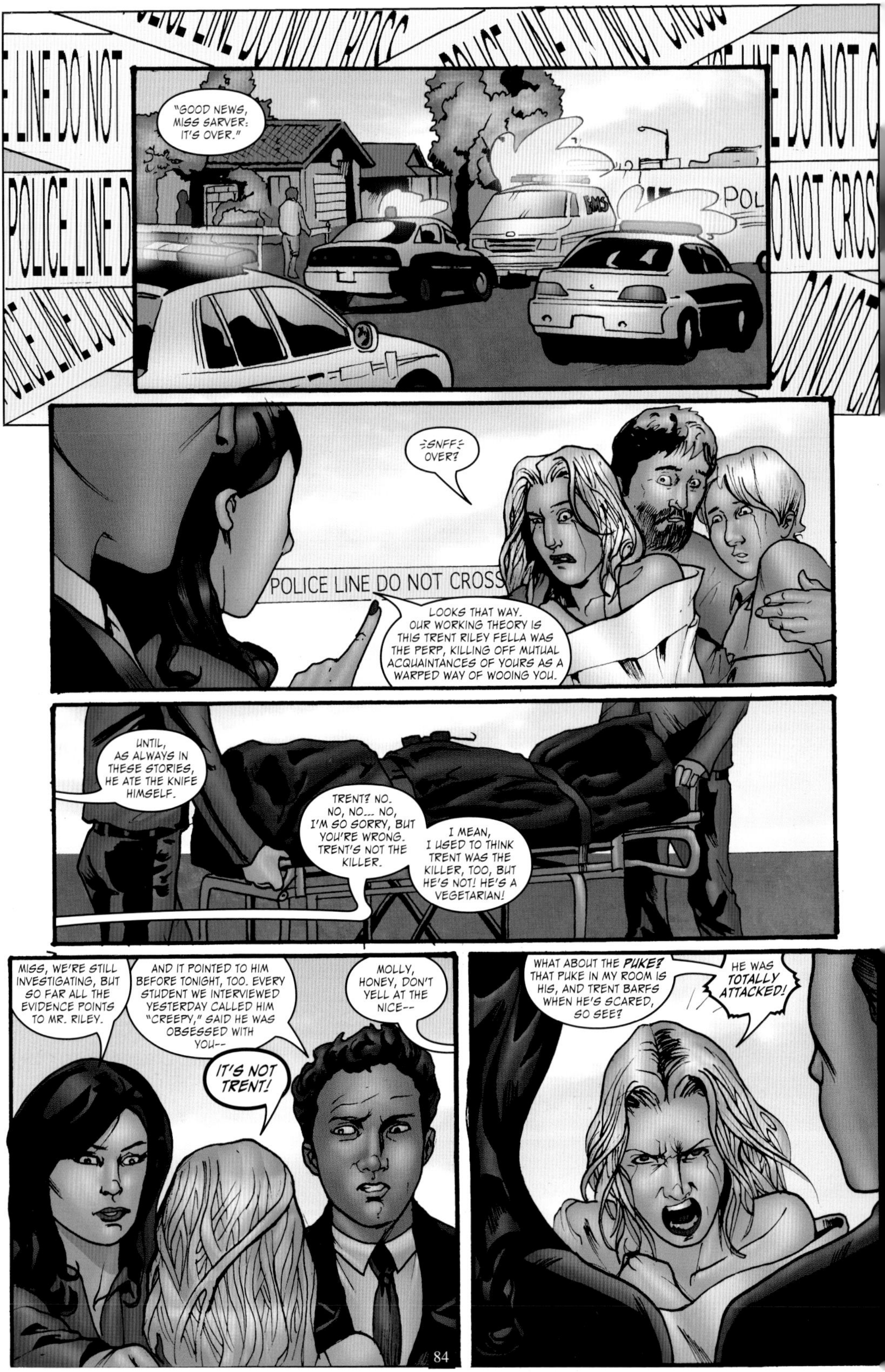
POLICE LINE DO NOT CROSS
"GOOD NEWS, MISS SARVER: IT'S OVER."
EMS
POLICE LINE DO NOT CROSS
-SNFF- OVER?
LOOKS THAT WAY. OUR WORKING THEORY IS THIS TRENT RILEY FELLA WAS THE PERP, KILLING OFF MUTUAL ACQUAINTANCES OF YOURS AS A WARPED WAY OF WOOING YOU.
UNTIL, AS ALWAYS IN THESE STORIES, HE ATE THE KNIFE HIMSELF.
TRENT? NO. NO, NO... NO, I'M SO SORRY, BUT YOU'RE WRONG. TRENT'S NOT THE KILLER.
I MEAN, I USED TO THINK TRENT WAS THE KILLER, TOO, BUT HE'S NOT! HE'S A VEGETARIAN!
MISS, WE'RE STILL INVESTIGATING, BUT SO FAR ALL THE EVIDENCE POINTS TO MR. RILEY.
AND IT POINTED TO HIM BEFORE TONIGHT, TOO. EVERY STUDENT WE INTERVIEWED YESTERDAY CALLED HIM "CREEPY," SAID HE WAS OBSESSED WITH YOU--
IT'S NOT TRENT!
MOLLY, HONEY, DON'T YELL AT THE NICE--
WHAT ABOUT THE PUKE? THAT PUKE IN MY ROOM IS HIS, AND TRENT BARFS WHEN HE'S SCARED, SO SEE?
HE WAS TOTALLY ATTACKED!

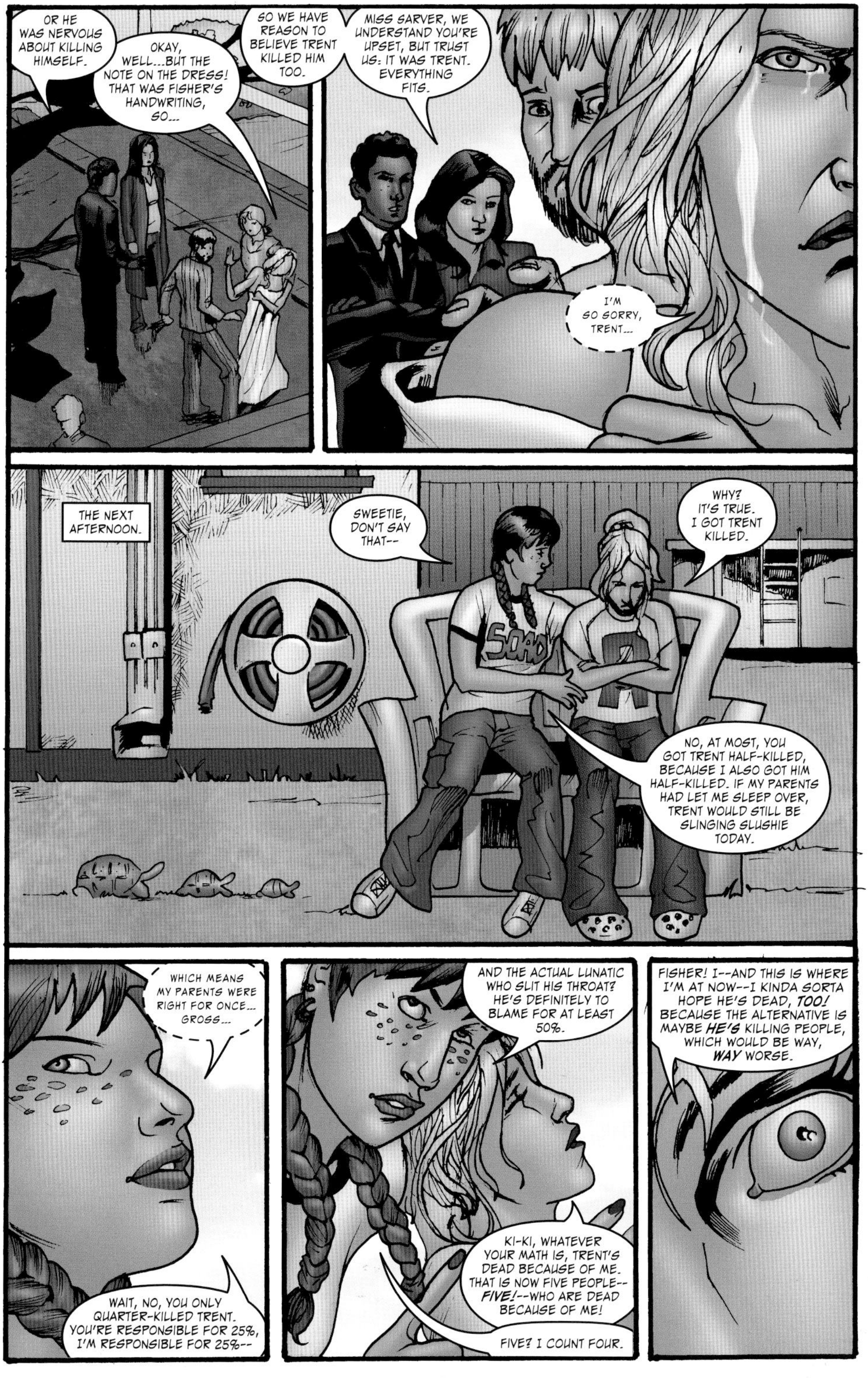
OR HE WAS NERVOUS ABOUT KILLING HIMSELF.
OKAY, WELL...BUT THE NOTE ON THE DRESS! THAT WAS FISHER'S HANDWRITING, SO...
SO WE HAVE REASON TO BELIEVE TRENT KILLED HIM TOO.
MISS SARVER, WE UNDERSTAND YOU'RE UPSET, BUT TRUST US: IT WAS TRENT. EVERYTHING FITS.
I'M SO SORRY, TRENT...
THE NEXT AFTERNOON.
SWEETIE, DON'T SAY THAT--
WHY? IT'S TRUE. I GOT TRENT KILLED.
NO, AT MOST, YOU GOT TRENT HALF-KILLED, BECAUSE I ALSO GOT HIM HALF-KILLED. IF MY PARENTS HAD LET ME SLEEP OVER, TRENT WOULD STILL BE SLINGING SLUSHIE TODAY.
WHICH MEANS MY PARENTS WERE RIGHT FOR ONCE... GROSS...
WAIT, NO, YOU ONLY QUARTER-KILLED TRENT. YOU'RE RESPONSIBLE FOR 25%, I'M RESPONSIBLE FOR 25%--
AND THE ACTUAL LUNATIC WHO SLIT HIS THROAT? HE'S DEFINITELY TO BLAME FOR AT LEAST 50%.
KI-KI, WHATEVER YOUR MATH IS, TRENT'S DEAD BECAUSE OF ME. THAT IS NOW FIVE PEOPLE-- *FIVE!*--WHO ARE DEAD BECAUSE OF ME!
FIVE? I COUNT FOUR.
FISHER! I--AND THIS IS WHERE I'M AT NOW--I KINDA SORTA HOPE HE'S DEAD, *TOO!* BECAUSE THE ALTERNATIVE IS MAYBE *HE'S* KILLING PEOPLE, WHICH WOULD BE WAY, *WAY* WORSE.

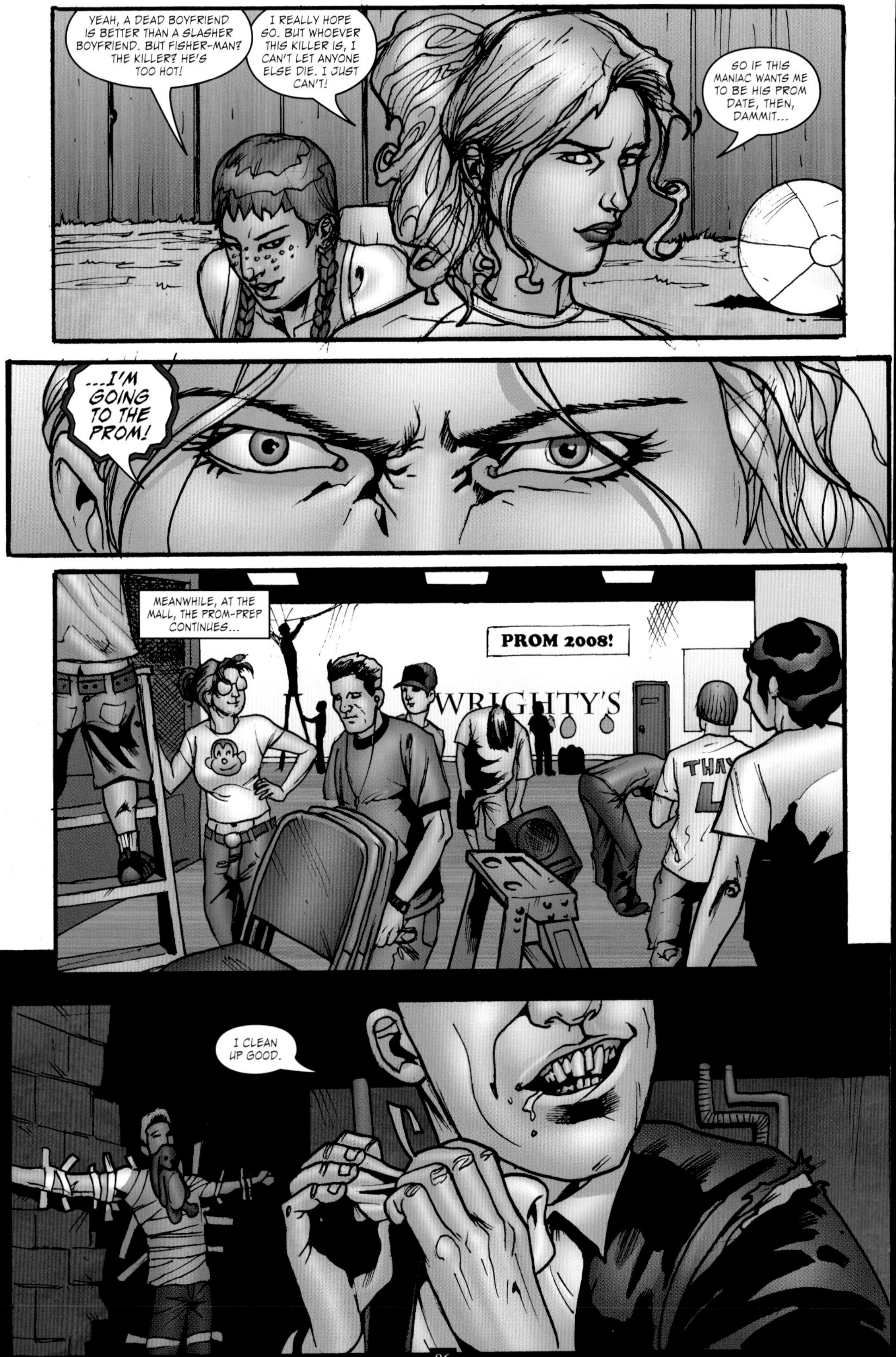
YEAH, A DEAD BOYFRIEND IS BETTER THAN A SLASHER BOYFRIEND. BUT FISHER-MAN? THE KILLER? HE'S TOO HOT!
I REALLY HOPE SO. BUT WHOEVER THIS KILLER IS, I CAN'T LET ANYONE ELSE DIE. I JUST CAN'T!
SO IF THIS MANIAC WANTS ME TO BE HIS PROM DATE, THEN, DAMMIT...
...I'M GOING TO THE PROM!
MEANWHILE, AT THE MALL, THE PROM-PREP CONTINUES...
PROM 2008!
WRIGHTY'S
I CLEAN UP GOOD.

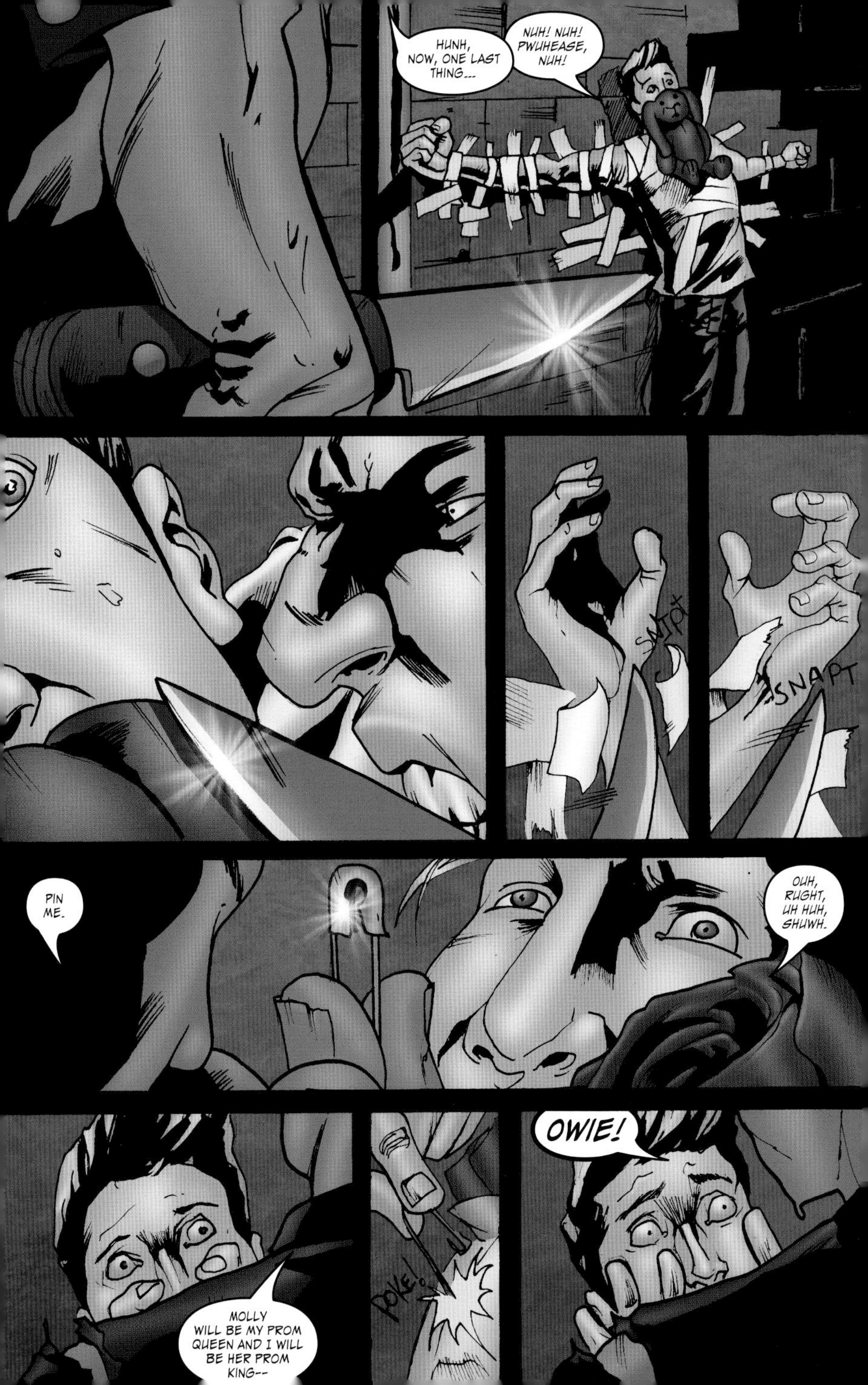
HUNH, NOW, ONE LAST THING...
NUH! NUH! PWUHEASE, NUH!
SNAPT
SNAPT
PIN ME.
OUH, RUGHT, UH HUH, SHUWH.
MOLLY WILL BE MY PROM QUEEN AND I WILL BE HER PROM KING--
POKE!
OWIE!

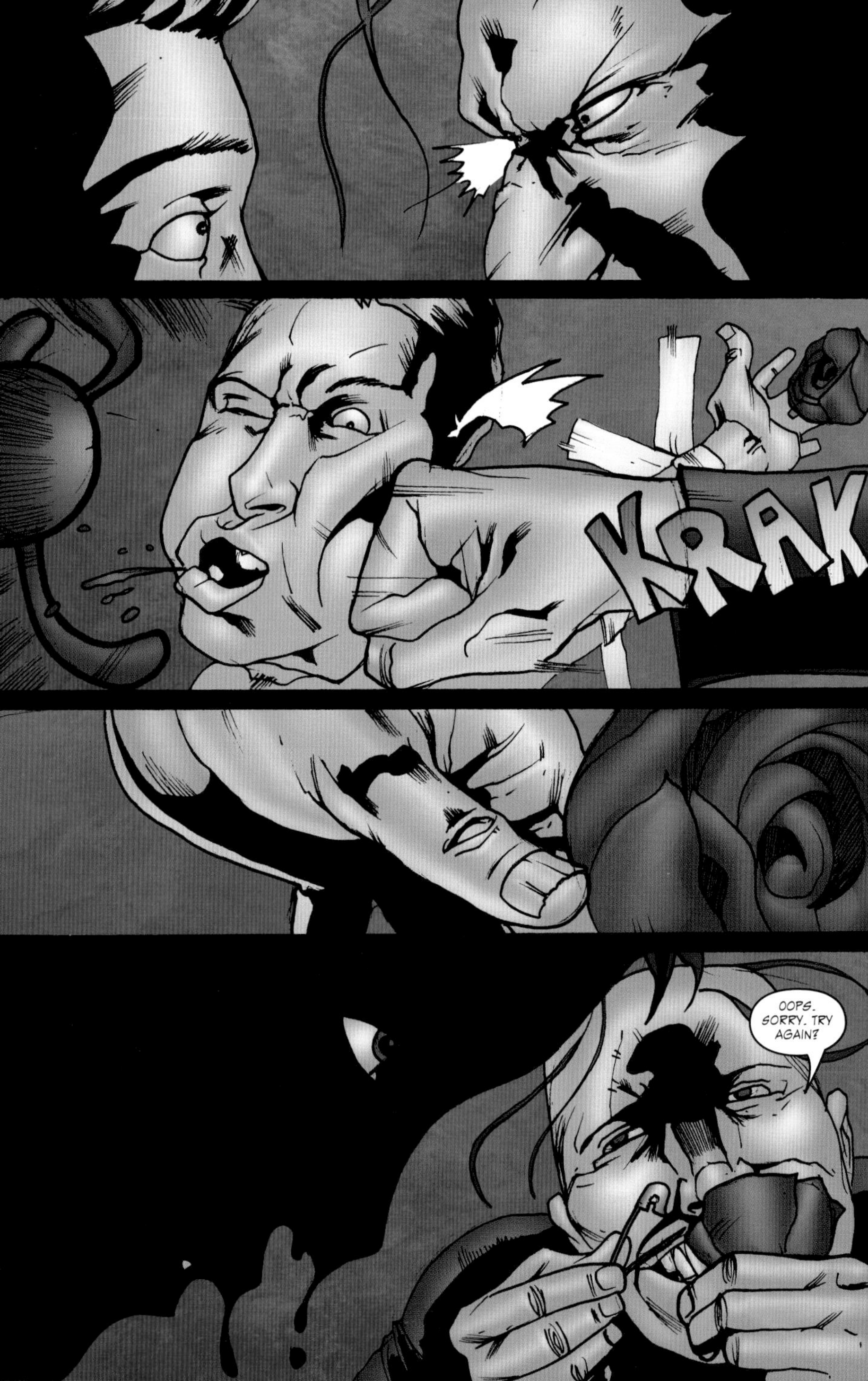
KRAK
OOPS. SORRY. TRY AGAIN?

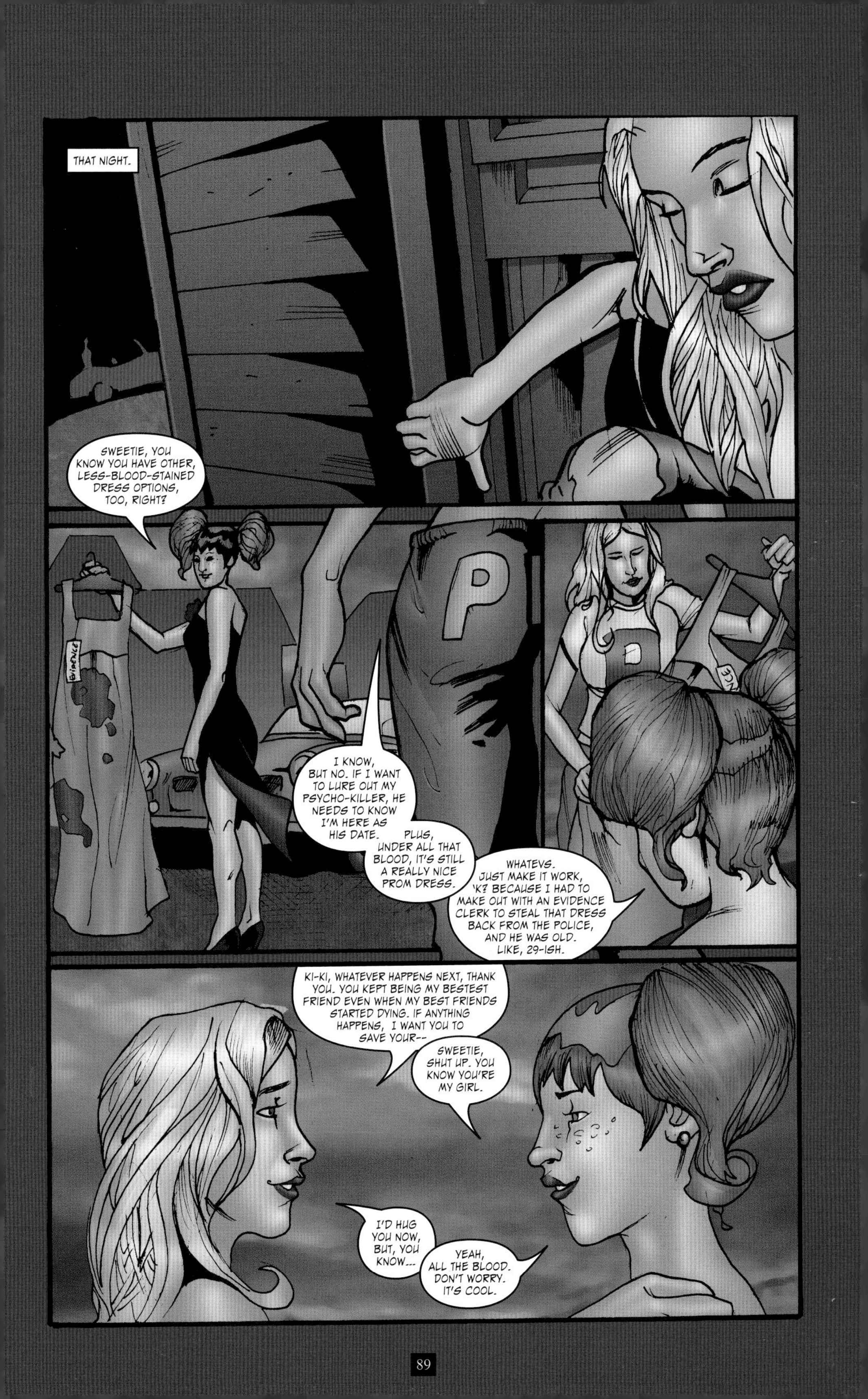
THAT NIGHT.
SWEETIE, YOU KNOW YOU HAVE OTHER, LESS-BLOOD-STAINED DRESS OPTIONS, TOO, RIGHT?
EVIDENCE
I KNOW, BUT NO. IF I WANT TO LURE OUT MY PSYCHO-KILLER, HE NEEDS TO KNOW I'M HERE AS HIS DATE.
PLUS, UNDER ALL THAT BLOOD, IT'S STILL A REALLY NICE PROM DRESS.
WHATEVS. JUST MAKE IT WORK, 'K? BECAUSE I HAD TO MAKE OUT WITH AN EVIDENCE CLERK TO STEAL THAT DRESS BACK FROM THE POLICE, AND HE WAS OLD. LIKE, 29-ISH.
KI-KI, WHATEVER HAPPENS NEXT, THANK YOU. YOU KEPT BEING MY BESTEST FRIEND EVEN WHEN MY BEST FRIENDS STARTED DYING. IF ANYTHING HAPPENS, I WANT YOU TO SAVE YOUR--
SWEETIE, SHUT UP. YOU KNOW YOU'RE MY GIRL.
I'D HUG YOU NOW, BUT, YOU KNOW...
YEAH, ALL THE BLOOD. DON'T WORRY. IT'S COOL.

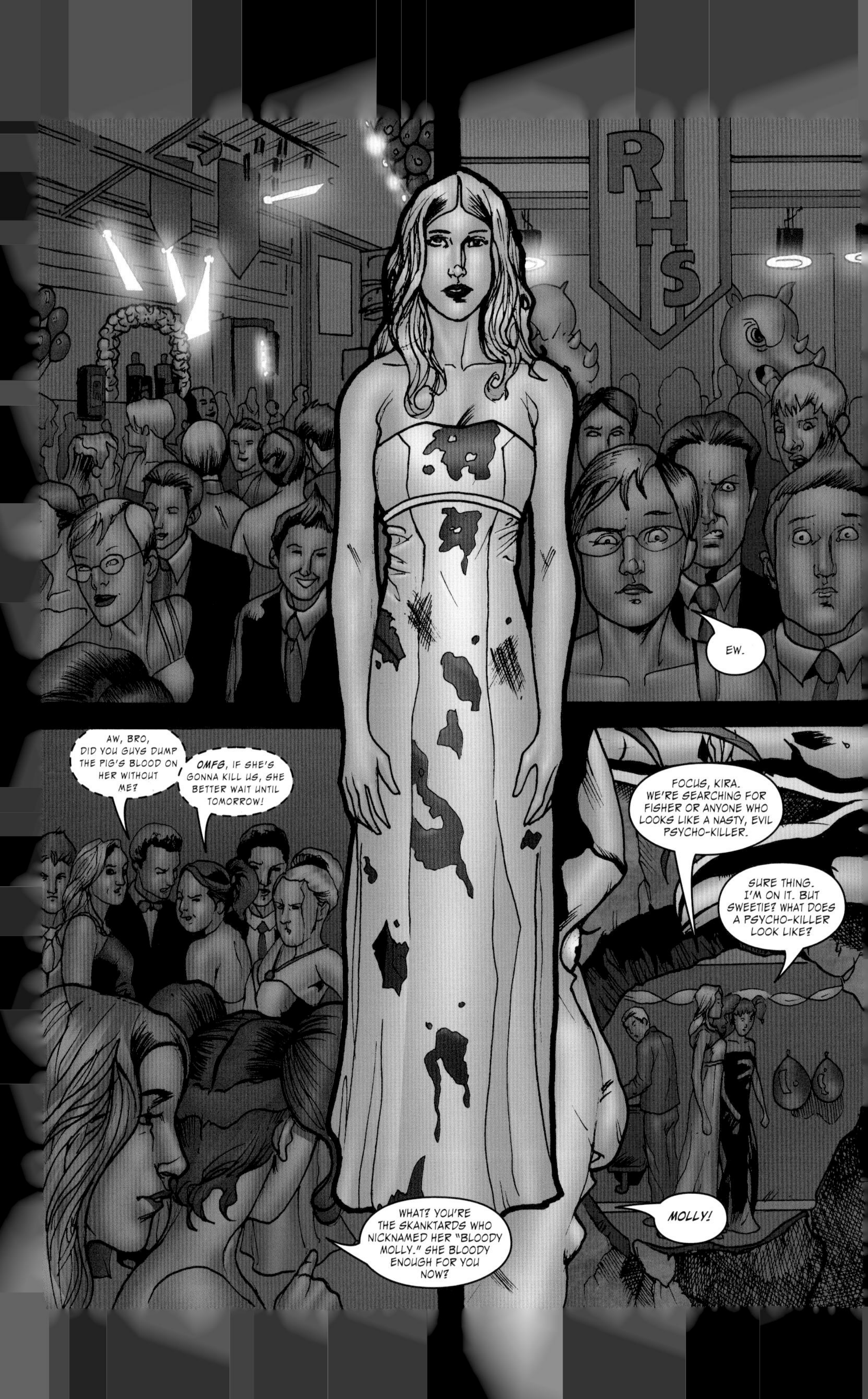
EW.
AW, BRO, DID YOU GUYS DUMP THE PIG'S BLOOD ON HER WITHOUT ME?
OMFG, IF SHE'S GONNA KILL US, SHE BETTER WAIT UNTIL TOMORROW!
FOCUS, KIRA. WE'RE SEARCHING FOR FISHER OR ANYONE WHO LOOKS LIKE A NASTY, EVIL PSYCHO-KILLER.
SURE THING. I'M ON IT. BUT SWEETIE? WHAT DOES A PSYCHO-KILLER LOOK LIKE?
WHAT? YOU'RE THE SKANKTARDS WHO NICKNAMED HER "BLOODY MOLLY." SHE BLOODY ENOUGH FOR YOU NOW?
MOLLY!

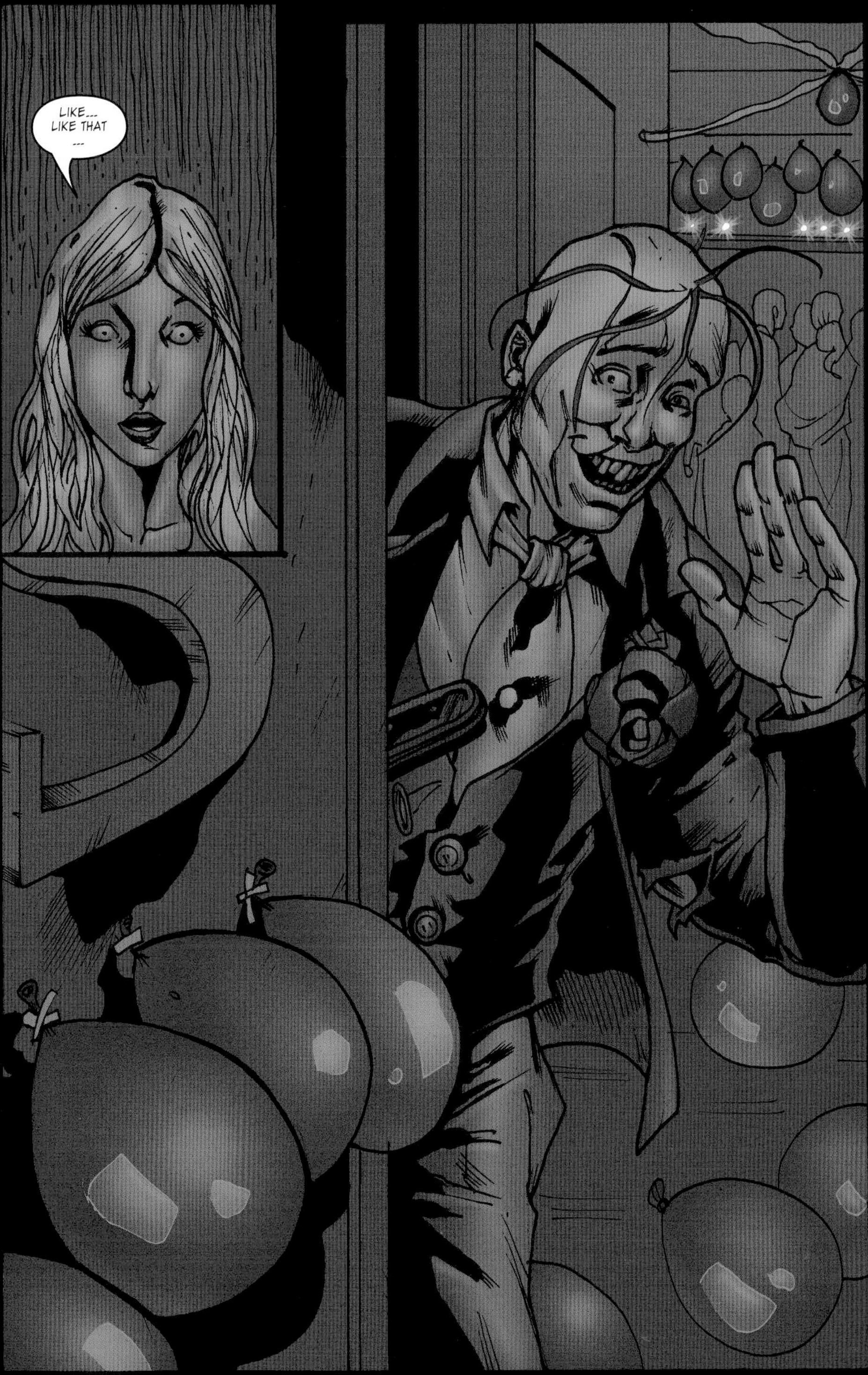
LIKE...
LIKE THAT
...

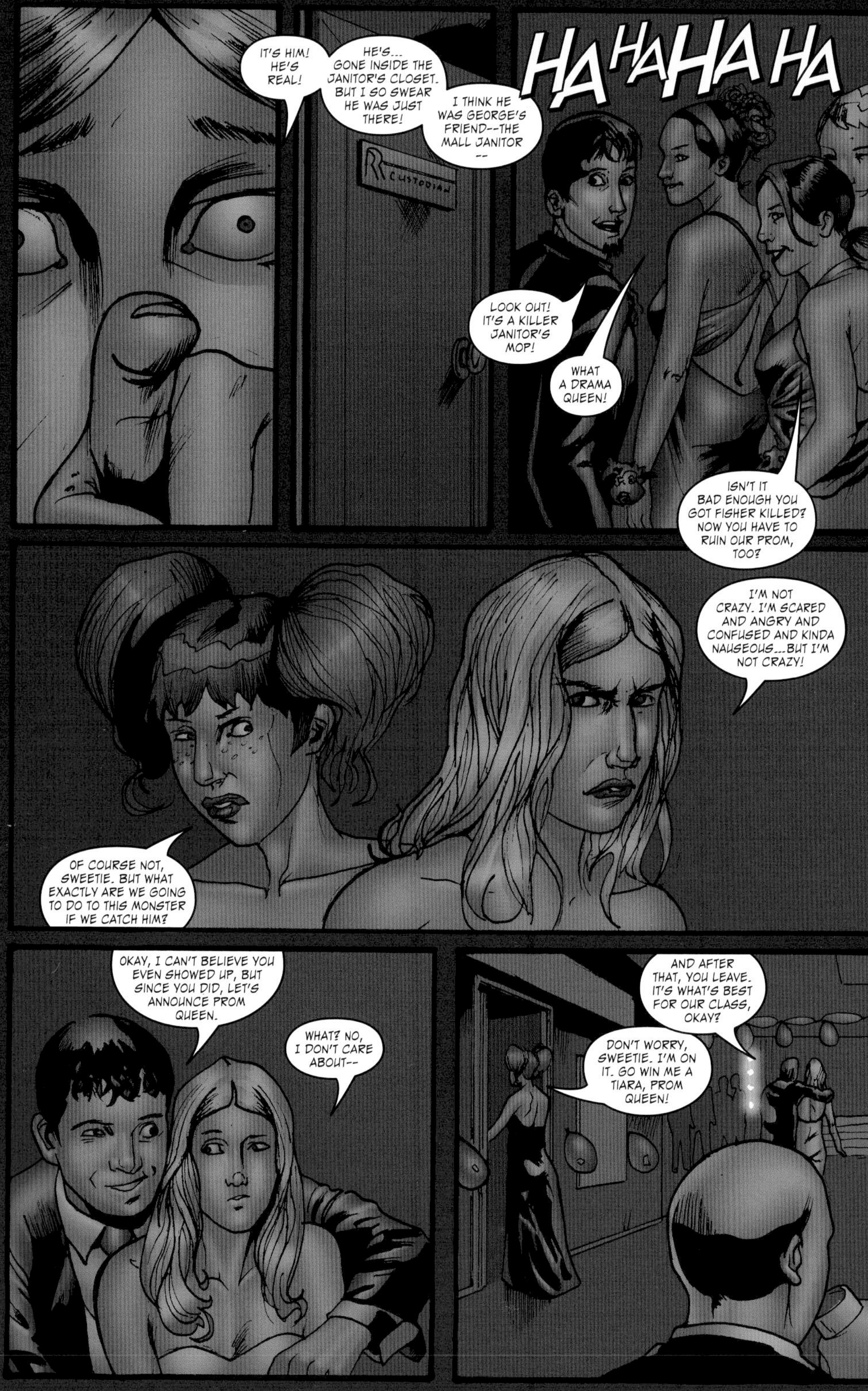
IT'S HIM! HE'S REAL!
HE'S... GONE INSIDE THE JANITOR'S CLOSET. BUT I SO SWEAR HE WAS JUST THERE!
CUSTODIAN
I THINK HE WAS GEORGE'S FRIEND--THE MALL JANITOR --
HA HA HA HA HA HA
LOOK OUT! IT'S A KILLER JANITOR'S MOP!
WHAT A DRAMA QUEEN!
ISN'T IT BAD ENOUGH YOU GOT FISHER KILLED? NOW YOU HAVE TO RUIN OUR PROM, TOO?
I'M NOT CRAZY. I'M SCARED AND ANGRY AND CONFUSED AND KINDA NAUSEOUS...BUT I'M NOT CRAZY!
OF COURSE NOT, SWEETIE. BUT WHAT EXACTLY ARE WE GOING TO DO TO THIS MONSTER IF WE CATCH HIM?
OKAY, I CAN'T BELIEVE YOU EVEN SHOWED UP, BUT SINCE YOU DID, LET'S ANNOUNCE PROM QUEEN.
WHAT? NO, I DON'T CARE ABOUT--
AND AFTER THAT, YOU LEAVE. IT'S WHAT'S BEST FOR OUR CLASS, OKAY?
DON'T WORRY, SWEETIE. I'M ON IT. GO WIN ME A TIARA, PROM QUEEN!

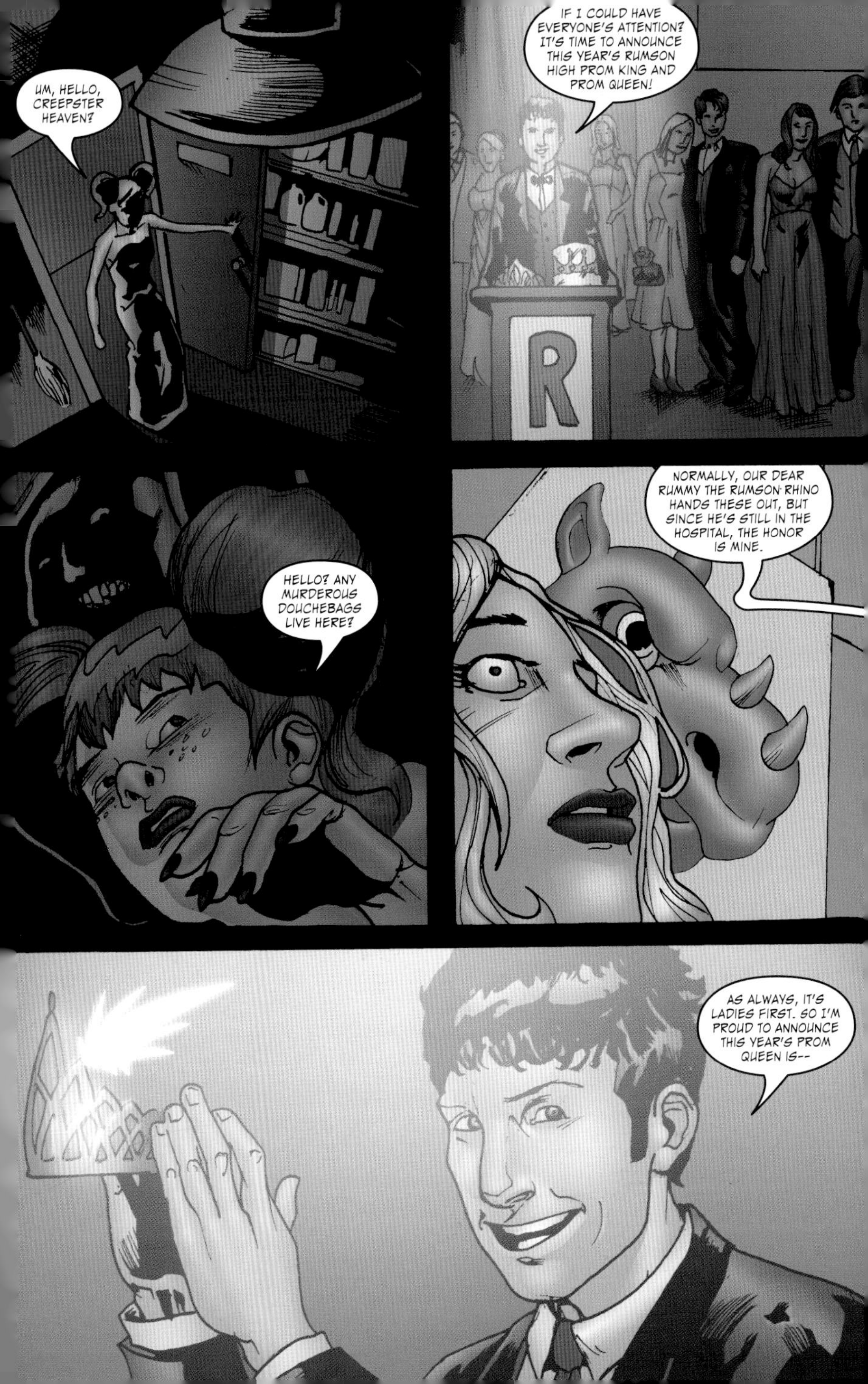
UM, HELLO, CREEPSTER HEAVEN?
IF I COULD HAVE EVERYONE'S ATTENTION? IT'S TIME TO ANNOUNCE THIS YEAR'S RUMSON HIGH PROM KING AND PROM QUEEN!
HELLO? ANY MURDEROUS DOUCHEBAGS LIVE HERE?
NORMALLY, OUR DEAR RUMMY THE RUMSON RHINO HANDS THESE OUT, BUT SINCE HE'S STILL IN THE HOSPITAL, THE HONOR IS MINE.
AS ALWAYS, IT'S LADIES FIRST. SO I'M PROUD TO ANNOUNCE THIS YEAR'S PROM QUEEN IS--

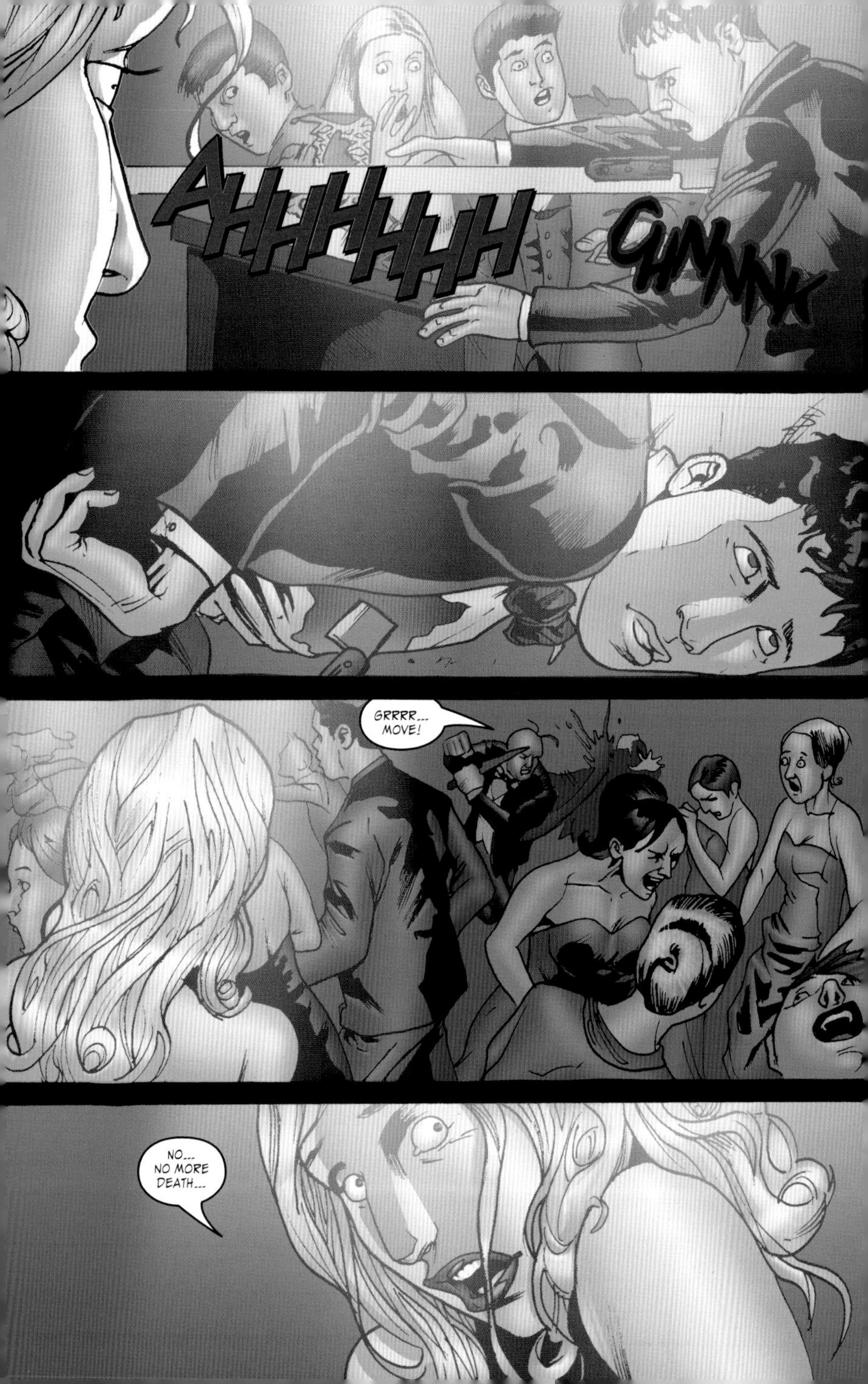
AHHHHHH
CHNNNK
GRRRR... MOVE!
NO... NO MORE DEATH...

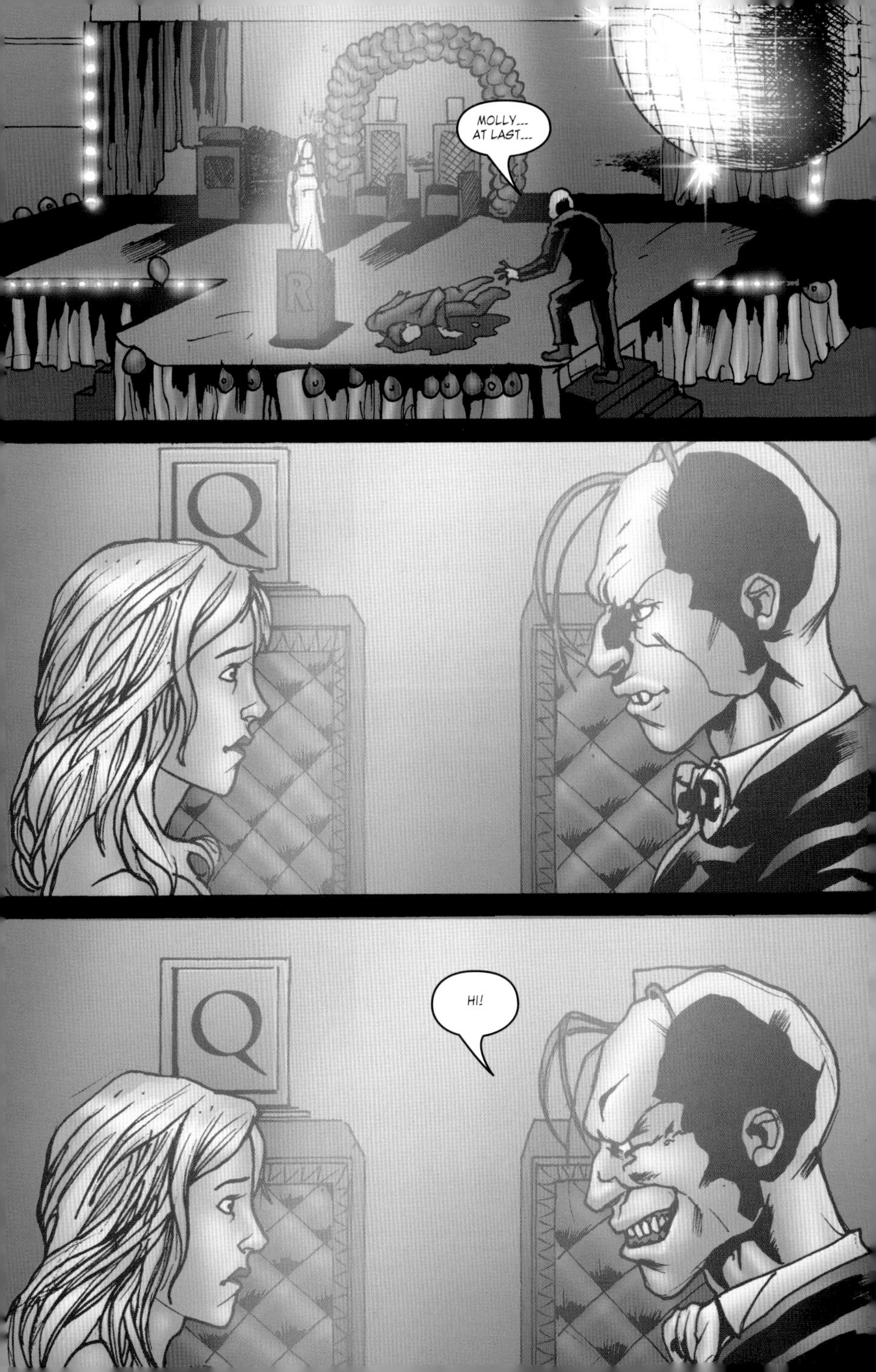
MOLLY...
AT LAST...
HI!

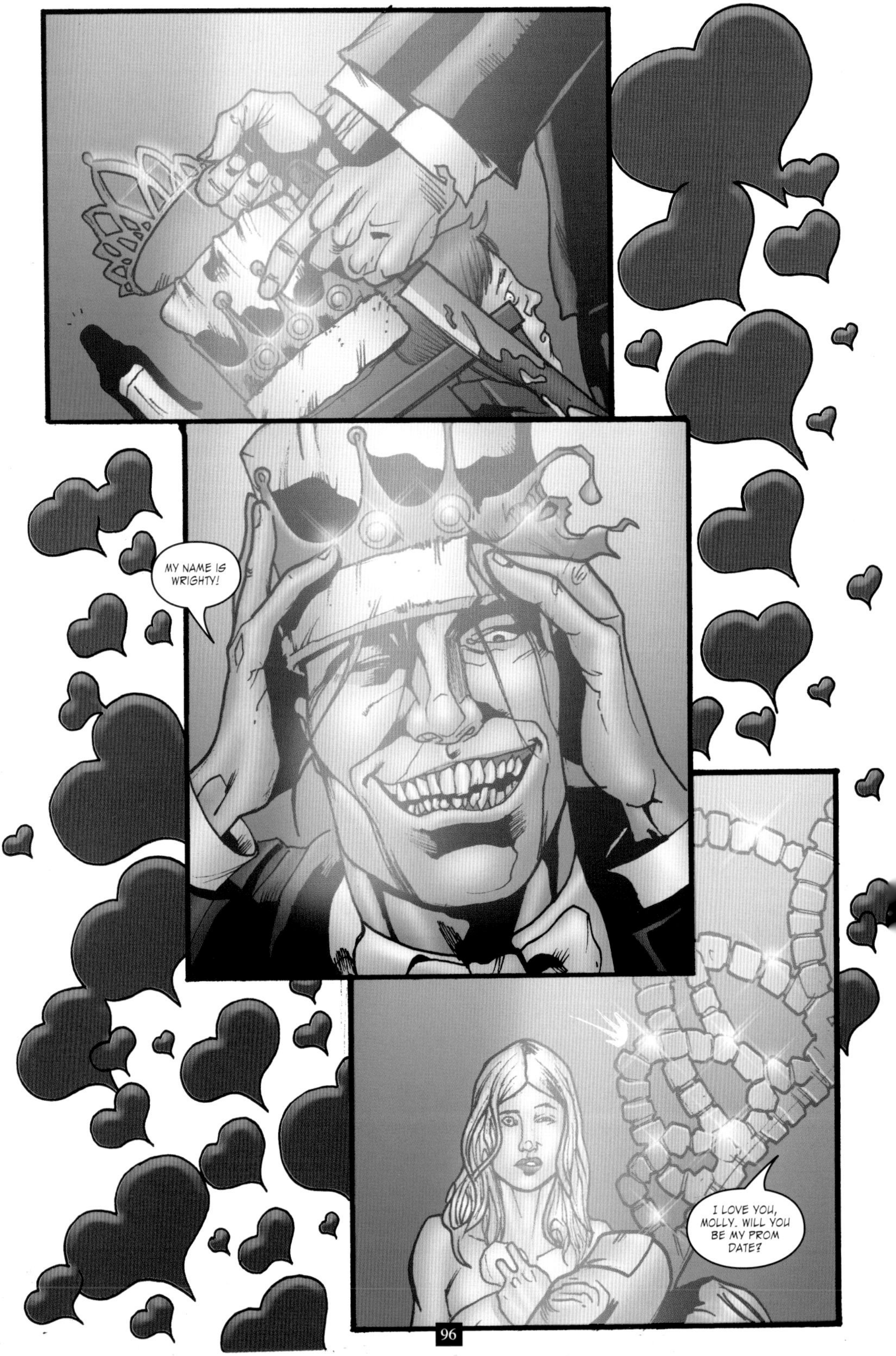
MY NAME IS WRIGHTY!
I LOVE YOU, MOLLY. WILL YOU BE MY PROM DATE?

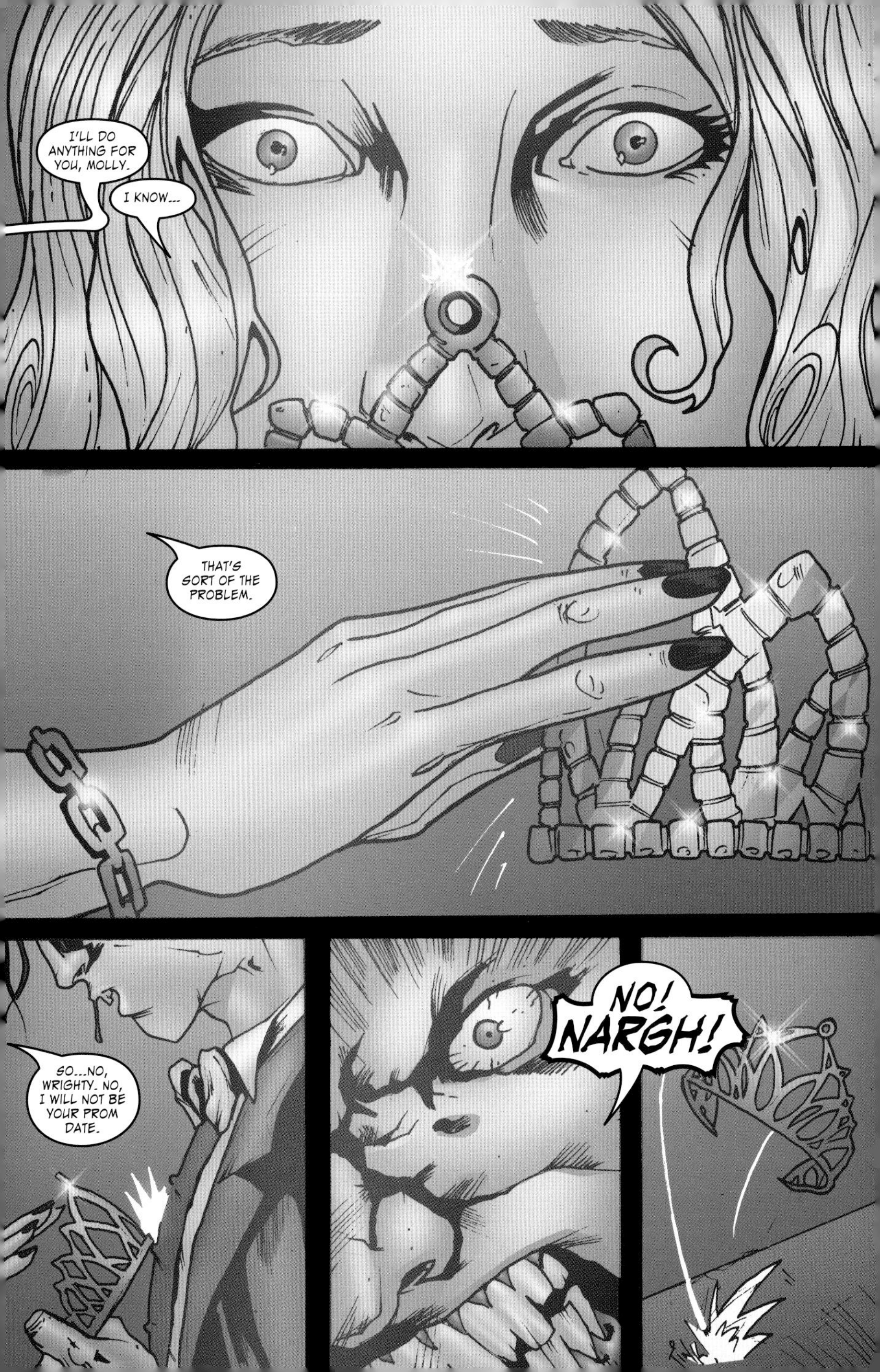
I'LL DO ANYTHING FOR YOU, MOLLY.
I KNOW...
THAT'S SORT OF THE PROBLEM.
SO...NO, WRIGHTY. NO, I WILL NOT BE YOUR PROM DATE.
NO! NARGH!

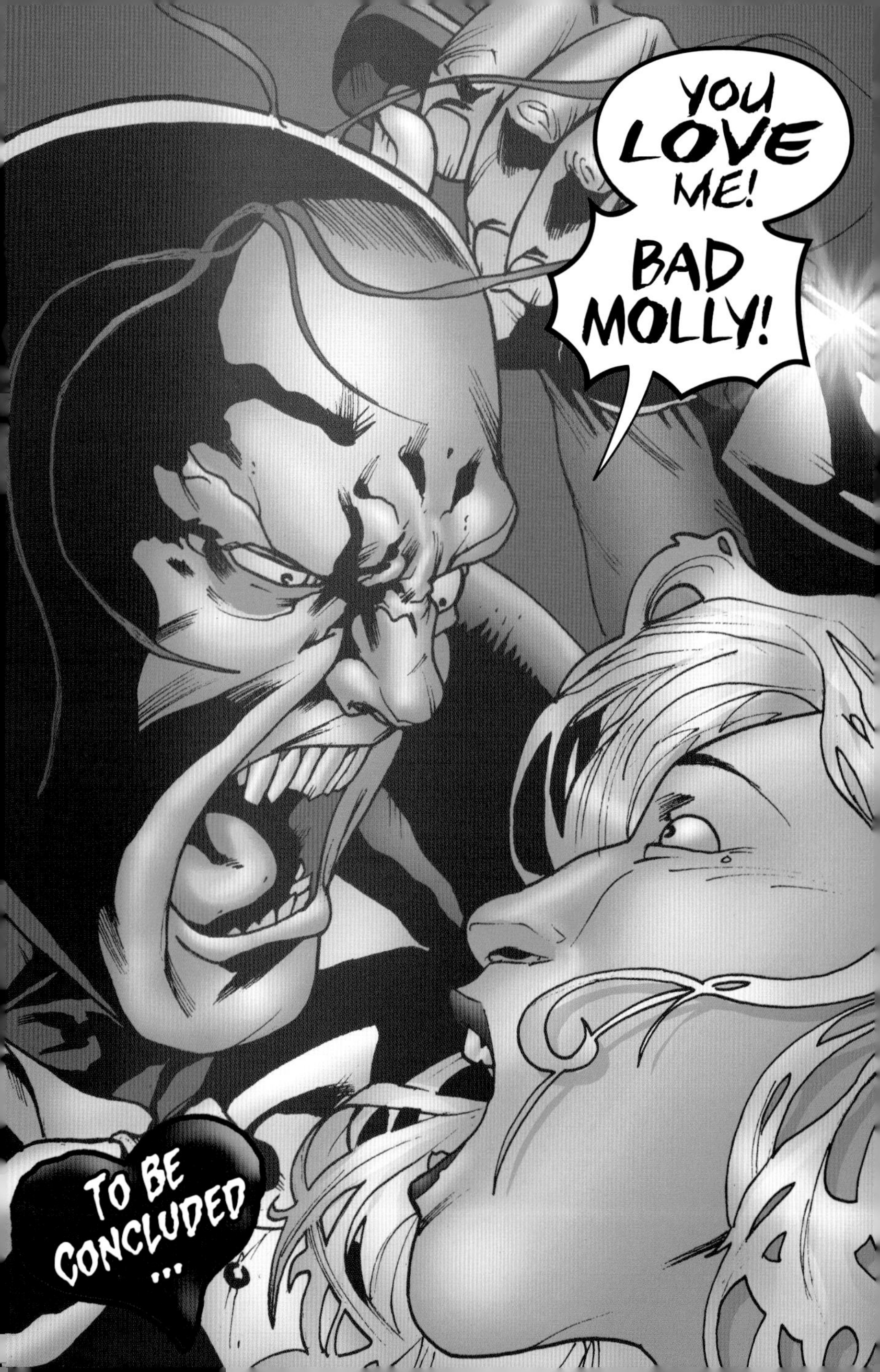
YOU LOVE ME!
BAD MOLLY!
TO BE CONCLUDED ...

CHAPTER 5

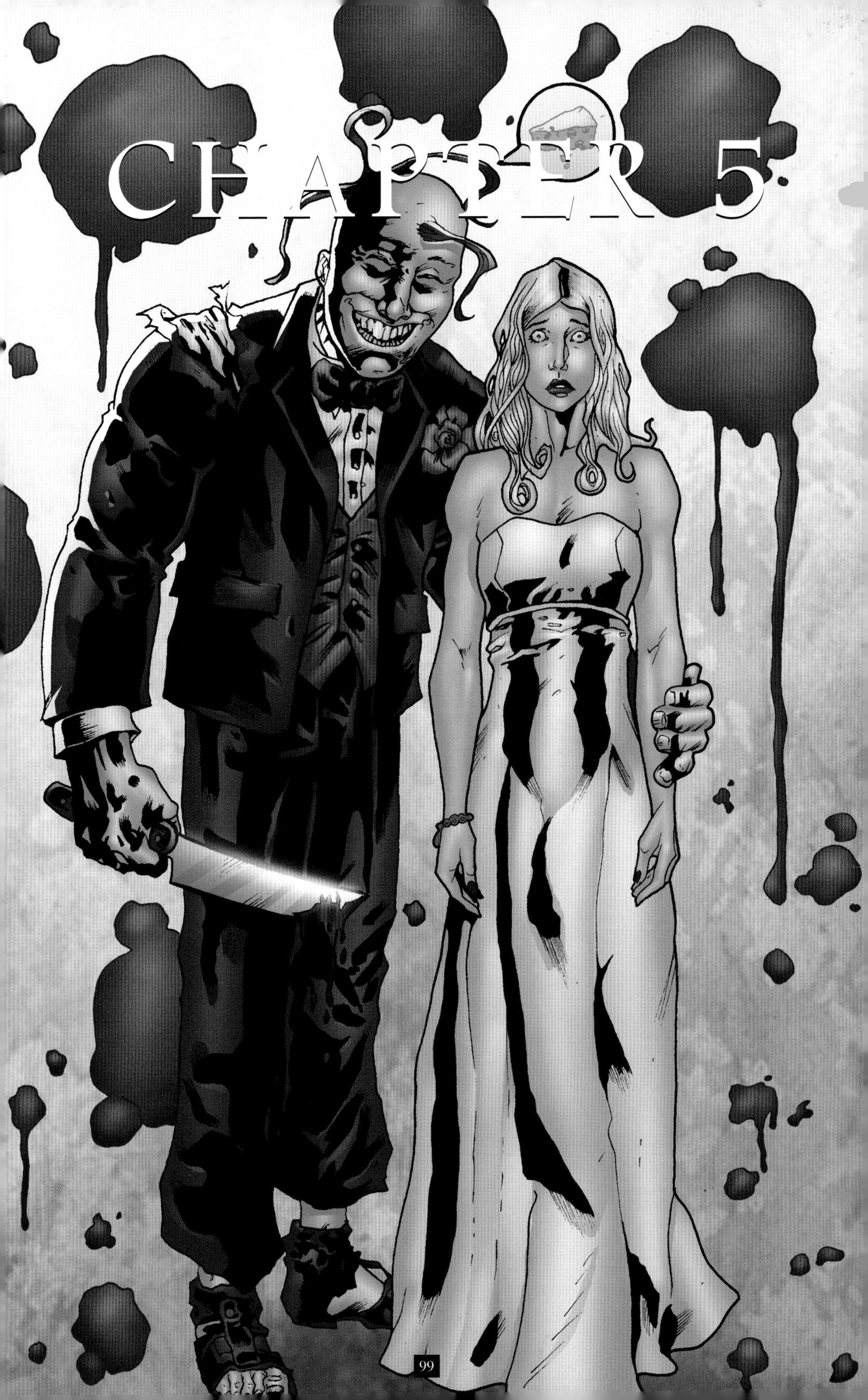

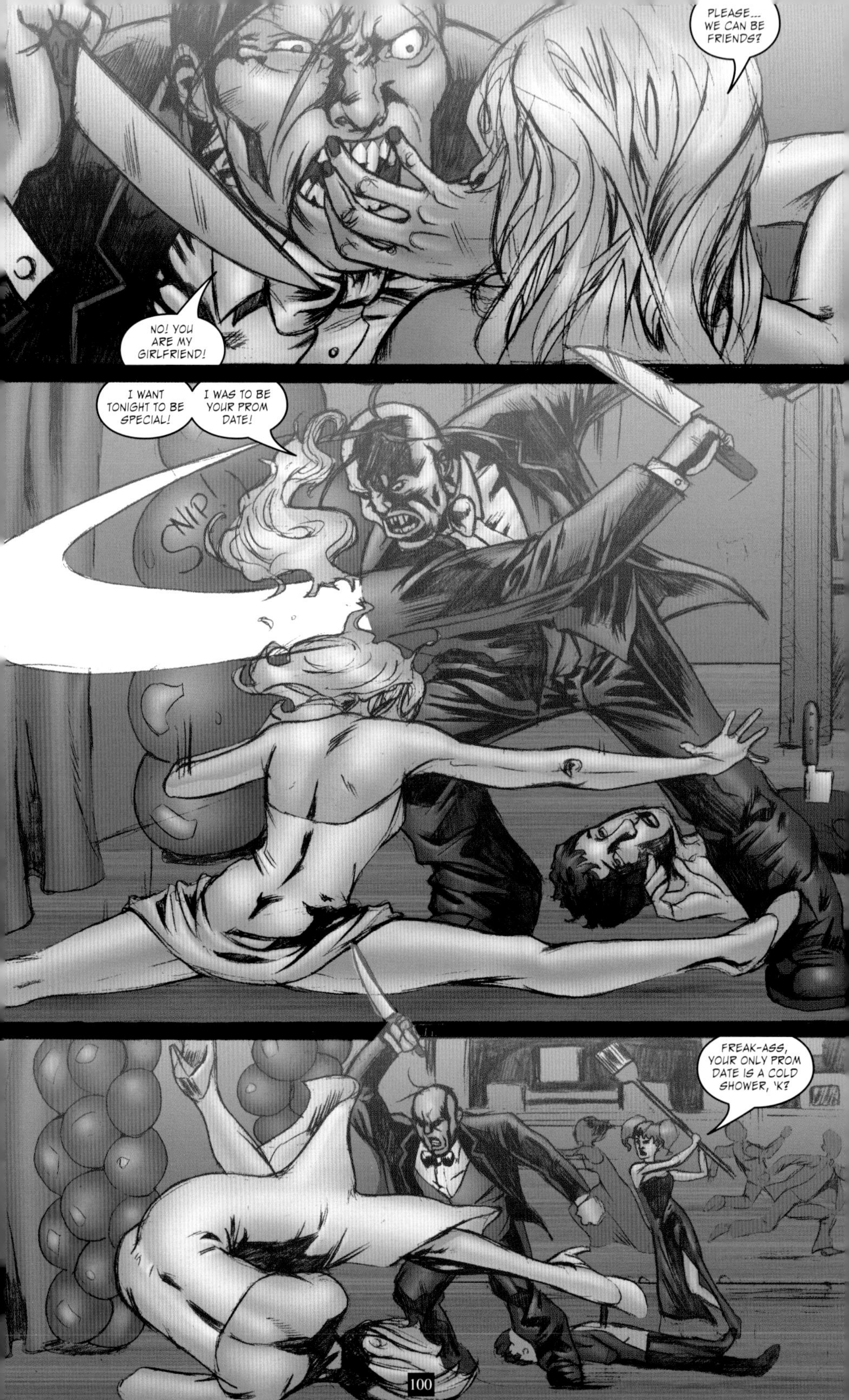
PLEASE... WE CAN BE FRIENDS?
NO! YOU ARE MY GIRLFRIEND!
I WANT TONIGHT TO BE SPECIAL!
I WAS TO BE YOUR PROM DATE!
SNIP!
FREAK-ASS, YOUR ONLY PROM DATE IS A COLD SHOWER, 'K?

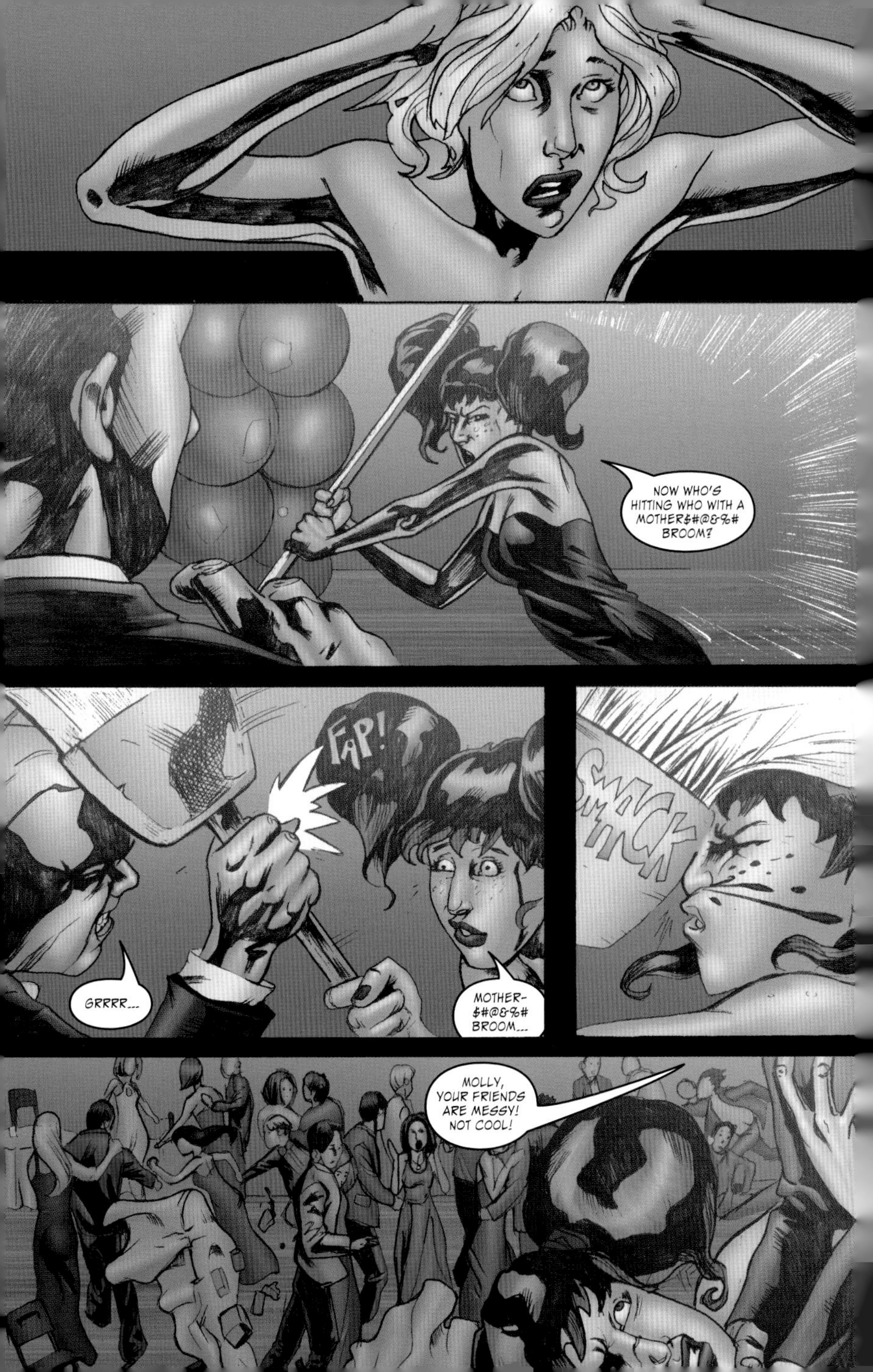
NOW WHO'S HITTING WHO WITH A MOTHER$#@&%# BROOM?
FAP!
GRRRR...
MOTHER-$#@&%# BROOM...
SMACK
MOLLY, YOUR FRIENDS ARE MESSY! NOT COOL!

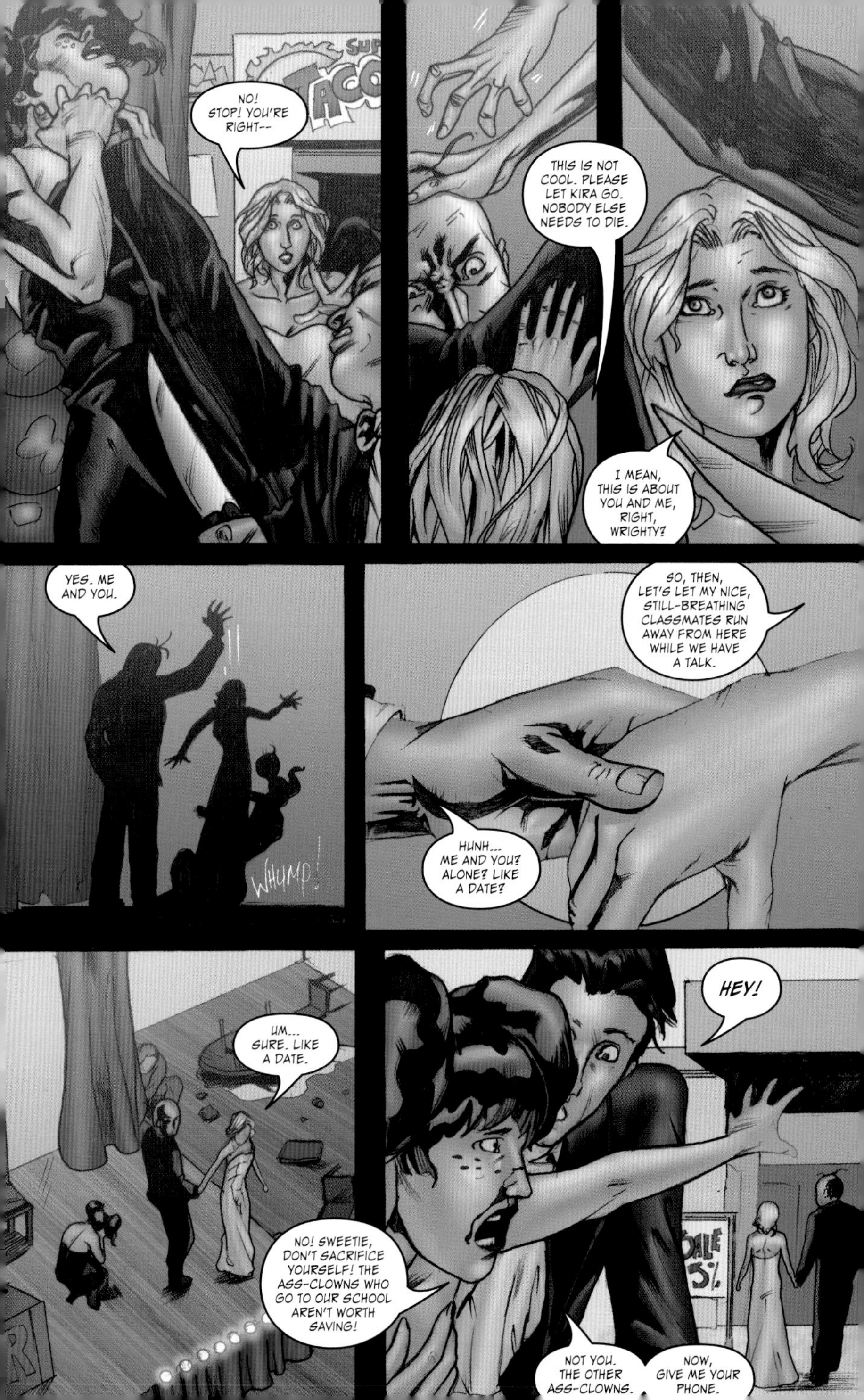

SUP
TACO
NO! STOP! YOU'RE RIGHT--
THIS IS NOT COOL. PLEASE LET KIRA GO. NOBODY ELSE NEEDS TO DIE.
I MEAN, THIS IS ABOUT YOU AND ME, RIGHT, WRIGHTY?
YES. ME AND YOU.
WHUMP!
SO, THEN, LET'S LET MY NICE, STILL-BREATHING CLASSMATES RUN AWAY FROM HERE WHILE WE HAVE A TALK.
HUNH... ME AND YOU? ALONE? LIKE A DATE?
UM... SURE. LIKE A DATE.
NO! SWEETIE, DON'T SACRIFICE YOURSELF! THE ASS-CLOWNS WHO GO TO OUR SCHOOL AREN'T WORTH SAVING!
HEY!
NOT YOU. THE OTHER ASS-CLOWNS.
NOW, GIVE ME YOUR PHONE.

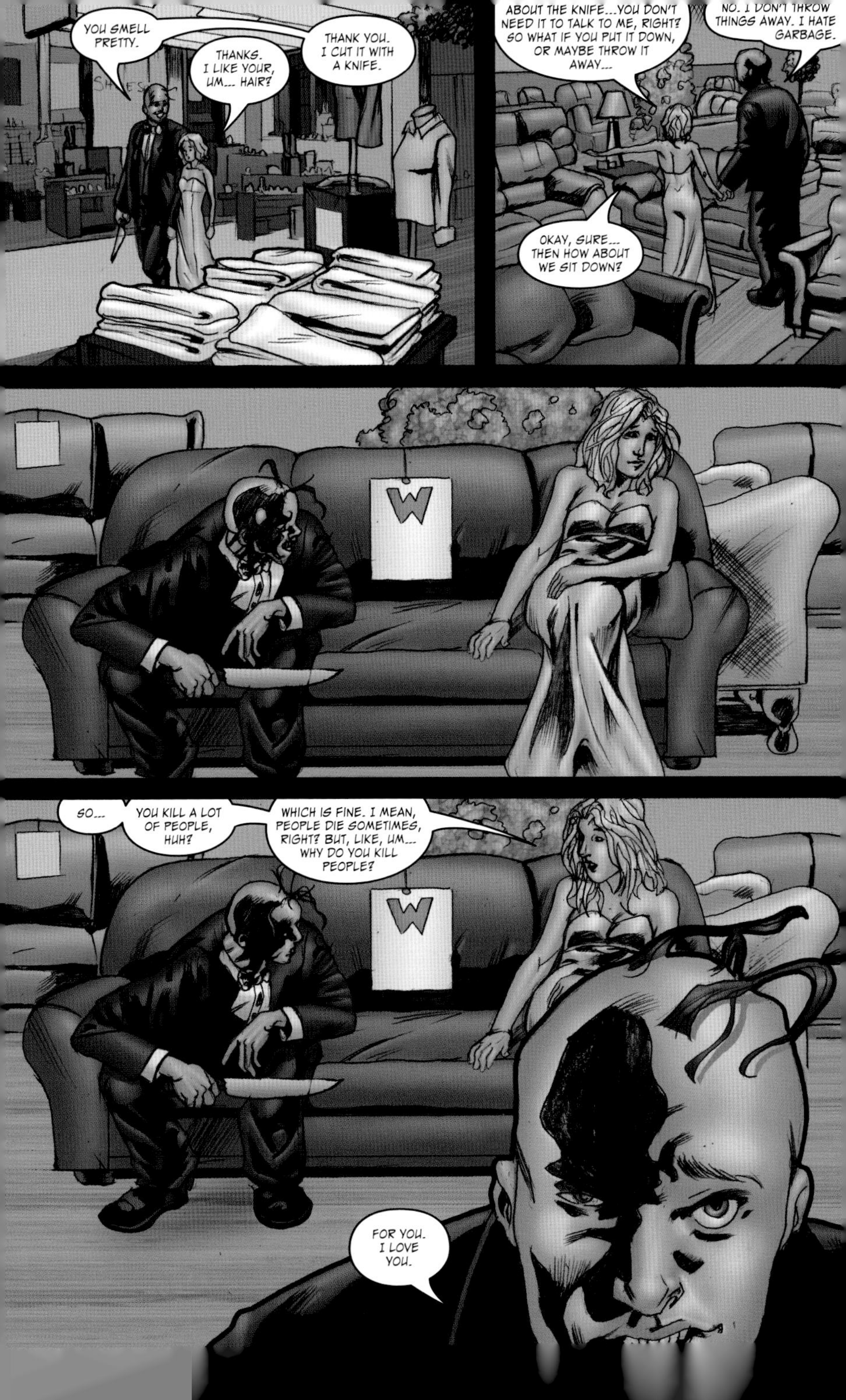
YOU SMELL PRETTY.
THANKS. I LIKE YOUR, UM... HAIR?
THANK YOU. I CUT IT WITH A KNIFE.
ABOUT THE KNIFE...YOU DON'T NEED IT TO TALK TO ME, RIGHT? SO WHAT IF YOU PUT IT DOWN, OR MAYBE THROW IT AWAY...
NO. I DON'T THROW THINGS AWAY. I HATE GARBAGE.
OKAY, SURE... THEN HOW ABOUT WE SIT DOWN?
W
SO...
YOU KILL A LOT OF PEOPLE, HUH?
WHICH IS FINE. I MEAN, PEOPLE DIE SOMETIMES, RIGHT? BUT, LIKE, UM... WHY DO YOU KILL PEOPLE?
W
FOR YOU. I LOVE YOU.

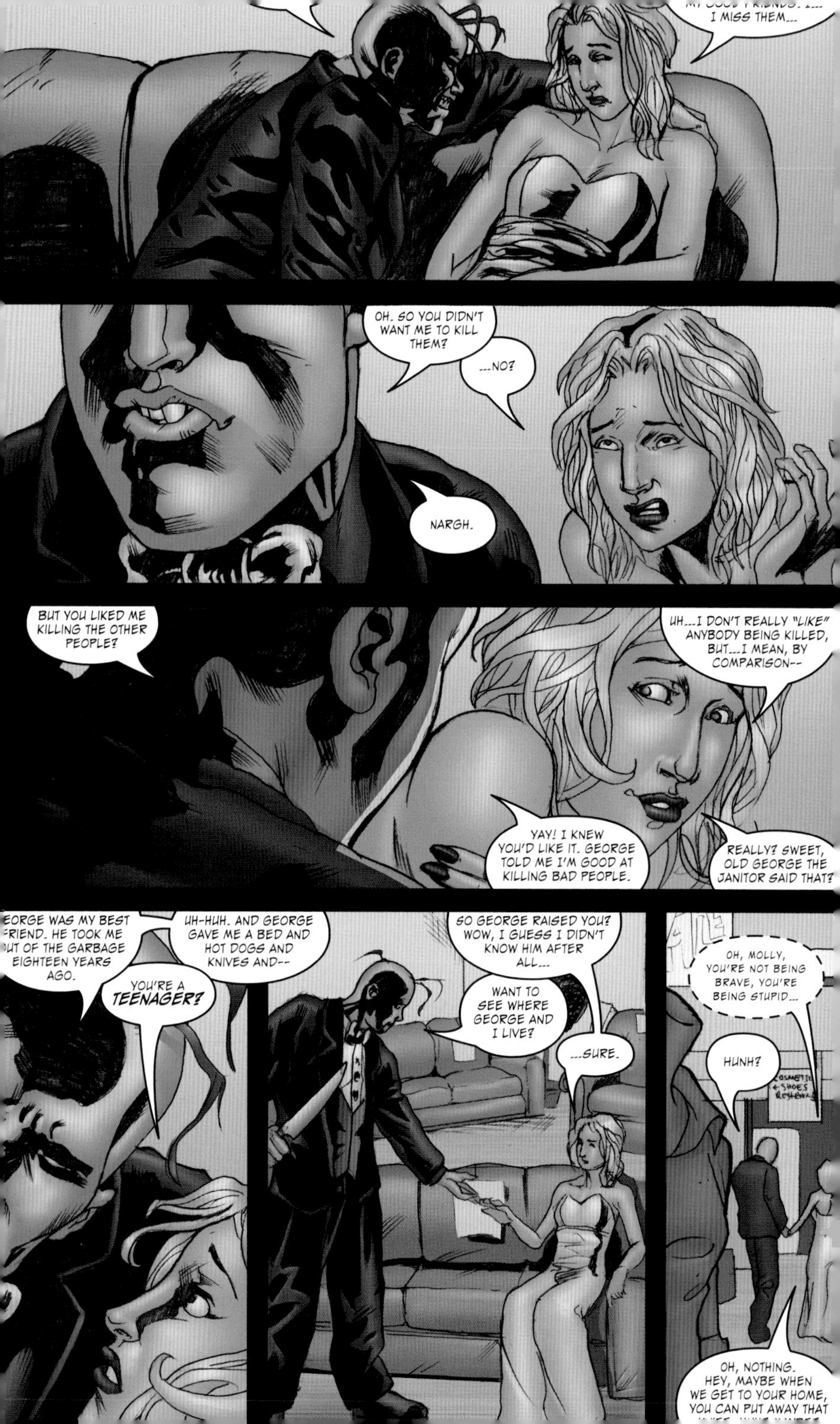
I MISS THEM...
OH. SO YOU DIDN'T WANT ME TO KILL THEM?
...NO?
NARGH.
BUT YOU LIKED ME KILLING THE OTHER PEOPLE?
UH...I DON'T REALLY "LIKE" ANYBODY BEING KILLED, BUT...I MEAN, BY COMPARISON--
YAY! I KNEW YOU'D LIKE IT. GEORGE TOLD ME I'M GOOD AT KILLING BAD PEOPLE.
REALLY? SWEET, OLD GEORGE THE JANITOR SAID THAT?
EORGE WAS MY BEST RIEND. HE TOOK ME UT OF THE GARBAGE EIGHTEEN YEARS AGO.
UH-HUH. AND GEORGE GAVE ME A BED AND HOT DOGS AND KNIVES AND--
YOU'RE A *TEENAGER?*
SO GEORGE RAISED YOU? WOW, I GUESS I DIDN'T KNOW HIM AFTER ALL...
WANT TO SEE WHERE GEORGE AND I LIVE?
...SURE.
OH, MOLLY, YOU'RE NOT BEING BRAVE, YOU'RE BEING STUPID...
HUNH?
OH, NOTHING. HEY, MAYBE WHEN WE GET TO YOUR HOME, YOU CAN PUT AWAY THAT

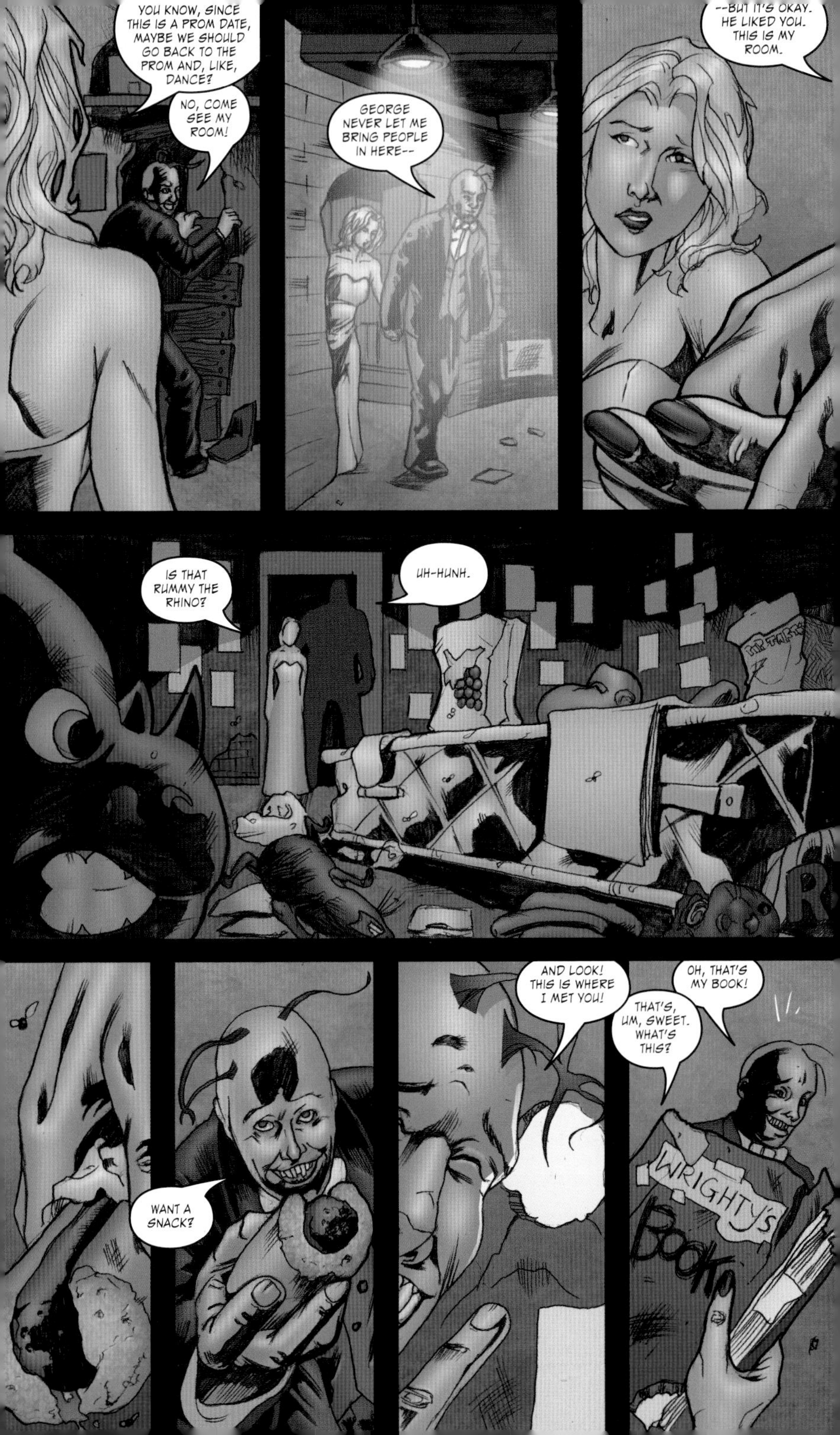
YOU KNOW, SINCE THIS IS A PROM DATE, MAYBE WE SHOULD GO BACK TO THE PROM AND, LIKE, DANCE?
NO, COME SEE MY ROOM!
GEORGE NEVER LET ME BRING PEOPLE IN HERE--
--BUT IT'S OKAY. HE LIKED YOU. THIS IS MY ROOM.
IS THAT RUMMY THE RHINO?
UH-HUNH.
WANT A SNACK?
AND LOOK! THIS IS WHERE I MET YOU!
THAT'S, UM, SWEET. WHAT'S THIS?
OH, THAT'S MY BOOK!
WRIGHTY'S Book

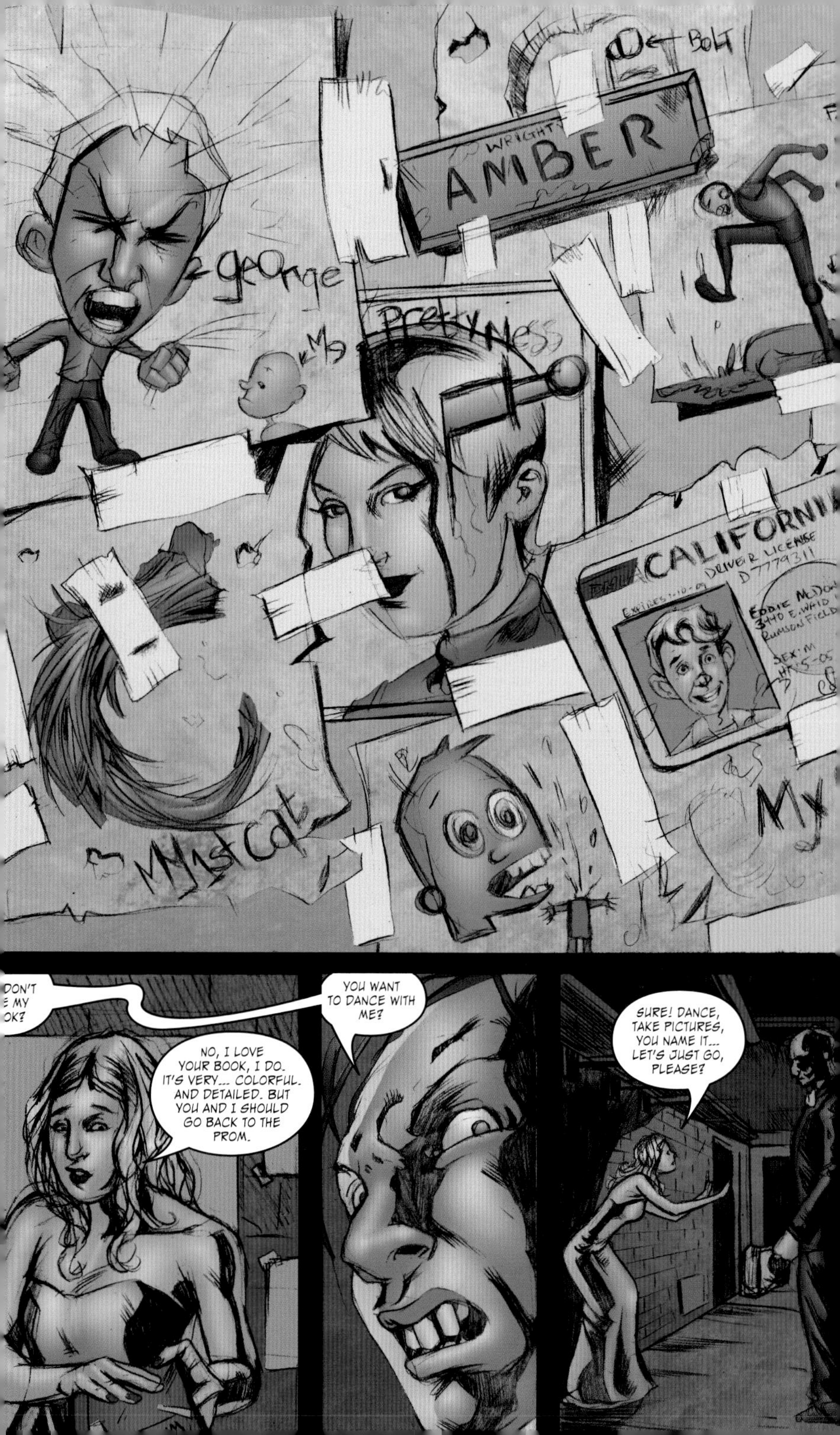
BOLT
WRIGHT
AMBER
george
My pretty ness
CALIFORNIA
DRIVER LICENSE
D7779311
Mist Cat
My
YOU WANT TO DANCE WITH ME?
NO, I LOVE YOUR BOOK, I DO. IT'S VERY... COLORFUL. AND DETAILED. BUT YOU AND I SHOULD GO BACK TO THE PROM.
SURE! DANCE, TAKE PICTURES, YOU NAME IT... LET'S JUST GO, PLEASE?

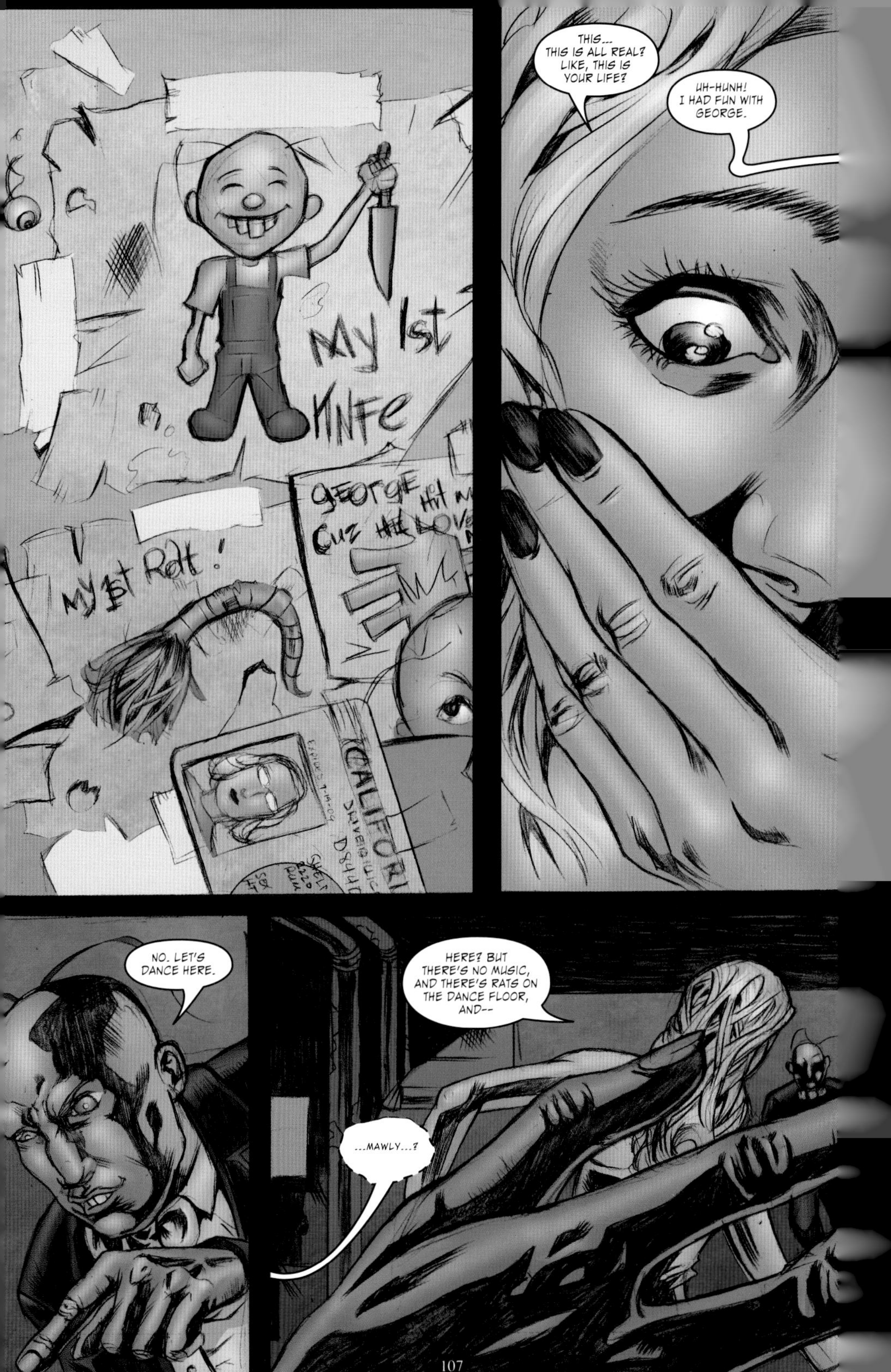
My 1st KnFe
george
My 1st Ratt!
THIS...
THIS IS ALL REAL? LIKE, THIS IS YOUR LIFE?
UH-HUNH! I HAD FUN WITH GEORGE.
NO. LET'S DANCE HERE.
HERE? BUT THERE'S NO MUSIC, AND THERE'S RATS ON THE DANCE FLOOR, AND--
...MAWLY...?

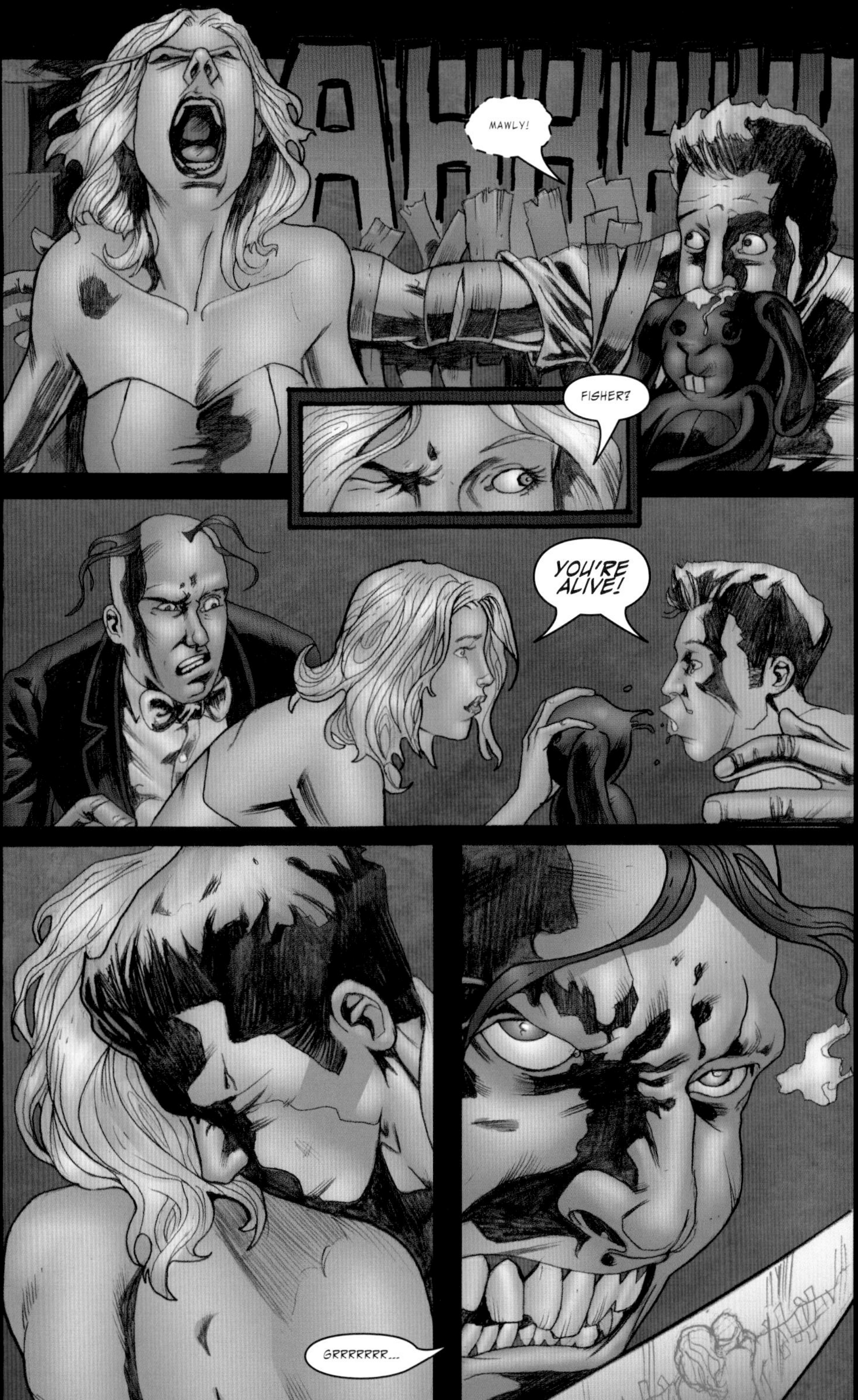
MAWLY!
FISHER?
YOU'RE ALIVE!
GRRRRRRR...

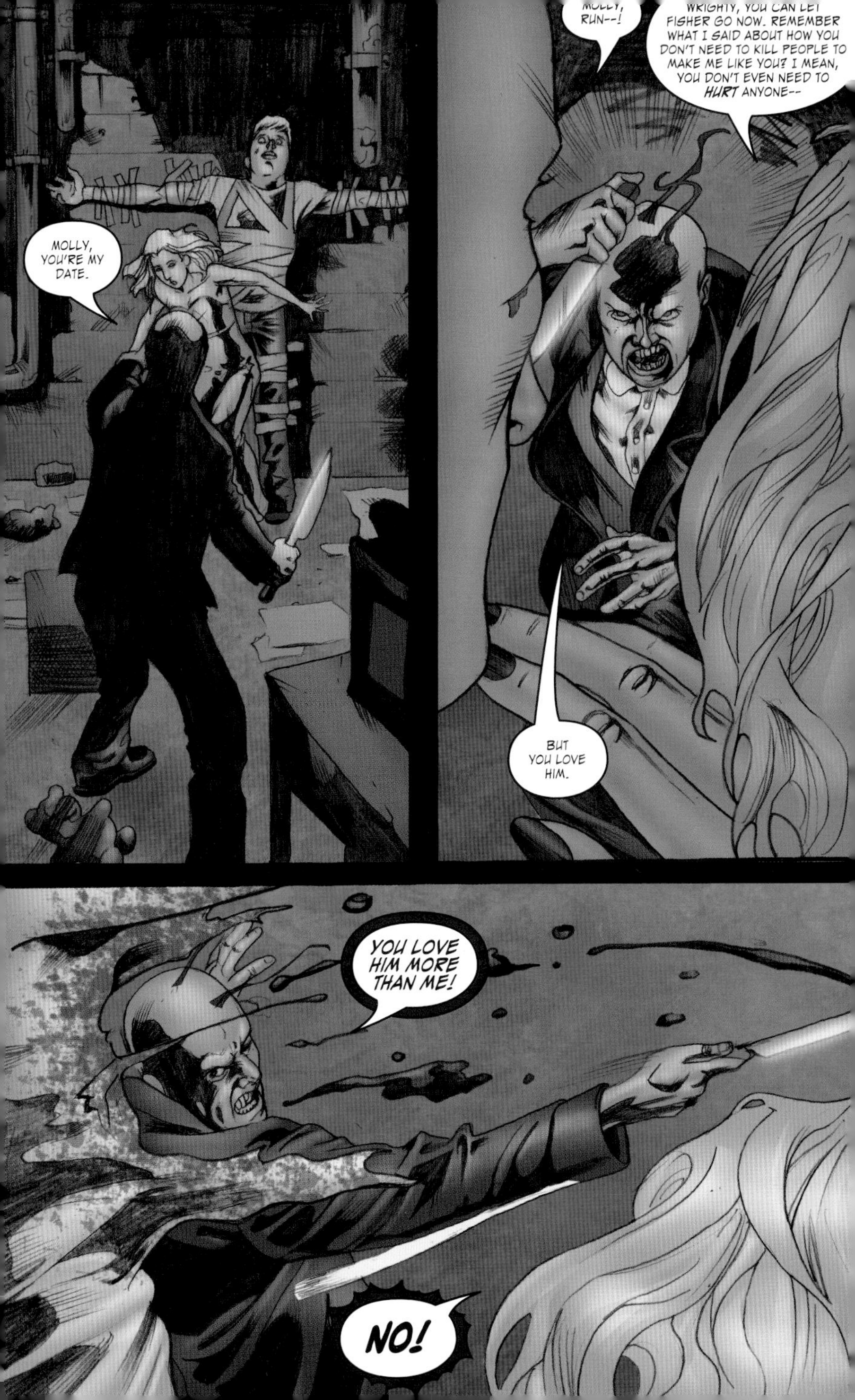

MOLLY, YOU'RE MY DATE.
MOLLY, RUN--!
WRIGHTY, YOU CAN LET FISHER GO NOW. REMEMBER WHAT I SAID ABOUT HOW YOU DON'T NEED TO KILL PEOPLE TO MAKE ME LIKE YOU? I MEAN, YOU DON'T EVEN NEED TO HURT ANYONE--
BUT YOU LOVE HIM.
YOU LOVE HIM MORE THAN ME!
NO!

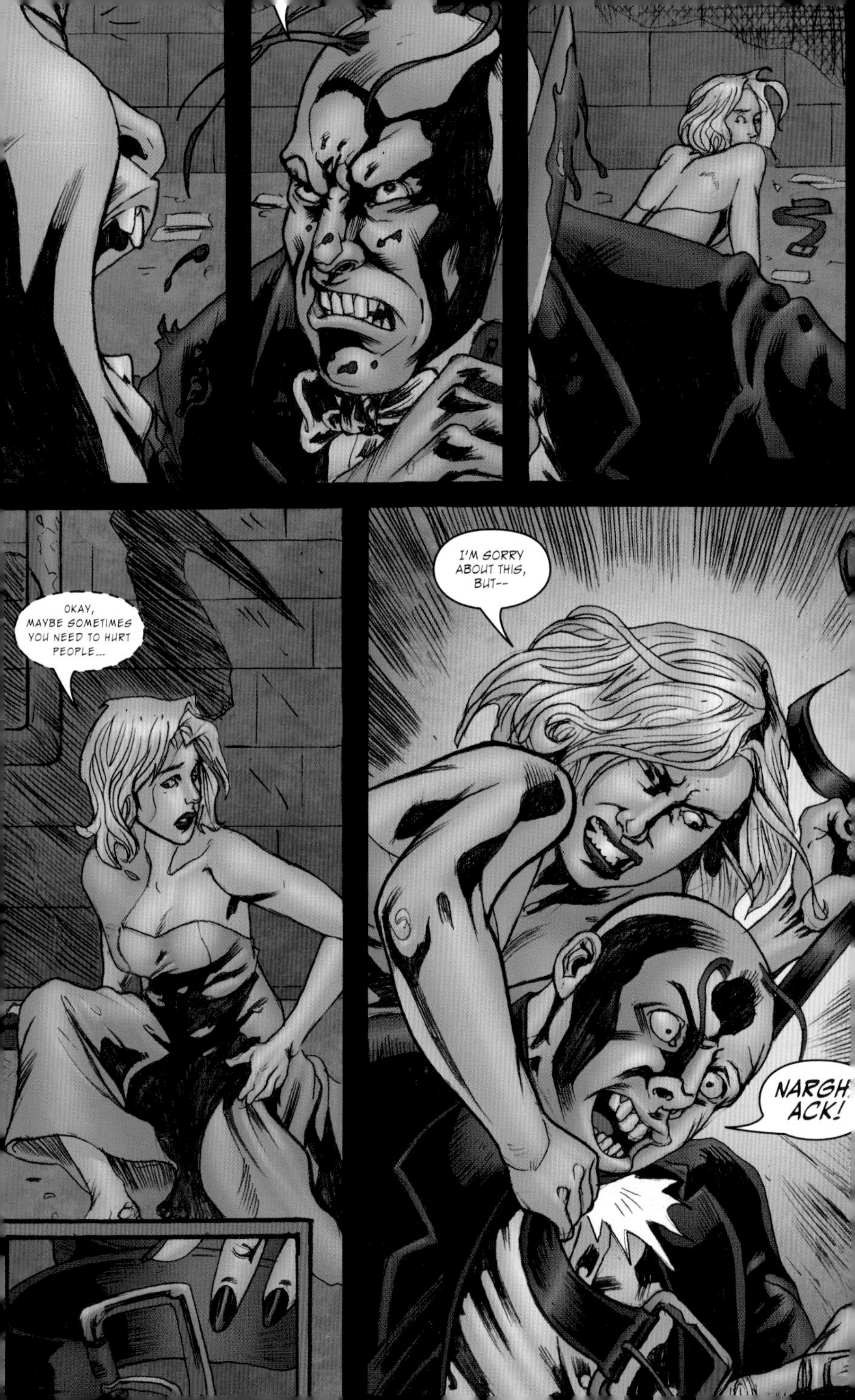
OKAY, MAYBE SOMETIMES YOU NEED TO HURT PEOPLE...
I'M SORRY ABOUT THIS, BUT--
NARGH. ACK!

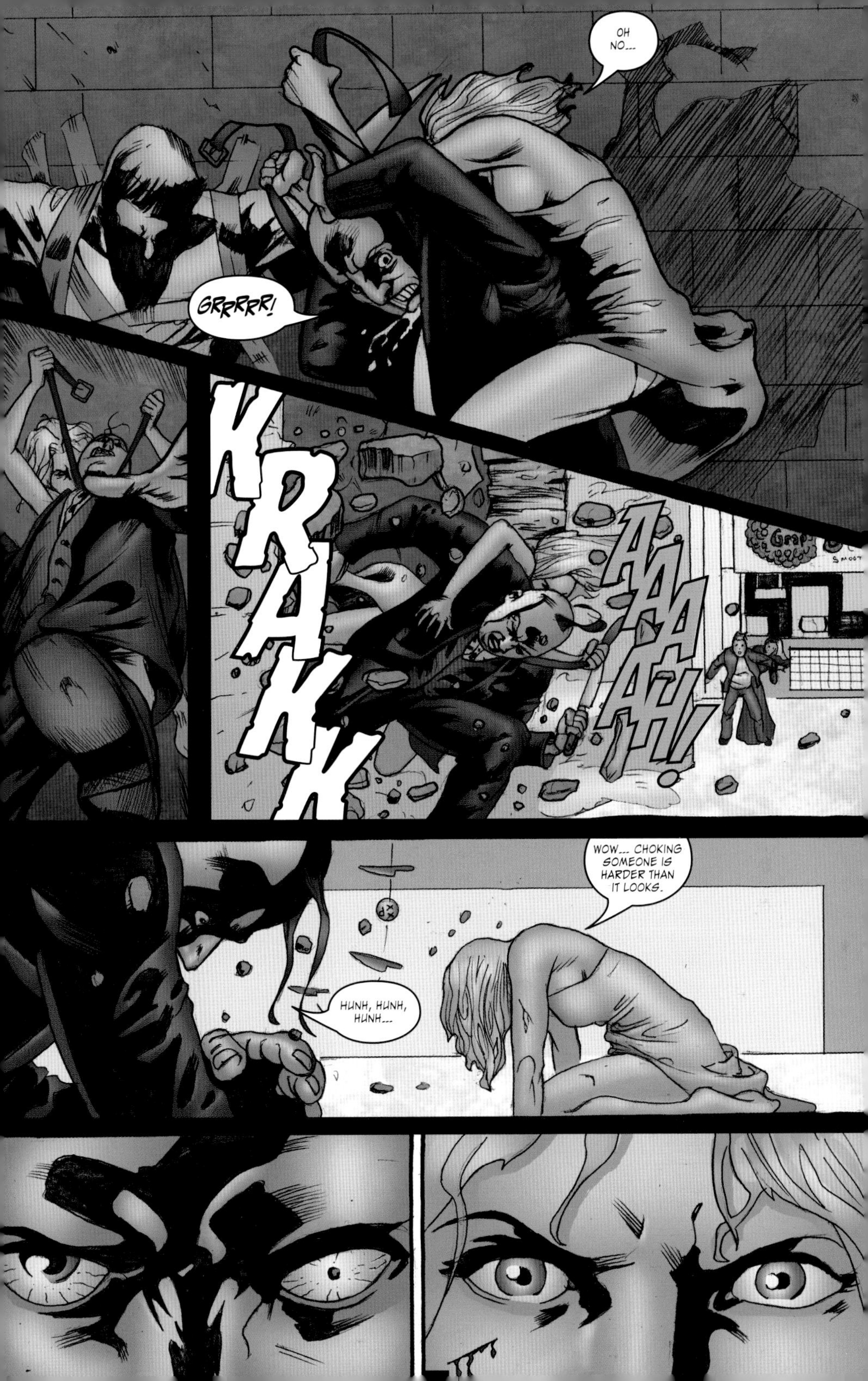
OH NO...
GRRRRR!
KRAKK
AAAAAH!
WOW... CHOKING SOMEONE IS HARDER THAN IT LOOKS.
HUNH, HUNH, HUNH...

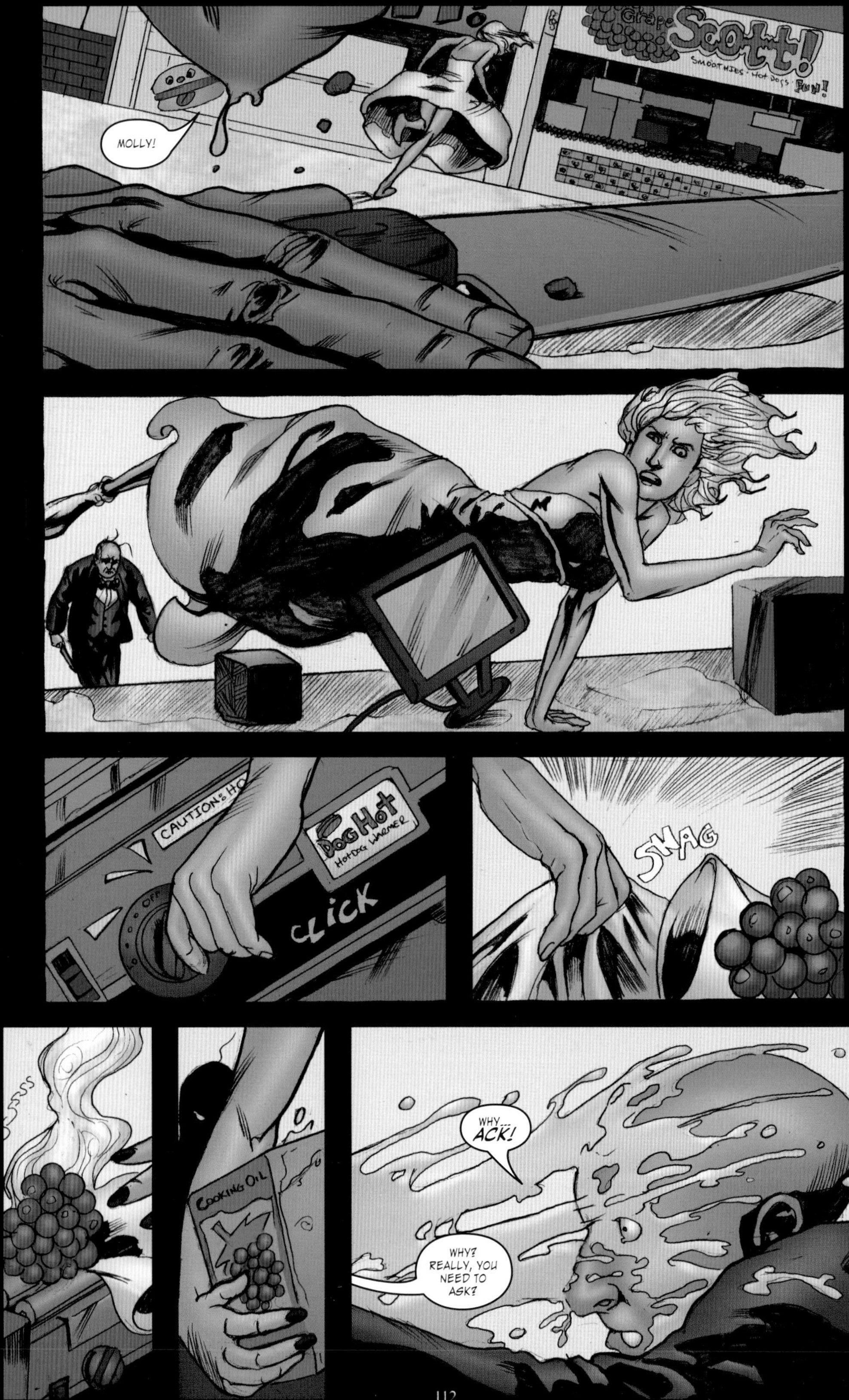
Grape Scott!
SMOOTHIES · HOT DOGS · FUN!
MOLLY!
CAUTION: HO
DOG HOT
HOTDOG WARMER
OFF
CLICK
SNAG
COOKING OIL
WHY... ACK!
WHY? REALLY, YOU NEED TO ASK?

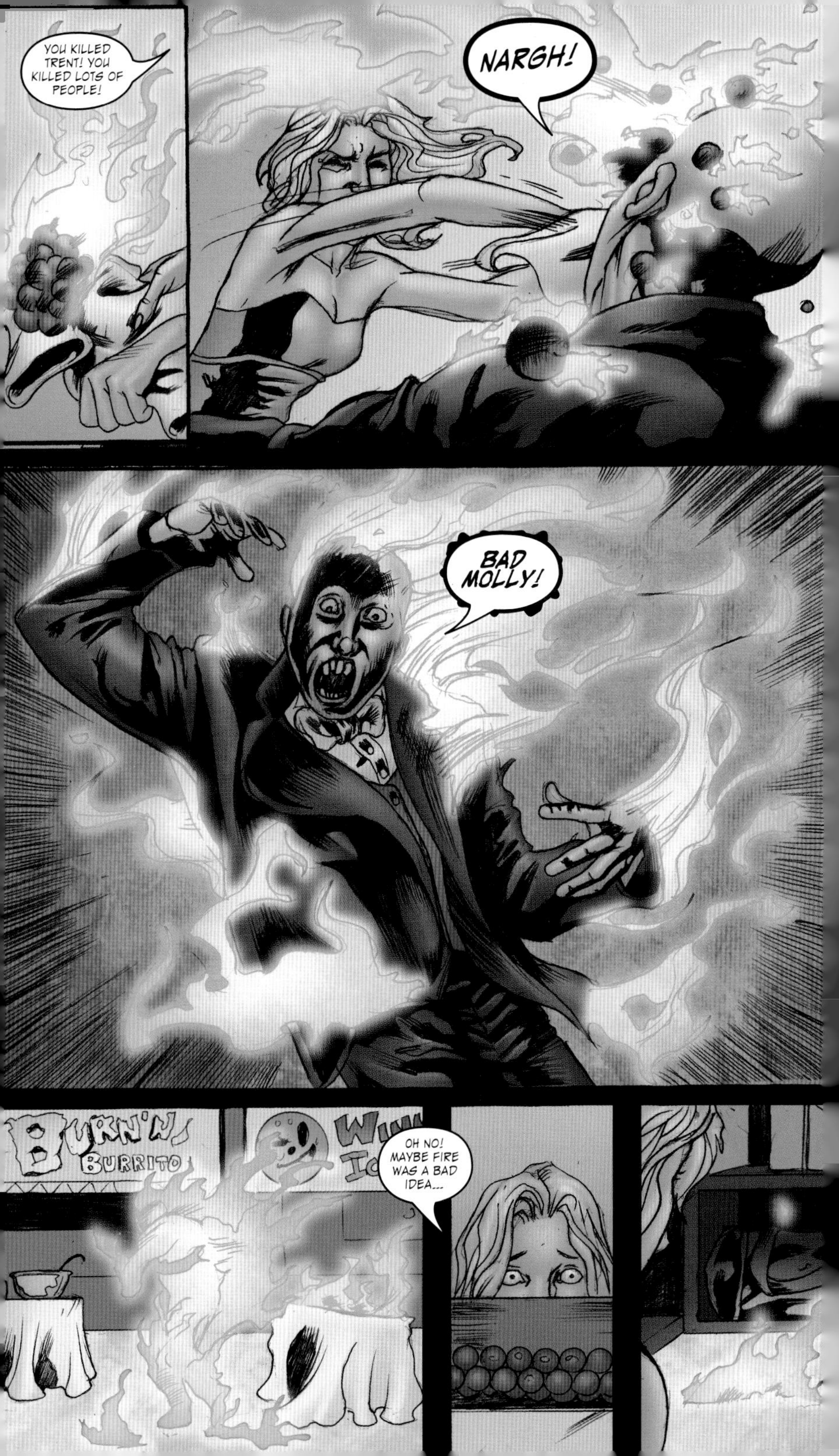
YOU KILLED TRENT! YOU KILLED LOTS OF PEOPLE!
NARGH!
BAD MOLLY!
BURN'N BURRITO
OH NO! MAYBE FIRE WAS A BAD IDEA...

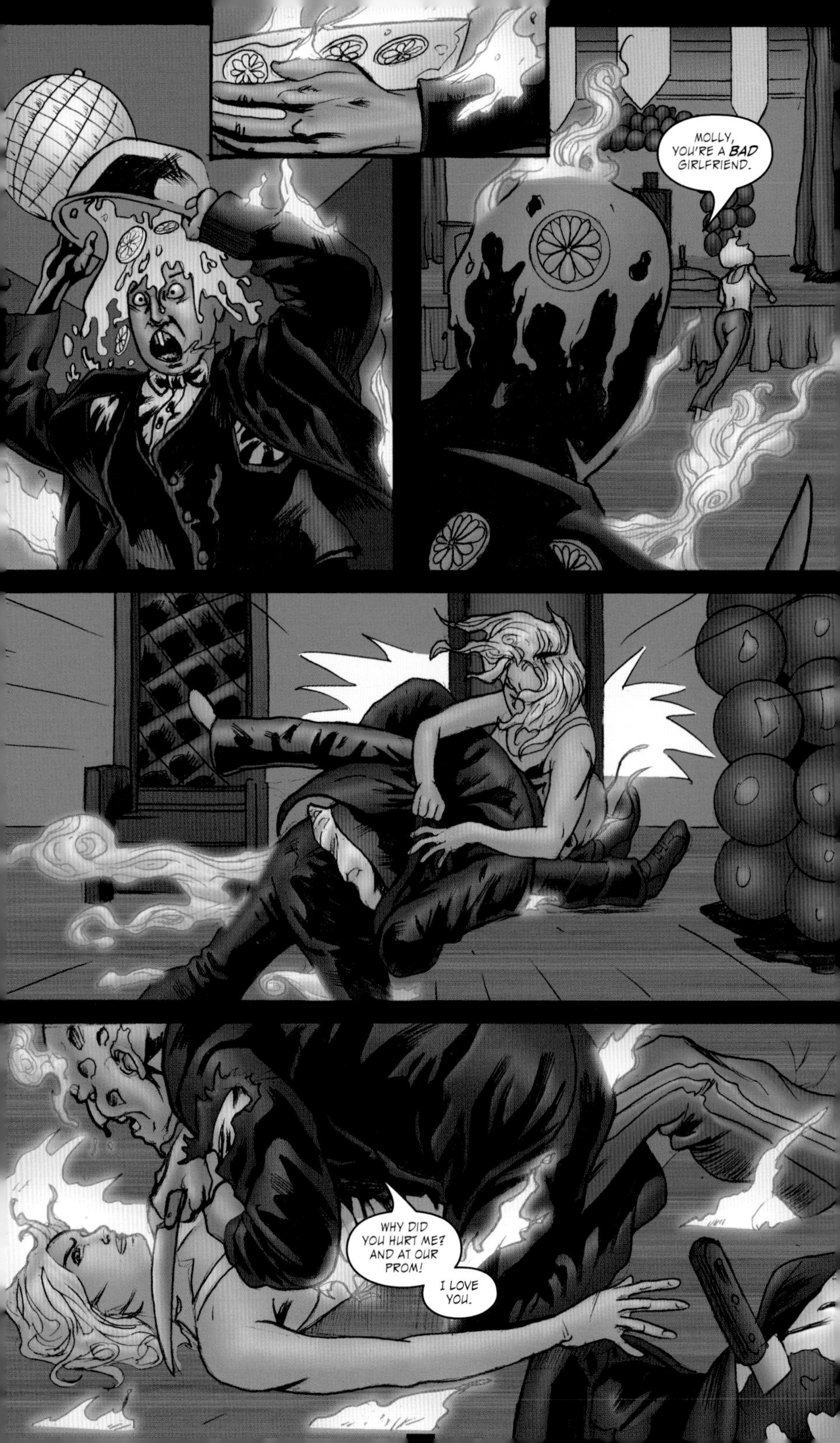
MOLLY, YOU'RE A BAD GIRLFRIEND.
WHY DID YOU HURT ME? AND AT OUR PROM!
I LOVE YOU.

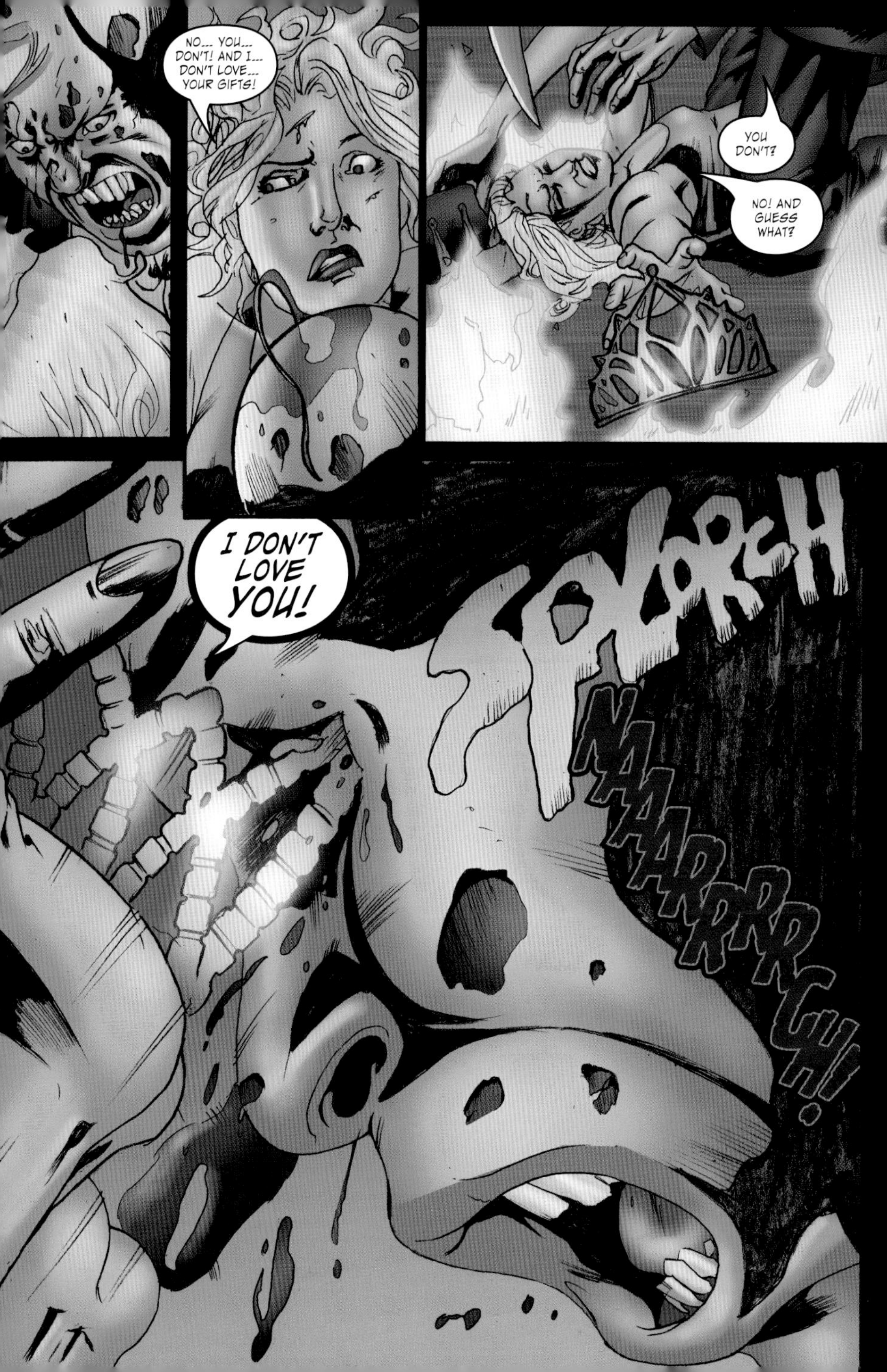
NO... YOU... DON'T! AND I... DON'T LOVE... YOUR GIFTS!
YOU DON'T?
NO! AND GUESS WHAT?
I DON'T LOVE YOU!
SKORCH
NAAARRRRGH!

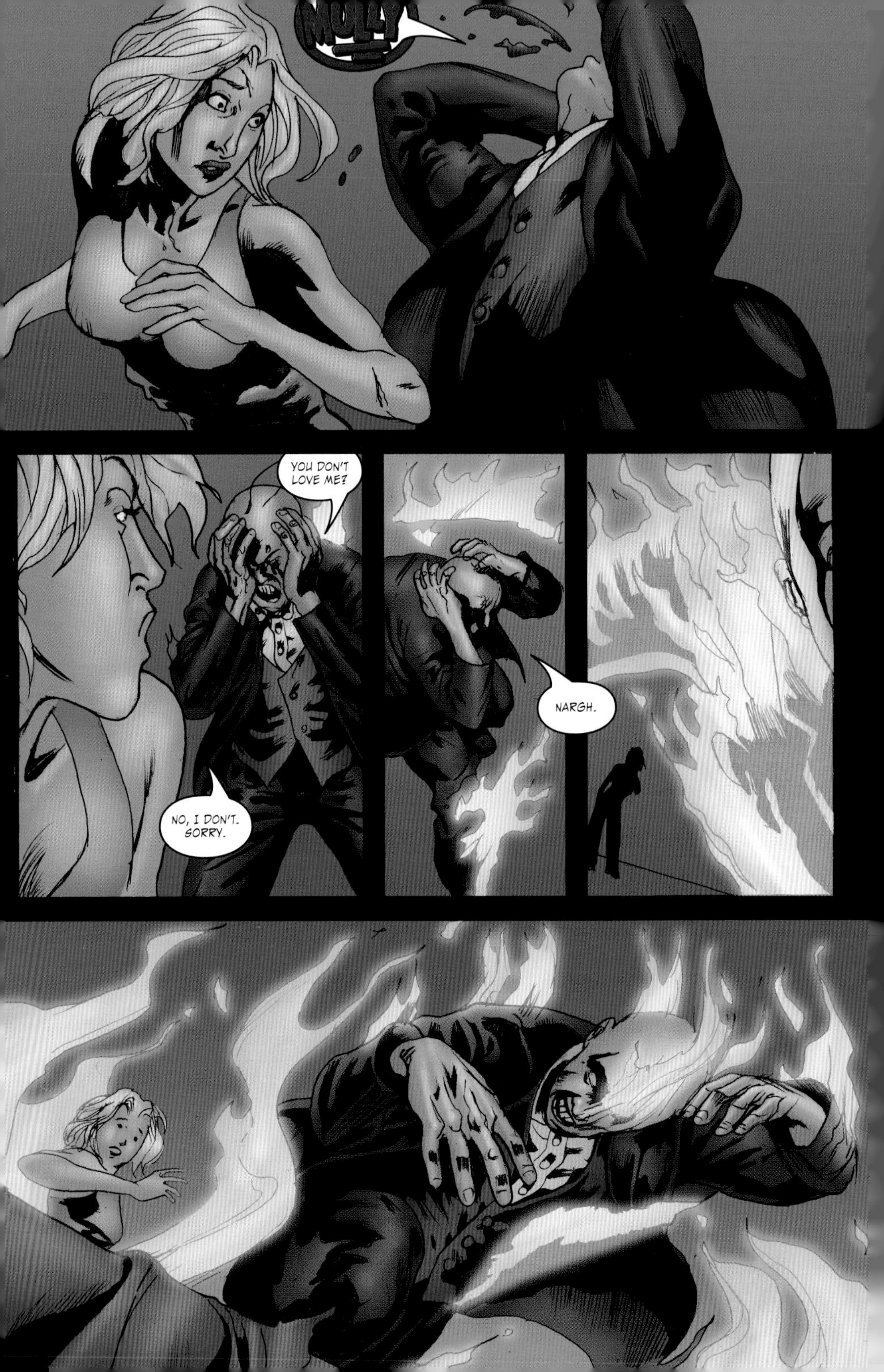
MULLY
YOU DON'T LOVE ME?
NO, I DON'T. SORRY.
NARGH.

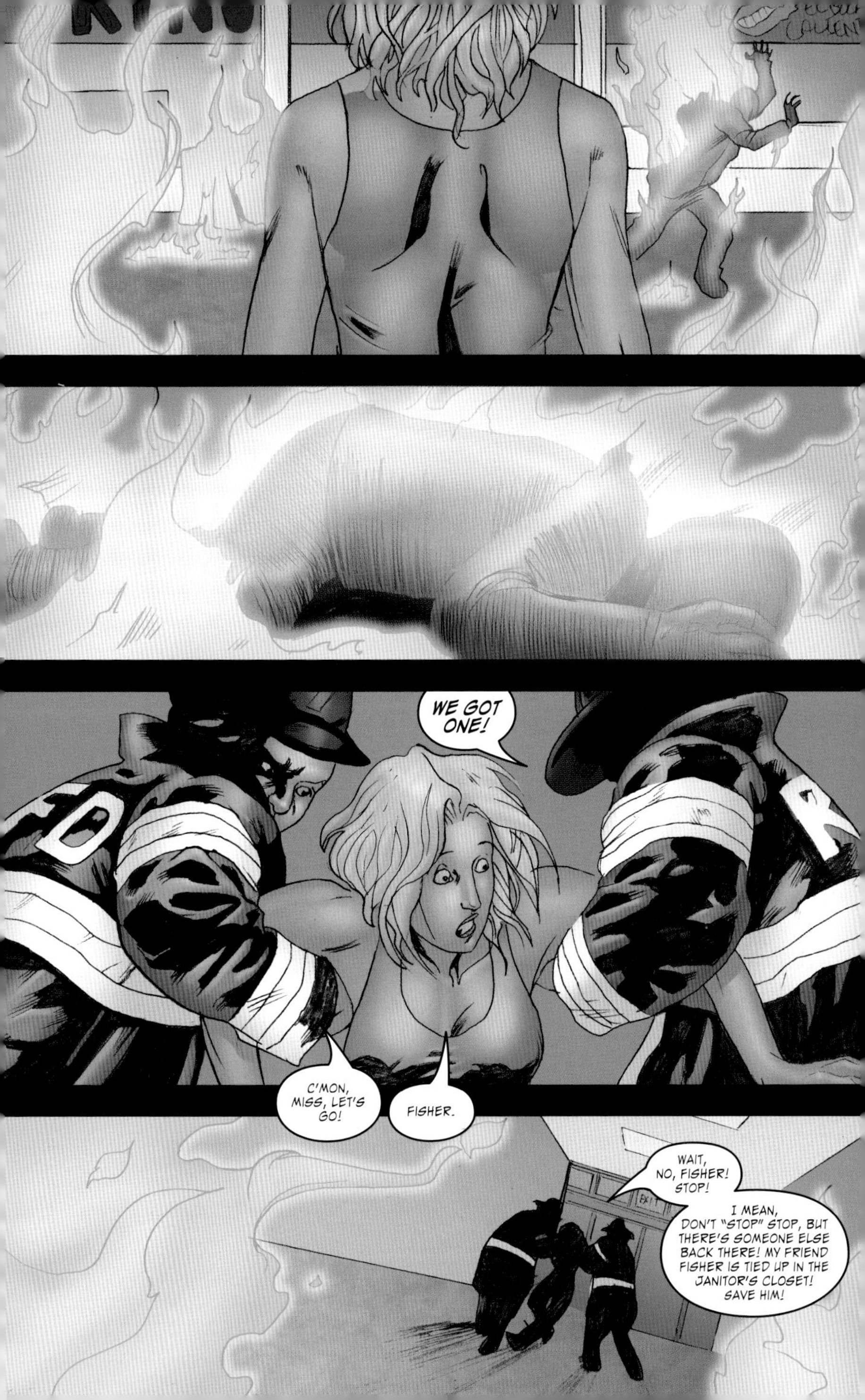
WE GOT ONE!
C'MON, MISS, LET'S GO!
FISHER.
EXIT
WAIT, NO, FISHER! STOP!
I MEAN, DON'T "STOP" STOP, BUT THERE'S SOMEONE ELSE BACK THERE! MY FRIEND FISHER IS TIED UP IN THE JANITOR'S CLOSET! SAVE HIM!

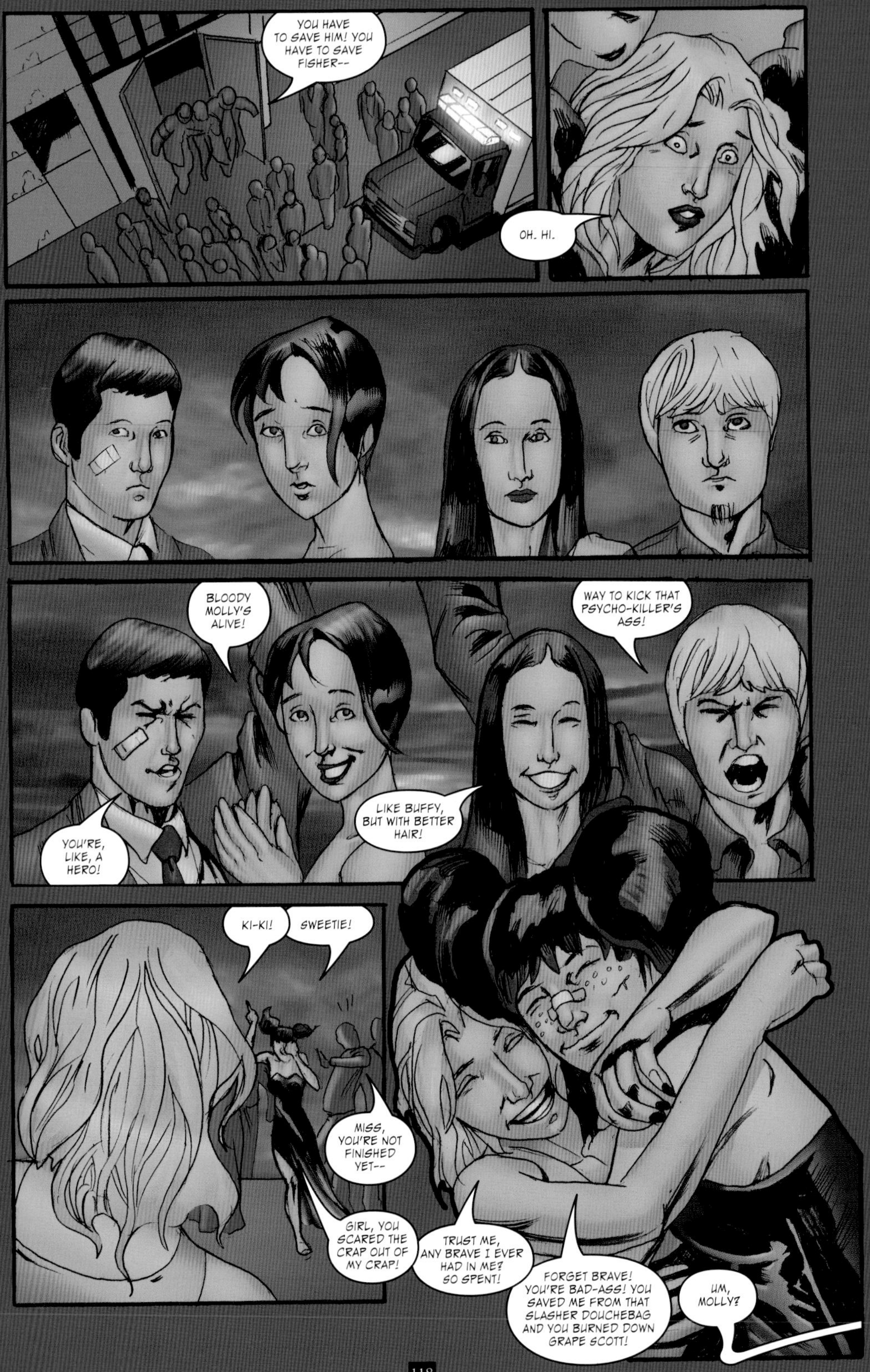
YOU HAVE TO SAVE HIM! YOU HAVE TO SAVE FISHER--
OH. HI.
BLOODY MOLLY'S ALIVE!
WAY TO KICK THAT PSYCHO-KILLER'S ASS!
YOU'RE, LIKE, A HERO!
LIKE BUFFY, BUT WITH BETTER HAIR!
KI-KI!
SWEETIE!
MISS, YOU'RE NOT FINISHED YET--
GIRL, YOU SCARED THE CRAP OUT OF MY CRAP!
TRUST ME, ANY BRAVE I EVER HAD IN ME? SO SPENT!
FORGET BRAVE! YOU'RE BAD-ASS! YOU SAVED ME FROM THAT SLASHER DOUCHEBAG AND YOU BURNED DOWN GRAPE SCOTT!
UM, MOLLY?

ME AND THE OTHER PROM QUEEN NOMINEES TALKED AND WE THINK YOU SHOULD BE PROM QUEEN.

YOU DID CATCH THE RUMSON SERIAL KILLER.

AND MADE VARSITY CHEERLEADING!

YOU'RE MOTHER*%&#* RIGHT SHE'S THE QUEEN!

WE'D GIVE YOU THE TIARA, BUT IT'S BURNING INSIDE THE MALL.

OH, DON'T WORRY. I ALREADY TOOK THE TIARA.

MISS, IS THIS YOUR FRIEND?

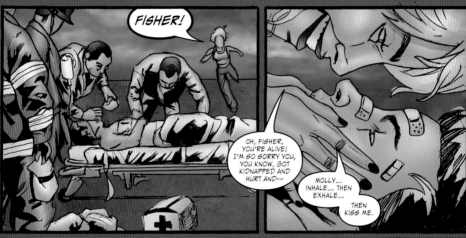

FISHER!

OH, FISHER, YOU'RE ALIVE! I'M SO SORRY YOU, YOU KNOW, GOT KIDNAPPED AND HURT AND--

MOLLY... INHALE... THEN EXHALE... THEN KISS ME.

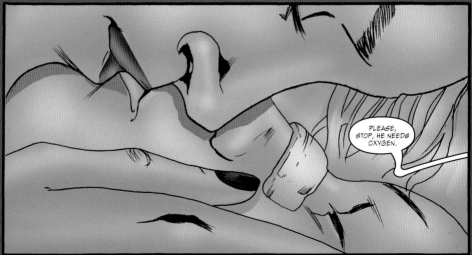

PLEASE, STOP, HE NEEDS OXYGEN.

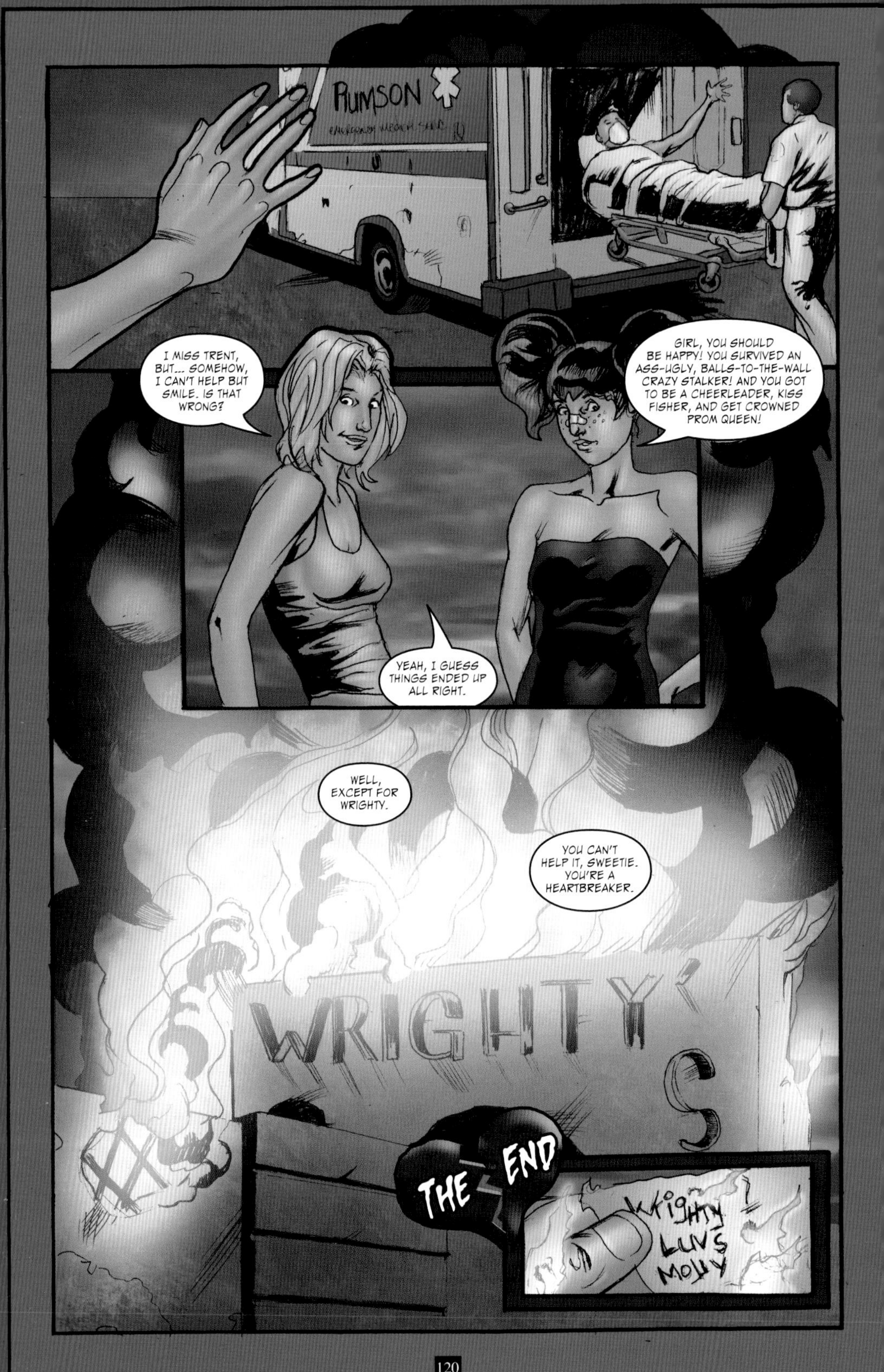
RUMSON
I MISS TRENT, BUT... SOMEHOW, I CAN'T HELP BUT SMILE. IS THAT WRONG?
GIRL, YOU SHOULD BE HAPPY! YOU SURVIVED AN ASS-UGLY, BALLS-TO-THE-WALL CRAZY STALKER! AND YOU GOT TO BE A CHEERLEADER, KISS FISHER, AND GET CROWNED PROM QUEEN!
YEAH, I GUESS THINGS ENDED UP ALL RIGHT.
WELL, EXCEPT FOR WRIGHTY.
YOU CAN'T HELP IT, SWEETIE. YOU'RE A HEARTBREAKER.
WRIGHTY'S
THE END
WRIGHTY LUVS MOLLY

TURN THE PAGE FOR THE
NEVER BEFORE SEEN
ALTERNATE ENDING

PAGE 20
PANEL ONE: THE OTHER PROM QUEEN NOMINEES CIRCLE AROUND MOLLY. THE OTHER GIRLS ARE SMILING, WHILE MOLLY LOOKS SURPRISED. KIRA'S RIGHT BEHIND MOLLY, EXCITED. A PARAMEDIC ATTENDS TO MOLLY'S NECK AS THIS HAPPENS.

1. PROM QUEEN NOMINEE #1: Me and the other prom queen nominees talked and we think you should be prom queen.

2. PROM QUEEN NOMINEE #2: You did catch the Rumson serial killer.

3. PROM QUEEN NOMINEE #3: And made Varsity Cheerleading!

4. KIRA: You're motherfingering right she's the queen!

PANEL TWO: MOLLY LAUGHS TO HERSELF AS PROM QUEEN NOMINEE #1 TOUCHES HER ARM, APOLOGETICALLY. IN THE BACKGROUND, ALL HER CLASSMATES CHEER AGAIN.

5. PROM QUEEN NOMINEE #1: We'd give you the tiara, but it's burning inside the mall.

6. MOLLY: Oh, don't worry. I already took the tiara.

PANEL THREE: MOLLY AND KIRA STAND SIDE-BY-SIDE, WATCHING THE MALL BURN DOWN. MOLLY TENTATIVELY SMILES, WHILE KIRA'S TOTALLY EXCITED. THE PARAMEDIC STILL WORKS ON HER NECK.

7. MOLLY: I miss Trent and I'm still worried about Fisher, but… I kinda want to smile. Is that wrong?

8. KIRA: Girl, you should be happy! You survived an ass-ugly, balls-to-the-wall crazy stalker!

9. PARAMEDIC/off: Miss, is this your friend?

PANEL FOUR: MOLLY RUNS TOWARDS TWO PARAMEDICS, ROLLING A BODY OUT ON A GURNEY. YOU CAN'T SEE WHO'S ON THE GURNEY YET, BUT YOU CAN TELL FROM THE WAY THE PARAMEDICS ARE WORKING THAT HE'S NOT DEAD.

10. MOLLY: FISHER!

PAGE 21
PANEL ONE: MOLLY ABURPTLY STOPS AT THE GURNEY'S SIDE, SCARED. AN ARM SHOOTS UP FROM THE GURNEY TOWARDS HER THROAT. IT LOOKS BADLY BURNED.

1. MOLLY: Fisher, I'm so… no!

PANEL TWO: WE SEE WRIGHTY LYING DOWN ON THE GURNEY. HE'S UGLIER THAN BEFORE: HIS FACE IS BLOODY AND HIS BODY IS BADLY BURNED. HE GRABS MOLLY BY HER THROAT. MOLLY IS TERRIFIED; THE PARAMEDICS ARE JUST STUNNED.

2. WRIGHTY: Molly… I'm sorry… I still love you…

3. WRIGHTY: I can change… give me one more try…

PANEL THREE: WRIGHTY PULLS MOLLY'S FACE DOWN TO HIS, KISSING HER ON THE LIPS. MOLLY FLINCHES WITH DISGUST. WRIGHTY IS IN HEAVEN… BLOODY, DISGUSTING HEAVEN.

PANEL FOUR: WE PULL BACK TO A WIDER SHOT, SHOWING KIRA AND THE POLICE TRYING TO PULL MOLLY AWAY FROM WRIGHTY. IN THE BACKGROUND, WE SEE THAT THE MALL IS ON FIRE AND SPECIFICALLY, WE SEE THE SIGN FOR "WRIGHTY'S" IN FLAMES.

4. CAPTION (in a heart-shaped-box): The End.

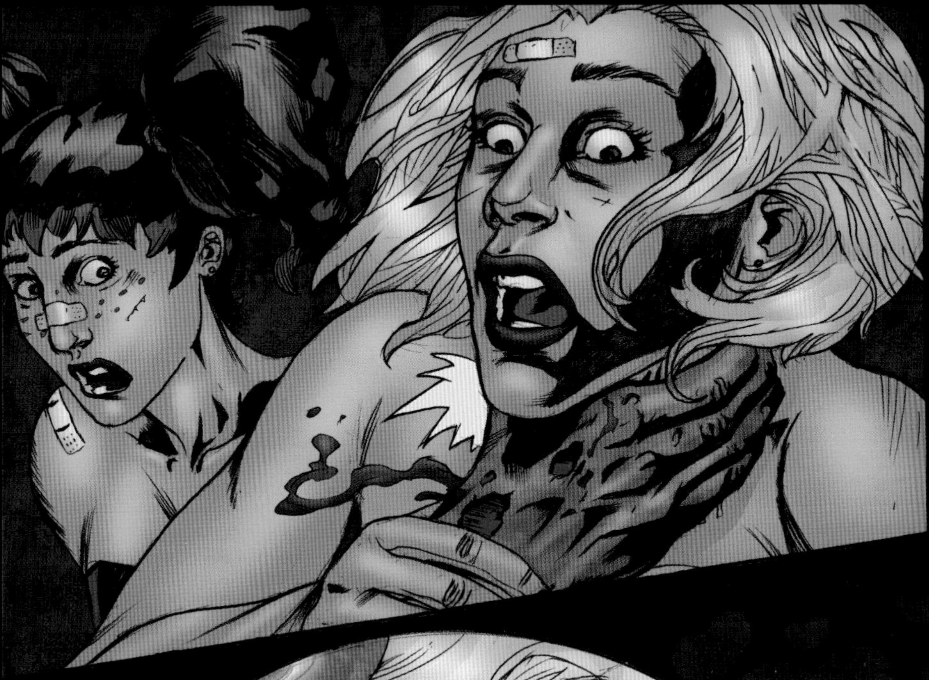

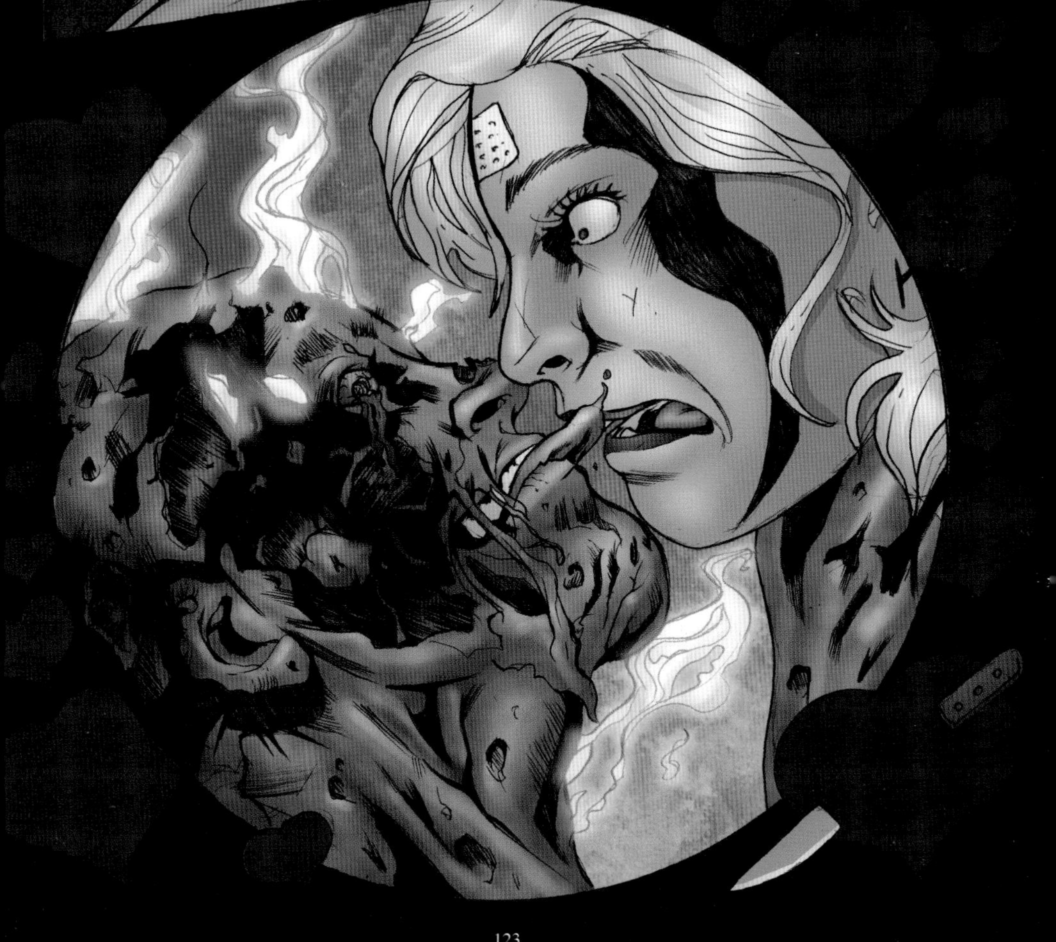

FAN ART BY
BRANDON BRACAMONTE

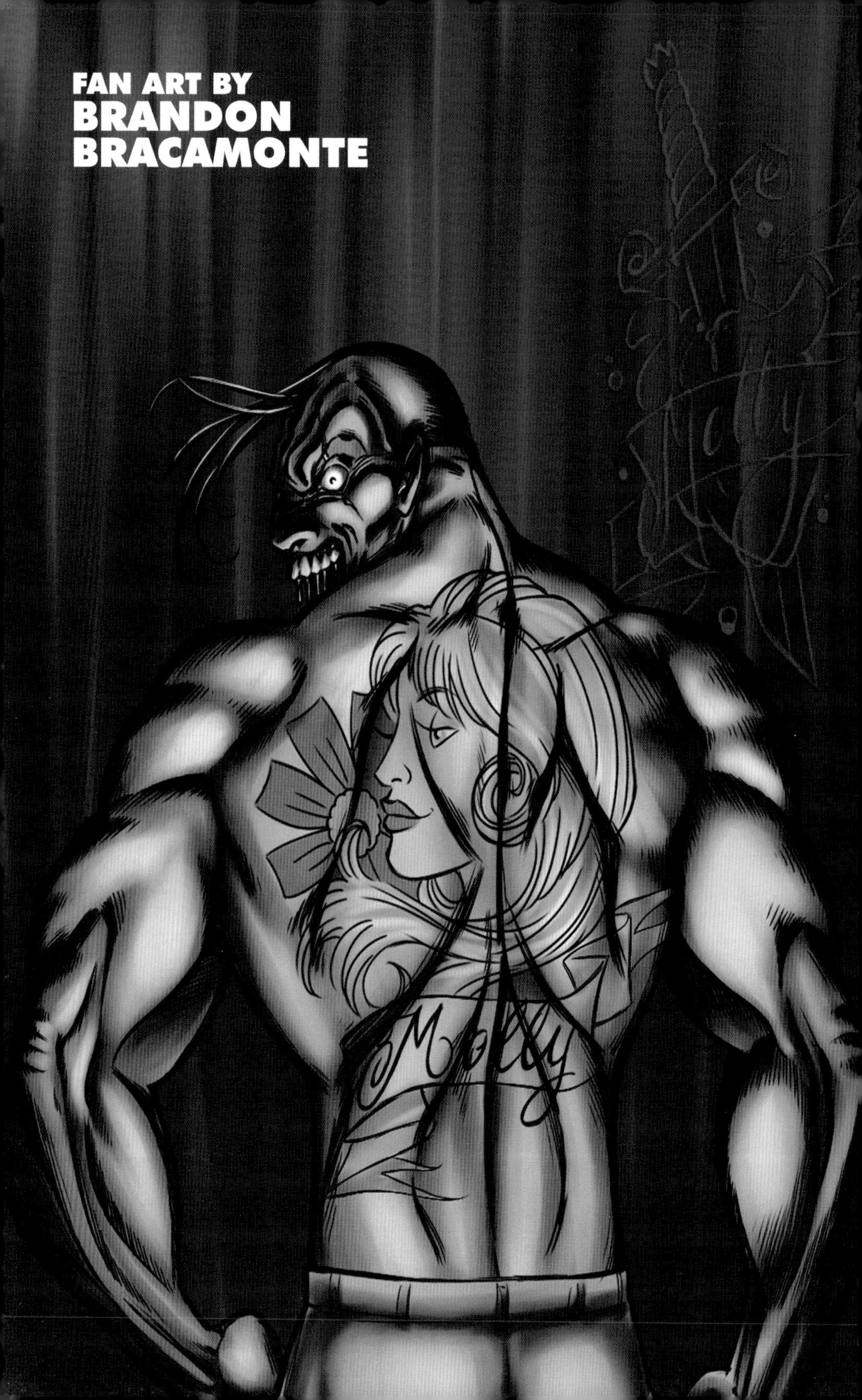
Molly

SKETCHBOOK

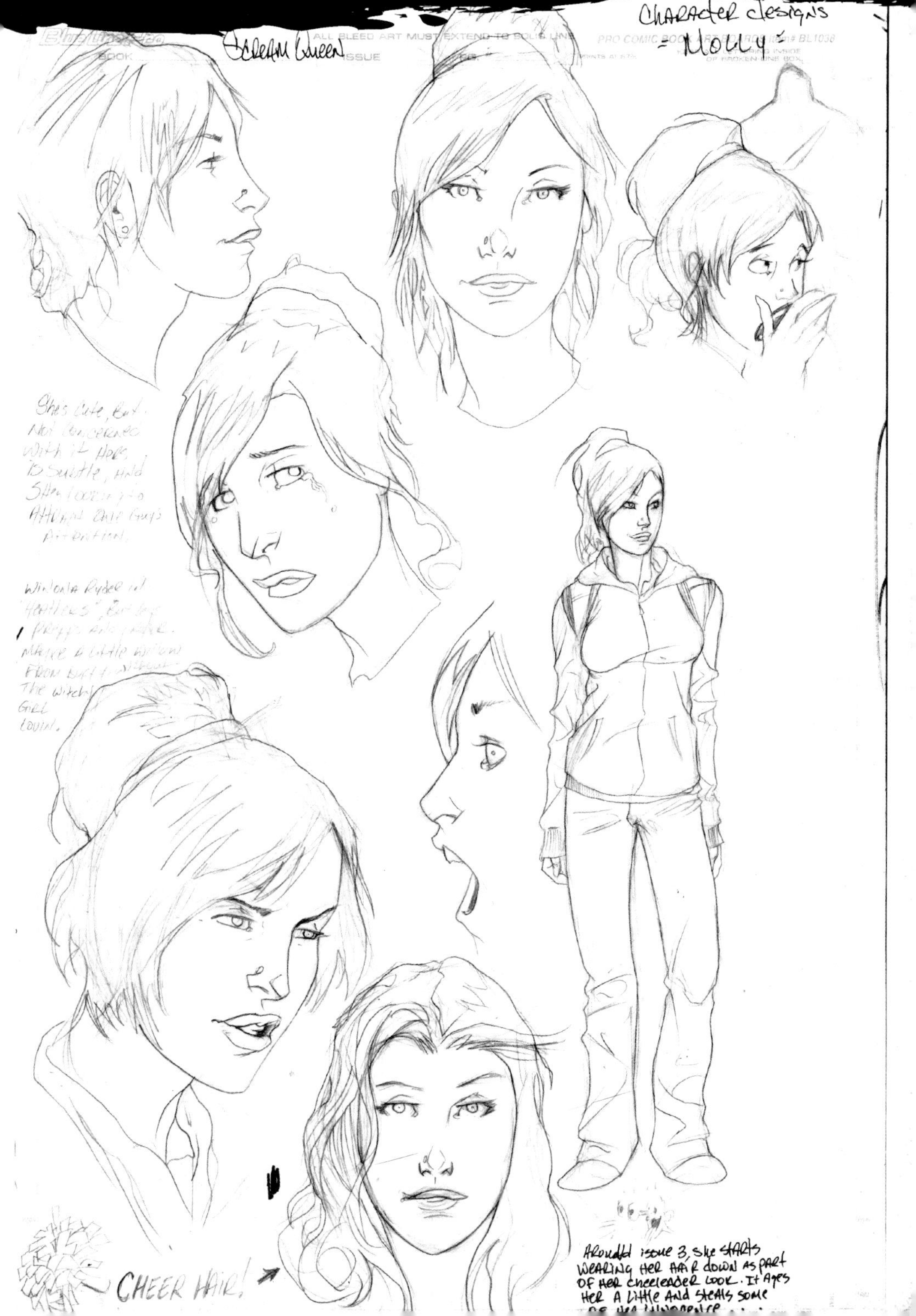
Scream Queen
Character designs
- Molly -
She's Cute, But Not Concerned With it. Hers Is Subtle, And She's looking to Attract One Guy's Attention.
CHEER HAIR!
Around issue 3, she starts wearing her hair down as part of her cheerleader look. It ages her a little and steals some

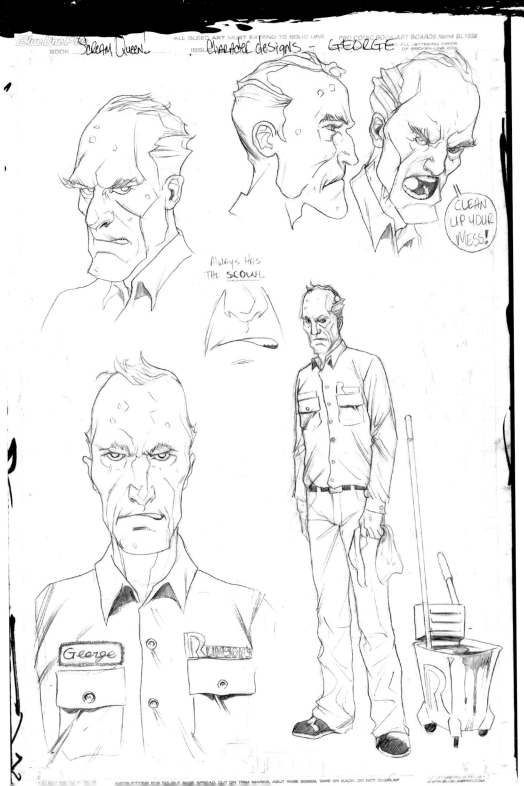

BlueLinePro

BOOK Scream Queen

ALL BLEED ART MUST EXTEND TO SOLID LINE

ISSUE Character designs - GEORGE

PRO COMIC BOOK ART BOARDS Item# BL1038

ALL LETTERING INSIDE OF BROKEN-LINE BOX

CLEAN UP YOUR MESS!

Always has the SCOWL.

George

RUMSON'S

SKETCHBOOK

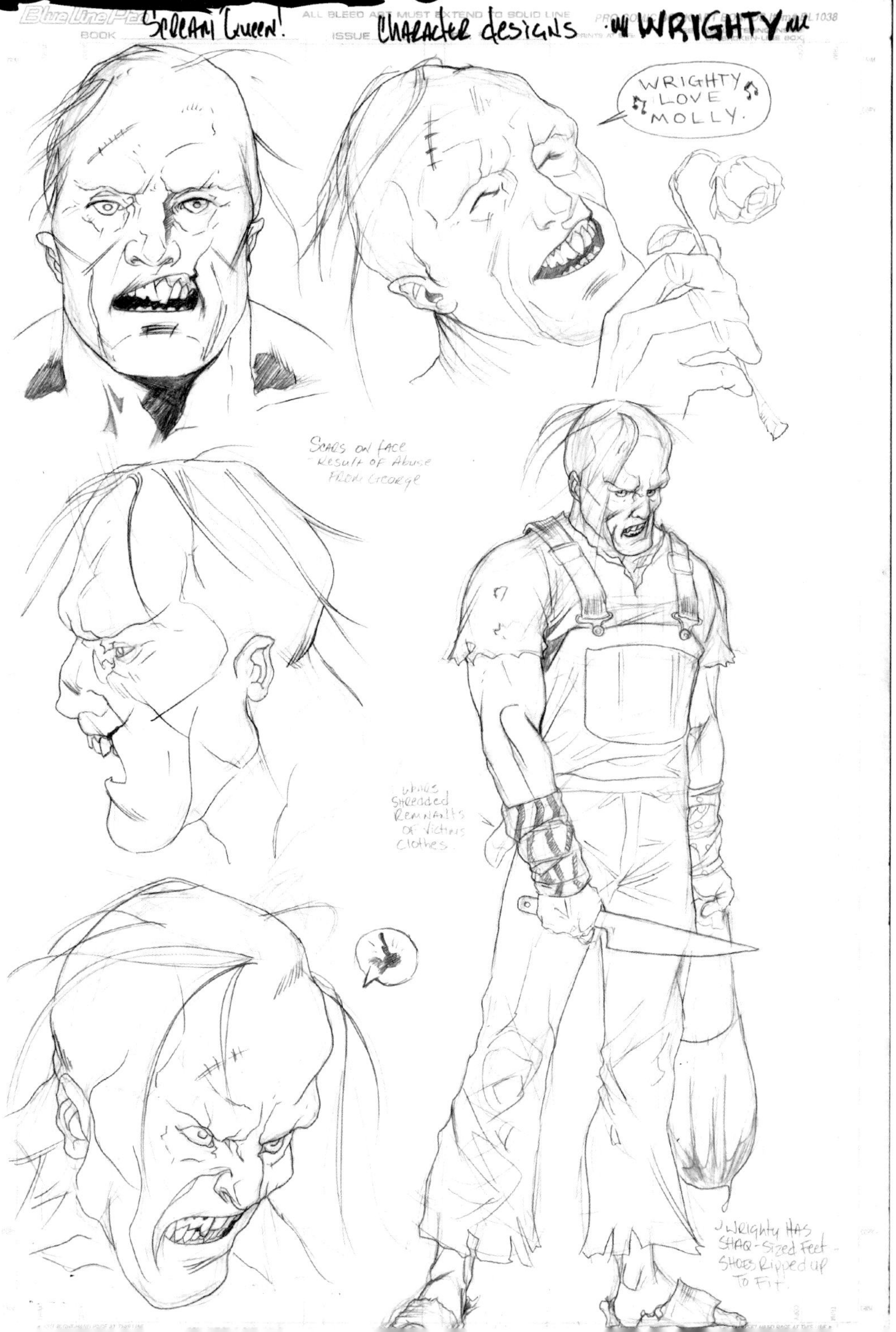
ALL BLEED ART MUST EXTEND TO SOLID LINE
BOOK Scream Queen!
ISSUE Character designs
WRIGHTY
WRIGHTY LOVE MOLLY.
Scars on face Result of Abuse from George
Wraps Shredded Remnants of Victims Clothes.
Wrighty Has SHAQ-Sized Feet - Shoes Ripped up To Fit.

SKETCHBOOK

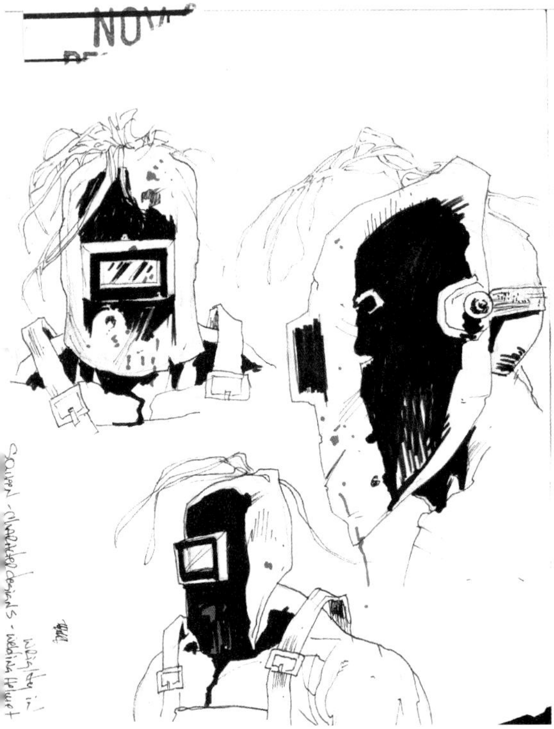

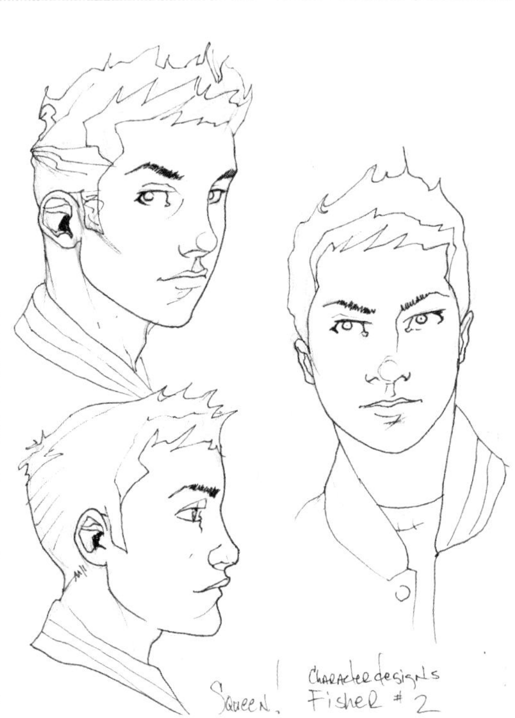
Squeen!
Character designs
Fisher # 2

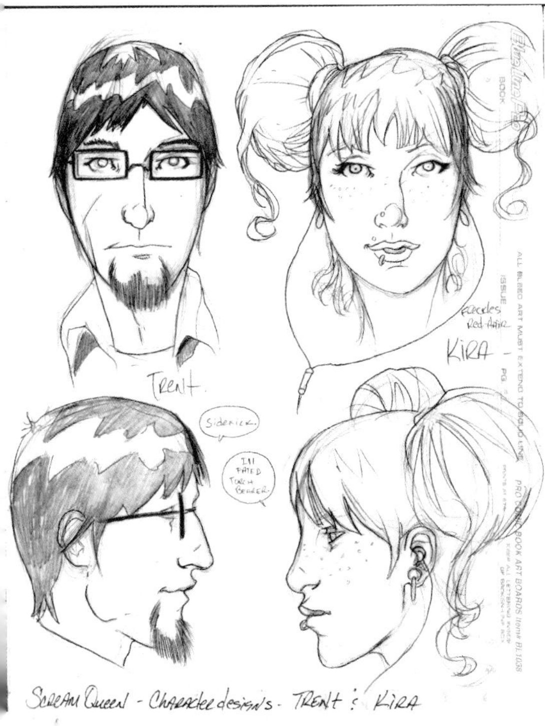
Trent
Freckles
Red hair
Kira -
Sidekick
Ill fated torch bearer
Scream Queen - Character designs - Trent & Kira

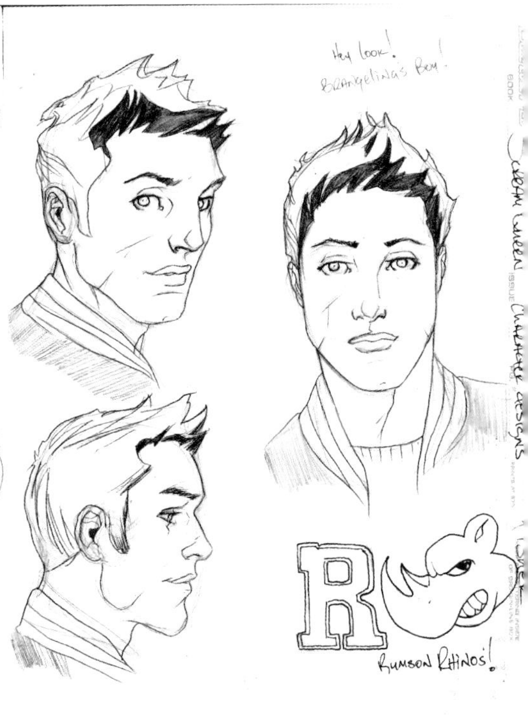
Hey look!
Brangelina's boy!
Scream Queen Character designs
R
Rumson Rhinos!